A LITERARY BIBLE SURVEY
FOR THE SECULAR SCHOOL

2ND EDITION

WRITTEN & PUBLISHED BY CARYN KIRK

Bible 101: A Literary Bible Survey for the Secular School
Second Edition
Author and editor: Caryn Crabb Kirk
Publisher: Caryn Crabb Kirk

© 2012 Lulu Author.
All rights reserved.
ISBN 978-1-304-40592-0

This book is dedicated to my
2011-2012 Honors English 9 class
at Hammond School.
Your diversity, intelligence, and enthusiasm
helped make this book what it is.
Thanks for being my test readers!

Awa Franklin
Ayan Dasgupta
Bailey DeLoache
Bristow Richards
Cantey Heath
Caroline Schraibman
Claire Harvin
Clara Castles
Cody Sims
Emma Ehreth
Frances Sadler
Isabelle Mikell
Jacob Burger
Katharyn Taylor
Maddy Wassermann
Margaret Banes Borden
Megan Ballew
Quinn Newman
Sara Stuart

Table of Contents

PART I: INTRODUCTION

A Word to the Student (Letters to Lexi, Fatima, and Scott)   8

Lesson One: **Backstage at the Bible**   13

PART II: ART & MYTH

Genesis 1-2:3 (Creation)   22

Lesson Two: **The Bible as Art**   24

Genesis 2:4-3 (Adam and Eve)   28

Lesson Three: **The Bible as Literature**   31

Lesson Four: **Genesis and Mythology**   39

"Pandora's Box"   43

Letter to Scott: Genealogies in Genesis   45

Lesson Five: **Genesis and Science**   46

Genesis 4 (Cain and Abel)   51

Genesis 6-9 (Noah and the Ark)   52

Genesis 11:1-9 (The Tower of Babel)   56

Lesson Six: **A History in Symbols**   57

"The Story of Utnapishtim" from The Epic of Gilgamesh   66

Lesson Seven: **Noah Like You've Never Seen Him Before**   67

PART III: HERO STORIES

Genesis 12-25 (Abraham)	78
Lesson Eight: **Father Abraham and the Covenant**	88
"The Muslim Abraham" excerpt from the Koran	97
Lesson Nine: **The Legacy of Abraham's Seed**	98
Letter to Lexi: Humanism and Abraham	102
Moses (excerpts from Exodus – Deuteronomy)	103
Lesson Ten: History of a Hero	119
Lesson Eleven: Go Down, Moses	122
Lesson Twelve: Epic Proportions	126
The Book of Jonah	132
Lesson Thirteen: **Jonah as Comic Anti-Hero**	135

PART IV: POETRY & PROPHECY

Psalms 100, 22, 23, 137 and 139	142
Lesson Fourteen: **Songs of Praise and Lament**	148
Proverbs 1, 10 and 31 (excerpts)	154
Ecclesiastes 1 and 3 (excerpts)	158
Lesson Fifteen: **Wisdom Literature**	161
Isaiah 9, 40, 53 and 65 (excerpts)	170
Lesson Sixteen: **Poet, Prophet, Prognosticator**	175

PART V: THE BIOGRAPHY OF JESUS

Matthew 1 and Luke 2 (The Nativity)	184
Lesson Seventeen: **Jesus: Fact or Fiction?**	186
Letter to Fatima: Gnostic gospels	191
Letter to Scott: Manuscript evidence	192
The Gospel of Mark (abridged)	195
Lesson Eighteen: **A Different Kind of Hero**	215

Letter to Lexi: Secular Allusions — 221

<u>Lesson Nineteen</u>: **Cross Culture** — 227

PART VI:
SERMON, EPISTLE & APOCALYPSE

Matthew 5-7 (Sermon on the Mount) — 234

<u>Lesson Twenty</u>: **Rhetoric on the Mount** — 239

Epistles: I Peter 1 and I Corinthians 13 — 247

<u>Lesson Twenty-One</u>: **Sincerely, Peter & Paul** — 249

Revelation 1, 13, 17 and 22 (excerpts) — 256

<u>Lesson Twenty-Two</u>: **Apocalypse!** — 262

INVENTORIES & APPENDICES

Inventory for Narrative (blank) — 270

Inventory for Poetry (blank) — 272

Inventory for Exposition (blank) — 274

Appearance/Format of the Biblical Text — 276

Annotated Bibliography — 277

Bible Versions and Translations — 279

Sidebar Topical Index — 280

Comprehensive Bible Timeline (diagram) — 281

A Verbal Overview of Bible History (list) — 281

Allusions to the Bible in Pop Culture — 282

Perspectives of Genesis and Evolution (chart) — 283

Image Credits — 284

A Word to the Teacher — 285

A Word from the Author — 286

A WORD TO THE STUDENT

"You'd be rightly written off as uncultivated if you knew nothing of the Bible."

Richard Dawkins, Darwinian biologist, atheist

You may be sitting in an English classroom with this book open on your desk, and you're asking yourself, "Why do I have to study the Bible in here?" This isn't a religious school, you say. Maybe you're not religious, and you don't see the point. Maybe you *are* religious, and you're afraid of having your faith devalued or insulted. And thus we begin our study by answering a few basic questions, posed by students like yourself, who want to know the *what*'s, *why*'s and *how*'s behind this study of the Bible.

 Lexi

I don't go to church and I'm not much interested in religion, so I never really planned on reading the Bible. Because, to be honest, I'm a little worried about "separation of church and state" here. Is this book going to assume I believe in God?

Dear Lexi,

This book is written for believers and nonbelievers alike, with sincere respect and consideration being given to both ends of the faith scale. My greatest hope is that you will come to see why the Bible stands up as landmark literature, even among the global greats like Shakespeare and Homer. The goal of our upcoming 22 lessons is to help you get familiar with the most famous stories and passages from the Bible, so that you are a better educated student and citizen. Along the way, you'll hear from multiple points of view and be asked to ponder religious and nonreligious interpretations, cultural facts, historical insights, and literary scholarship. You will be free to like or dislike, believe or disbelieve, as you see fit. In the same way that you don't have to be French to enjoy French films, and that city-dwellers often enjoy country music, I think that the Bible can be fascinating study material for a diverse assortment of readers.

Along the way, I will speak a fair amount about "literary scholars." When I use that term, you might imagine a group of college professors who study literature for a living and are experts in all sorts of books. Literary scholars do not necessarily read the Bible as a holy book, but they certainly consider it an important book and a book of complex artistry. If you don't agree with the "scholars," that's okay. Consider it an opportunity to find out what other people think.

You will also be reading about the opinions of "theologians." When I use that term, you can imagine a group of pastors or rabbis who study the Bible for its moral and spiritual ideas. It is impossible to look closely at the Bible without encountering a little bit of theology along the way. Some students (perhaps you) might find these ideas old-fashioned or uninteresting. If you don't agree with the theological explanations presented in this book, that's okay too – you won't find sermons here, just summaries of mainstream points of view. Again, consider it an opportunity to find out what other people think.

The most pervasive opinion you will encounter in this book is, simply, that the Bible is good art. I will talk about Abraham, Solomon, and Jesus as if I like them very much, and I do. If we were studying <u>To Kill a Mockingbird</u>, I'd sing the praises of Atticus as well. Whether you align more closely with a secular scholar or a conservative theologian, or if you're just a fan of good stories and poems, the assumption throughout all our upcoming lessons is that the Bible is rich and complex and worth a few weeks in your English class. I hope you find something to admire and enjoy!

 Fatima

I'm not for or against religion, but I'm not sure Bible reading at school is quite fair. I mean, I don't see the Koran being assigned, or the Hindu Gitas. Why the Bible and not these other spiritual books?

Dear Fatima,

Studying the Bible is significantly important in a Western/American English class. I hope you will have a chance to study these other books in other contexts; both of the works you mention should appear during world literature and/or social studies classes at some point during high school. But the Bible, and in particular the King James Bible, has had such a profound effect on Western, English-speaking culture that to ignore it in an English class in the United States or Europe would be as problematic as ignoring Shakespeare. Take a look at a list of literary concepts you need to know for the Advanced Placement English Literature Exam, and you'll see Bible passages from Genesis and Psalms. Study Western culture with an eye for political and social trends, and you'll find Bible-based ideas everywhere. Listen to the radio for a couple of hours and you're bound to hear a biblical allusion – if you recognize it, that is. This textbook is designed to help you understand those biblical ideas, stories, characters, phrases and details in many contemporary contexts, from songs to politics to school.

The Bible is, in fact, the number one best seller in the world, and there is good reason for that. For one thing, it has profuse amounts of blood, sex, supernatural pyrotechnics, battle intrigue, flashy heroes, beautiful women, dramatic poetry, song lyrics, love letters, history, and, of course, some fiery preaching. The themes of the Bible resound all over literature: good guys defeating evil villains, the grandeur of nature, the clash of war, sons in search of fathers, revenge upon enemies, redemption from sin, journeys through dark lands, and, finally, the big three: faith, hope, and love…"with the greatest of these being love" (I Cor. 13:13). It's seriously hard to be born in the West, make a life of writing or composing or designing, and never find yourself influenced by some aspect of the Bible. It is an important topic for any arts-related classroom in the Western hemisphere.

 Scott

I am a Christian and I already know a lot about the Bible. Frankly, my parents and I are afraid that if the school gets into teaching the Bible, they are going to twist it into something it's not.

Dear Scott,

Hopefully this unit of study will enhance what you already know – it is not designed to change what you believe, and the sanctity of the Bible will be treated with great respect. However, you will very likely encounter some interpretations of the text that are new and different. I think everyone in your class will find this to be true. Here are three principles that governed the presentation and analysis of the Bible throughout the writing of this textbook:

1) Words from the King James Version of the Bible appear verbatim – but with paragraph breaks, quotation marks, and footnotes to help with comprehension.

Many students find the language of the KJV to be difficult, particularly since it does not use the modern conventions of paragraphing and quoting; these were incorporated to ease the reading process, and they do not alter or add to the meaning of the text. Please refer to page 276 (in the appendices) for further information about the appearance and format of the KJV text in this book. Footnotes have also been provided to assist with vocabulary, sentence structure, and ancient cultural background. These footnotes are usually based on factual information, like word definitions (from a Hebrew or Greek lexicon) and historical knowledge (from an encyclopedia, a map, or the NIV <u>Archaeological Study Bible</u>). Feel free to fact check. You are also free, if you prefer, to read from your own personal copy of a King James or New King James Bible.

2) Lessons will analyze the text using standard "English class" literary methods, often presenting more than one point of view when there are interpretive options.

In each of the lessons, you will find not only factual and historical information, but also literary analysis. Our primary mode of study will be to apply literary principles to the biblical text. We will analyze concepts like theme, character, metaphor, and irony, just like you would do with any classic work of literature in any English Language Arts class. For instance, God will be analyzed as a character in the same way you'd analyze Romeo or Juliet. When reading the Psalms, we will learn about Hebrew poetry characteristics, in the same way you would learn about sonnets or haiku. We will also consider each biblical book's genre, point of view, and intended audience. As mentioned in my letter to Lexi, I will present to you the perspective of a "literary scholar." Literary analysis is often interpretive and subjective, so it's OK if you don't agree.

Throughout the lessons, you will find additional ideas presented in the gray "sidebars." This feature will sometimes highlight related factual information and will sometimes acknowledge a specific critical or religious perspective, ranging from evangelical to skeptical. The sidebars are there to supplement the reader's interests and curiosities, and you can read the ones you like and ignore the ones you don't. At the end of each lesson, you will find a list of terms you can study (**Objective Identification**) as well as some analytical questions (**Subjective Expression**) you can answer *in whatever fashion you choose*. I hope, Scott, that your critical thinking skills will be encouraged, and that your questions and religious convictions will be welcomed in an environment of respectful discussion.

3) While remaining respectfully neutral about spiritual interpretations, I will sometimes lean toward traditional points of view when addressing issues of culture and authorship.

For instance, we will treat Moses as the author of Genesis, Solomon as the author of Proverbs, and Mark the Apostle as the author of the Gospel of Mark. When discussing Jewish points of view, information has been drawn from general reference books and the website <u>Judaism 101</u> (not affiliated in any way with <u>Bible 101</u>). When analyzing the New Testament, summations of Christian theological principles are traditional and mainstream – points that most Catholics, Baptists, Methodists, and Episcopalians (etc.) would agree on. For more information about my personal approach to biblical scholarship, read **A Word from the Author** at the end of the book.

LESSON ONE:
BACKSTAGE AT THE BIBLE

Eliza Codex 23 - Ethiopian biblical manuscript (Early 20th Century)

Let's begin by taking a bird's-eye view of what the Bible is – its contents, its history, its language, its geography. We will be looking specifically at the King James Version of the Bible (more on why later in this lesson). The KJV Bible is a collection of 66 individual books. They are grouped into two sections, one called the Old Testament and one the New Testament.

CONTENT & COMPOSITION

The Old Testament is also known as the Hebrew Bible[a] (Tanakh), and it contains stories, prophecies, and poetry that are considered sacred to the Jewish faith. It was concluded before the "zero" point on the timeline. Historical scholars and traditional religious scholars disagree somewhat about when it was put into writing and how reliable the historical details are. It may have taken anywhere from 500 to around 1000 years for its entire composition to take place, and there were numerous authors involved.

---

[a] The KJV Old Testament has the same content as the Tanakh, but the books are arranged differently.

The New Testament story begins around the year "zero." It chronicles the life and teachings of Jesus Christ, who became the central figure in what the world now knows as Christianity. The New Testament was written over a 40-60 year period in the late First Century. Let's take a look at the historical placement of the Bible by using a general time line:

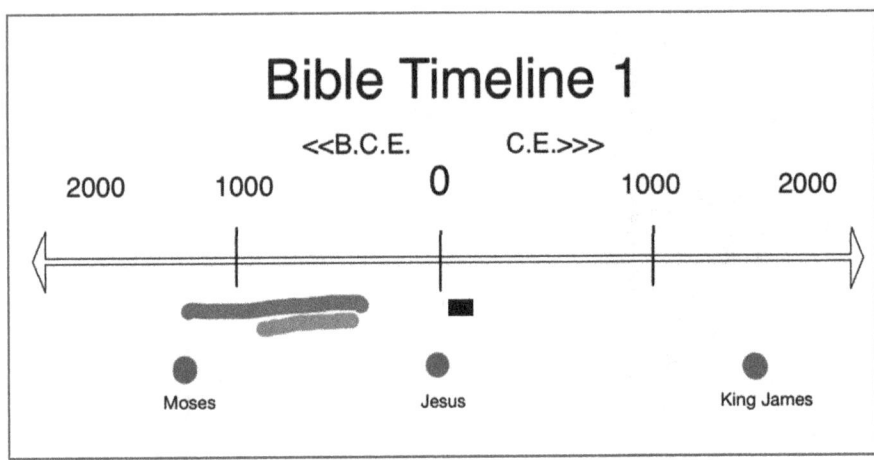

In this diagram the gray stripes represent the time frame of the composition of the Old Testament – the darker top stripe being the traditional estimation, and the lighter bottom stripe the more modern estimation. The small black line represents the 40-60 year composition of the New Testament.

GEOGRAPHY

The Old and New Testaments are both centered around the same geographical region, what we might call the ancient Near East or Middle East: the Mediterranean Sea, Egypt, Jerusalem/Israel, the Arabic Peninsula, and modern day Turkey and Iraq. New Testament expansion of Christianity extended up through southern Europe, starting in Greece and eventually headquartering in Rome.

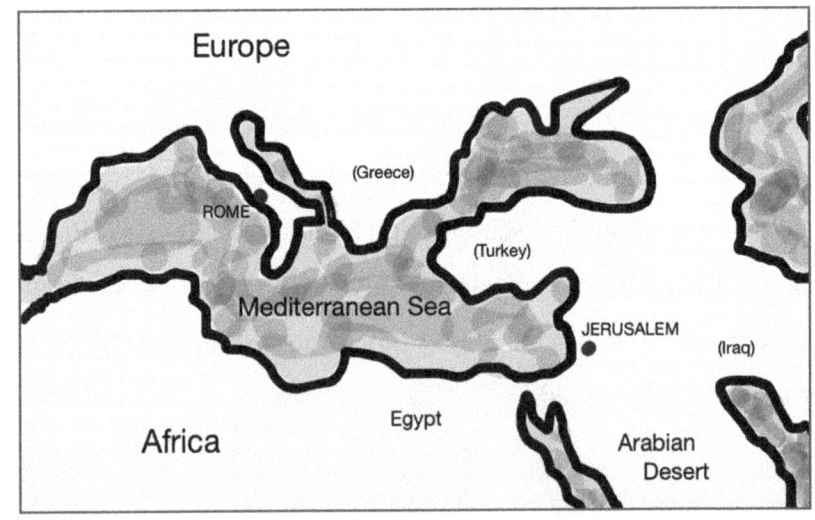

LANGUAGE & CULTURE

The two testaments were written in different languages and from different cultural points of view. Although the original manuscripts are long lost, the completed Old Testament was written in Hebrew[b] and it speaks from the unique perspective of ancient Jews; tradition asserts that it was written by Jewish prophets and kings over the course of a thousand years. The New Testament was written in Greek.[c] Its 27 books tell of the life and legacy of Jesus Christ, whom Christians believe to be the literal incarnation of the Jewish God. The cultural setting of the New Testament is the Roman Empire during the reigns of Augustus Caesar and ten other emperors. Its original audience therefore included both Jews and Gentiles of the First Century.

OLD TESTAMENT OVERVIEW

The first book of the Bible is Genesis, which starts "In the beginning…" and then moves quickly to the stories of the Jewish founding fathers: Abraham and his sons and grandsons. Due to famine in their homeland, the Jews end up in Egypt, enslaved by Egyptian pharaohs. Then the great Jewish hero Moses emerges, who leads his people out of bondage. Eventually, they reach the "Promised Land." They are given a king, the kingdom splits, the people are conquered and transplanted, and although many Jews return to the Promised Land, the Israelites are to some extent permanently dispersed throughout other lands and countries. It is an expansive, epic story laid out over the course of 39 separate books of many different genres.

> **Israel / Israelite**: political and ethnic terms for the nation fathered by Abraham, whose grandson Jacob was re-named "Israel," which means "one who wrestles with God"
>
> **Jew / Jewish**: religious and ethnic terms deriving from Judaism
>
> **Judaism:** the Jewish religion, derived from the name of Jacob's eldest son, Judah
>
> **Hebrew:** literally means "one from the other side" (referring to either the Euphrates or the Jordan) and used primarily to indicate the language or the alphabet of the Israelites
>
> **Semitic:** adjective referring to the Jews and ethnically-related peoples including the Arabs
>
> **Gentile:** a non-Jew

---

[b] Technically, a few passages in the Old Testament were written in Aramaic. The Bible Gateway Blog describes the relationship between Hebrew and Aramaic as similar "to that between modern Spanish and Portuguese: they're distinct languages, but sufficiently closely related that a reader of one can understand much of the other." ("What Was the Original Language of the Bible?" posted 1 June 2012.)

[c] Some contemporary scholars believe that the original versions of some New Testament books were written in Aramaic, but since all original manuscripts are lost, this is purely theoretical. Jesus' native tongue was Aramaic.

Tradition asserts that Moses is the writer of the first five books of the Old Testament (Genesis, Exodus, Leviticus, Numbers, Deuteronomy – called the *Torah*). After Moses, a series of many Jewish prophets and kings are said to have authored the remaining books. One of these writers was the great King David, a warrior poet who is credited with most of the Psalms. Other Old Testament authors you may be familiar with include King Solomon and the prophet Isaiah. All the books of the Hebrew Bible were completed by around 400 BCE.

NEW TESTAMENT OVERVIEW

New Testament composition probably began about 30 years after the death of Jesus Christ, who was born around the year "zero" and, according to most biblical scholars, lived for 33 years. Let's take a moment to define Jesus Christ himself. First of all, "Christ" is not his last name! It is the Greek form of the Hebrew word for *Messiah*. Many books of the Tanakh predict the eventual appearance of a Messiah, or "Anointed One," who will usher in a new kingdom, a new age of prosperity and goodness. Persons of the Jewish faith do not accept Jesus' claim to be that Messiah; Christians do. The New Testament positions itself as the fulfillment and continuation of God's word through Jesus "the Christ," a Jew born in the lineage of Abraham and King David. Many verses in the New Testament demonstrate Jesus' claims to be not only the foretold Messiah but also the incarnation of God himself (see John 5:18). When Jesus is quoted in the New Testament, he refers to God as his "Father" and asserts that he, the "Son," is one with the Father. The followers of Jesus, beginning with Saint Peter and Saint Paul, established what we now know as the Christian church. For the next 2000 years and up to today, people have been interpreting New Testament texts and re-defining the church: Catholic, Orthodox, Protestant, Progressive, etc. But it all began with the events recorded in the New Testament and has, ever since, been built upon the words of the New Testament.

The first four books of the New Testament contain overlapping stories of the life of Jesus: they are called the Gospels of Matthew, of Mark, of Luke, and of John. Following the gospels, another narrative book (Acts) tells the continuing story of the early Christians and what happened to them after Jesus' departure from earth. The rest of the New Testament is made up of letters (epistles) written from First Century missionaries to First Century churches. It ends with an apocalyptic book (Revelation) that describes a vision of what will happen at the end of the world.

BOOKS OF THE BIBLE
BOOKS IN BOLD WILL BE SURVEYED IN THIS TEXT

OLD TESTAMENT	NEW TESTAMENT
Genesis	**Matthew**
Exodus	**Mark**
Leviticus	**Luke**
Numbers	John
Deuteronomy	Acts
Joshua	Romans
Judges	**1 Corinthians**
Ruth	2 Corinthians
1 Samuel	Galatians
2 Samuel	Ephesians
1 Kings	Philippians
2 Kings	Colossians
1 Chronicles	1 Thessalonians
2 Chronicles	2 Thessalonians
Ezra	1 Timothy
Nehemiah	2 Timothy
Esther	Titus
Job	Philemon
Psalm	Hebrews
Proverbs	James
Ecclesiastes	**1 Peter**
Song of Solomon	2 Peter
Isaiah	1 John
Jeremiah	2 John
Lamentations	3 John
Ezekial	Jude
Daniel	**Revelation**
Hosea	
Joel	**KJV**
Amos	**APOCRYPHA**
Obadiah	1 Maccabees
Jonah	2 Maccabees
Micah	Tobit
Nahum	Judith
Habakkuk	Baruch
Zephaniah	Wisdom
Haggai	Sirach
Zechariah	
Malachi	

All 27 New Testament books were written within the century surrounding Jesus' death, allegedly composed by authors who either knew him directly (primary sources) or knew his friends and family (secondary sources). The identities of most New Testament authors have been part of church tradition dating back to the First Century and built largely on word of mouth across the ancient world, as handwritten copies of these documents made their way from city to city. Modern scholarship challenges the notion of authentic primary and secondary source authorship; however, in this textbook, we will speak of biblical authors in a traditional way, i.e. Saint Mark as the secondary-source writer of Mark's gospel and Saint John as the primary-source writer of Revelation.

THE BIBLE ON YOUR BOOKSHELF

By the year 200, the church in Rome was using a collection of 25 Christian texts, (23 of which are in today's New Testament, plus two books that eventually lost favor with church scholars[d]). By the year 400, there was broad and firm approval of exactly 27 books. The same 27 books still compose any New Testament you can buy in a store today (see the list to the left). It should be noted, however, that among the surviving New Testament manuscripts from ancient Rome, Alexandria, Byzantium, and elsewhere, there are numerous (yet mostly minor) discrepancies that have caused some variations among different Bible translations. For example, there are around 50 verses in the King James version

---

[d] The two books that were eventually rejected were the Revelation of Peter and the Wisdom of Solomon. This group of 25 books was known as the Muratorian Canon. (Eerdman's Handbook to the History of Christianity, p.94)

that are omitted or altered in the New International Version, due to differences in the manuscripts that were available to scholars at the times of their translations.

As for the Old Testament, we are talking about 39 books that have been considered holy for more than 2000 years. However, an additional set of books called the *Apocrypha* has been the subject of much debate. The seven Apocryphal books are important in Jewish culture (for example, the book of Maccabees contains the story behind Hanukkah), but these books are not in the Tanakh. However, they were included in some of the early manuscripts of the Greek Old Testament.[e] Several popes and Catholic councils approved their inclusion in the Bible, but the Protestants, specifically Martin Luther, did not (1500's). For this reason, the Protestant Bible includes 39 Old Testament books, whereas the Catholic Bible, as approved at the Council of Trent (1546), includes 46. The King James Version, printed in 1611 and sponsored by the Catholic King James, originally included the Apocryphal books in a separate section inserted between the Old and New Testaments. During the 1800's, the Apocrypha were totally removed from KJV Bibles but are still readily available for readers today, both online and in print.[f]

AVAILABLE TRANSLATIONS

Over the centuries, different translations of the Bible have been made from ancient Hebrew and Greek manuscripts into many languages around the globe. The King James Version (KJV) has been the most influential version in the English-speaking world, and that is why we are using it in this textbook. It is considered the most poetically beautiful of the English translations. However, many modern readers find the KJV to be a challenging text since it was written during the Renaissance and uses language that sounds "Shakespearean" in quality. It also has no quotation marks, no paragraph divisions, and no poetic line divisions (since these conventions are not present in the original Hebrew or Greek). You might find that other translations, with more modern English and

> **BIBLICAL CANON**
>
> The official church-approved collection of books is called the "canon." The word canon means "measuring rod" and can refer to any type of standard rule or authoritative collection.
>
> Today's KJV bible has 66 canonical books, whereas it used to have 73, including 7 Apocrypha.

---

[e] The Greek Old Testament was called the Septuagint. The word *Septuagint* means 70 and refers to the group of 70 Jewish scholars who produced the translation, probably sometime during the third and second centuries B.C.E.
[f] See the official King James Bible Online.org for information and copies of all Apocryphal books.

more conventional formatting, can be of help as you make sense of assigned Bible passages. This textbook adds paragraph breaks and quotation marks to the KJV text for ease of reading.

One popular alternative to the KJV is the New International Version (NIV), which is the best-selling contemporary English translation. Another trendy version, called The Message, is currently in demand for its easy-to-understand vernacular, but please note that it is not a straight translation; rather, it is an interpretive paraphrase that takes many liberties in figurative language, imagery, and interpretation. On the other end of the scale, the New Revised Standard Version (NRSV) is considered one of the most literally precise translations available today and is favored by many Bible scholars. And if you appreciate the King James literary style but just can't get used to reading without paragraphs and quotation marks, the New King James Version (1982) preserves the artistic qualities of the 1611 text while updating format and vocabulary. More detailed descriptions of these alternative Bible versions can be found in the Bible Versions and Translations list on pages 279. If you choose to read textbook assignments from an alternate translation, be sure to return to the King James before class time. The language of the KJV has long been preferred by literary scholars due to its devotional formality and ear-pleasing musicality.

A TRANSLATION COMPARISON
Matthew 6:9-10 (from the Lord's Prayer)

King James Version:
[9] After this manner therefore pray ye: Our Father which art in heaven, Hallowed be thy name.
[10] Thy kingdom come, Thy will be done in earth, as it is in heaven.

New King James Version:
"In this manner, therefore, pray:
    Our Father in heaven,
    Hallowed be Your name.
    Your kingdom come.
    Your will be done..."

New International Version:
"This, then, is how you should pray:
    "'Our Father in heaven,
    hallowed be your name.
    your kingdom come,
    your will be done...'"

The Message:
"...pray very simply. Like this:
    Our Father in heaven,
    Reveal who you are.
    Set the world right;
    Do what's best..."

New Revised Standard Version:
"Pray then in this way:
    Our Father in heaven,
    hallowed be your name.
    Your kingdom come.
    Your will be done..."

INTRO & LESSON ONE STUDY GUIDE

Objective Identification:

Mediterranean region, Old Testament, Hebrew Bible, Tanakh, Genesis, Moses, King David, New Testament, Jesus Christ, gospels, Apocrypha, canon, King James Version (KJV)

Subjective Expression:

1) Recall: What are two good reasons for studying the Bible in your English class?

2) Opinion: How do you feel about the fact that this textbook may present some ideas that you might disagree with? Do you think it is important to learn about a broad spectrum of diverse ideas, even regarding the Bible? Or would you prefer that Bible opinions be kept at home?

3) Comparison: Compare and contrast the Old and New Testaments – when they were written, how long it took to complete each collection, the original languages, and their differing cultural settings. You could answer this question with a comparative chart.

4) Further Research: Look up the Dead Sea Scrolls and find out how this discovery confirmed the reliability of the Old Testament manuscripts.

5) Opinion: Which Bible version would you prefer to read, and why?

QUOTABLE QUOTES

> The influence of the King James Bible is so great that the list of idioms from it that have slipped into everyday speech, taking such deep root that we use them all the time without any awareness of their biblical origin, is practically endless: sour grapes; fatted calf; salt of the earth; drop in a bucket; skin of one's teeth; apple of one's eye; girded loins; feet of clay; whited sepulchers; filthy lucre; pearls before swine; fly in the ointment; fight the good fight; eat, drink and be merry.

Charles McGrath
"Why the King James Bible Endures"
The New York Times
April 23, 2011

ART & MYTH

*of the Tree of
Knowledge of Good and Evil,
thou shalt not eat of it*

GENESIS 1 - 2:3   CREATION

Chapter 1

[1]In the beginning God created the heaven and the earth. [2]And the earth was without form, and void; and darkness was upon the face of the deep. And the Spirit of God moved upon the face of the waters. [3]And God said, "Let there be light": and there was light. [4]And God saw the light, that it was good: and God divided the light from the darkness. [5]And God called the light Day, and the darkness he called Night. And the evening and the morning were the first day.

[6]And God said, "Let there be a firmament[g] in the midst of the waters, and let it divide the waters from the waters." [7]And God made the firmament, and divided the waters which were under the firmament from the waters which were above the firmament: and it was so. [8]And God called the firmament Heaven. And the evening and the morning were the second day.

[9]And God said, "Let the waters under the heaven be gathered together unto one place, and let the dry land appear": and it was so. [10]And God called the dry land Earth; and the gathering together of the waters called he Seas: and God saw that it was good. [11]And God said, "Let the earth bring forth grass, the herb yielding seed, and the fruit tree yielding fruit after his kind, whose seed is in itself, upon the earth": and it was so. [12]And the earth brought forth grass, and herb yielding seed after his kind, and the tree yielding fruit, whose seed was in itself, after his kind: and God saw that it was good. [13]And the evening and the morning were the third day.

[14]And God said, "Let there be lights in the firmament of the heaven to divide the day from the night; and let them be for signs, and for seasons, and for days, and years: [15]And let them be for lights in the firmament of the heaven to give light upon the earth": and it was so. [16]And God made two great lights; the greater light to rule the day, and the lesser light to rule the night: he made the stars also. [17]And God set them in the firmament of the heaven to give light upon the earth, [18]And to rule over the day and over the night, and to divide the light from the darkness: and God saw that it was good. [19]And the evening and the morning were the fourth day.

[20]And God said, "Let the waters bring forth abundantly the moving creature that hath life, and fowl that may fly above the earth in the open firmament of heaven." [21]And God created great whales, and every living creature that moveth, which the waters brought forth abundantly, after their kind, and every winged fowl after his kind: and God saw that it was good. [22]And God blessed them, saying, "Be fruitful, and multiply, and fill the waters in the seas, and let fowl multiply in the earth." [23]And the evening and the morning were the fifth day.

[24]And God said, "Let the earth bring forth the living creature after his kind, cattle, and creeping thing, and beast of the earth after his kind": and it was so. [25]And God made the beast of the earth after his kind, and cattle after their kind, and every thing that creepeth upon the earth after his kind: and God saw that it was good.

[26]And God said, "Let us make man in our image, after our likeness: and let them have dominion over the fish of the sea, and over the fowl of the air, and over the cattle, and over all the earth, and over every creeping thing that creepeth upon the earth." [27]So God created man in his own

---

[g] Firmament = sky (often imagined as a dome over the earth) (FI)

image, in the image of God created he him; male and female created he them. [28]And God blessed them, and God said unto them, "Be fruitful, and multiply, and replenish the earth, and subdue it: and have dominion over the fish of the sea, and over the fowl of the air, and over every living thing that moveth upon the earth." [29]And God said, "Behold, I have given you every herb bearing seed, which is upon the face of all the earth, and every tree, in the which is the fruit of a tree yielding seed; to you it shall be for meat. [30]And to every beast of the earth, and to every fowl of the air, and to every thing that creepeth upon the earth, wherein there is life, I have given every green herb for meat": and it was so. [31]And God saw every thing that he had made, and, behold, it was very good. And the evening and the morning were the sixth day.

Chapter 2

[1]Thus the heavens and the earth were finished, and all the host of them. [2]And on the seventh day God ended his work which he had made; and he rested on the seventh day from all his work which he had made. [3]And God blessed the seventh day, and sanctified it: because that in it he had rested from all his work which God created and made.

LESSON TWO:
THE BIBLE AS ART

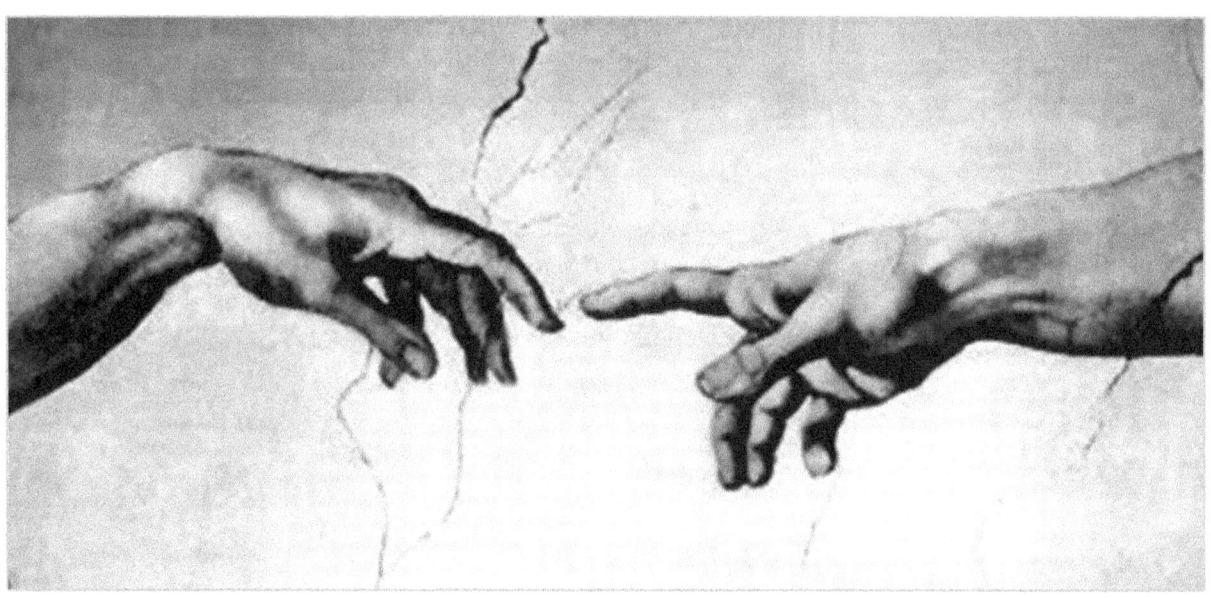

Do you recognize this image? Can you tell what is going on here? This is one of the most famous images of creation in the world, painted by Michelangelo on the ceiling of the Sistine Chapel. It was inspired by the events described in Genesis 1-3 and depicts God giving life to his first human creature, Adam. Go to the Internet and find "The Creation of Adam" so you can see the full picture, in color.

Look more closely at the hands in the detail above. Can you tell which one belongs to God, and which belongs to Adam? Adam's hand seems more limp, more passive, as if he is receiving the spark of life. God's hand is more muscularly engaged. With your own hands, imitate these positions and "feel" the characters of God and Adam as expressed through these tiny details. Then, once you've found a full-size color image, look at what else is going on in the picture. Do the bodily postures and surrounding details add information to the story? Do you think any colors or other details may be symbolic? Are there different opinions in your class concerning symbolism? Spend some time translating the images into character and plot ideas.

The observations that you have made over the past few minutes are examples of the interpretive process that is common to all works of art. The purpose of this lesson is to show you that the same types of artistic interpretations you did with the painting are applicable to the stories and poems of the Bible. We'll get started with Genesis 1 in particular, what I've called the "Creation Song." This passage is just as much a complex and expressive work of art as Michelangelo's famous painting. Stories in the Bible which may seem very simple actually hold the same type of artistic subtlety as the creations of Michelangelo, Shakespeare, or Beethoven.

You may be surprised to find that Genesis 1 has many qualities in common with music. If you read it aloud and listen carefully, it sounds very much like a song and in fact has many qualities in common with Hebrew poetry (like you find in the Psalms). Yes, it looks like a paragraph, but its poem-like elements actually cause literary scholars to call it "elevated prose" – elevated prose is more grand, patterned, and musical than ordinary prose. Let's take a look at those poetic qualities. First of all, can you spot a "refrain" in the passage? A set of words that the speaker comes back to again and again? Yes, there are many refrains, for example "and God saw that it was good." Many lines also begin with the words "And God said, let there be…" Using these repetitions alone, we could re-structure the paragraphs in Genesis 1 into something that looks a lot like a poem:

And God said, Let there be light: and there was light.
    And God saw the light, that it was good:
        and God divided the light from the darkness.
And God called the light Day, and the darkness he called Night.
    And the evening and the morning were the first day.

And God said, Let there be a firmament in the midst of the waters, and let it divide the waters from the waters.
    And God made the firmament, and divided the waters which were under the firmament
        from the waters which were above the firmament: and it was so.
And God called the firmament Heaven.
    And the evening and the morning were the second day.

Continuing in this fashion, we could format the entire passage into lines that reflect the repetitive patterns inherent in the language. Look back at what we've already done with these five verses, and note that there are two stanzas, each one beginning with "And God said…" and ending with the conclusion of one day. How many stanzas would be formed if we continued our process with the rest of the passage? In the context of Hebrew poetry, we would call these stanzas "strophes." A strophe is a set of phrases or sentences that are generally parallel to each other, but not identical, like you hear in a church hymn. The strophes in Genesis 1 go along with the six days of the creation story, each day being told like a verse in a song.

All these features seem to indicate a poetic form and intent for Genesis 1 – and poetry is of course the highest level of language. Imagine trying to speak in poetry or rhyme all day! Poetry requires careful attention to every word, and the presence of poetic language generally indicates an elevated or emotional purpose. Genesis 1 clearly has a grand, important purpose: describing how the entire world came into being!

But even before I called your attention to its musical and poetic qualities, it was still a work of art – narrative art. It tells a story in the same basic pattern in which all good stories are told. The conflict is presented immediately: a dark, empty world of chaos. The protagonist, God, appears right away to start solving the conflict. He conquers the darkness by creating light. He conquers the formlessness by separating out the sky, the water, and the land. He conquers the void by filling the new earth with life. These creative acts continue rising until they reach a climax. When do you think the climax of the story is? The climax, or turning point, of a story is the moment when everything changes. It is a point of high intensity.

Study the sixth strophe (the sixth day) closely. It is the longest strophe. It also has lines and ideas that do not run parallel to anything else in the passage, namely the details about God creating man in his own image. This is a unique detail. Another unique aspect of the sixth day is that God grants control of the earth to his newest creation, his most personal image-bearing creation. Yes, this is the climax of the story, the making of men and women. The sixth strophe is unique, the point of highest intensity when everything changes. After the climax, resolution comes on day seven, when God rests and pronounces that everything is complete and good. This story is tightly structured and full of subtle craftsmanship.

So we can see that Genesis 1 is both an artistic story as well as a poem and a song. Furthermore, some scholars have noted that the arrangement of the chapter is also very visual, almost like a painting or a diagram. To understand this, let's draw it out in chart form:

Day 1: Light	Day 4: Sun, Moon and Stars
Day 2: Sky and Water	Day 5: Birds and Fish
Day 3: Land	Day 6: Animals and Mankind

Note how in the left column, God is creating spaces, and on the right, he systematically fills those spaces. Some critics think this is a poetic storytelling technique that was designed as a memory aid, given that the story existed long before writing was invented and had to be passed down orally for many centuries. It is definitely more aesthetically appealing than something like a journalist's report. The way this story is told has structure and balance, artistry and elegance.

Some readers, noting this artistic structural device in addition to the other poetic elements we've been discussing, have concluded that the "Creation Song" should be read as a work of artistic design rather than a literal historical account. Such readers see the seven days of creation as a figurative representation of God's handiwork, not a journalistic report or scientific description. On the other hand, conservative theologians believe that the meaning of the passage is obvious and literal, and that symbolic interpretation is not called for. Regardless of your point of view on this matter, we should all be able to agree that the text is rich in artistic value. Perhaps it has more artistic value than you expected to find. Genesis 1 in particular is highly crafted, highly structured, highly poetic… and that's just the first chapter of the Bible! The rest of this textbook will explore the complex art of many biblical books (and excerpts) that are best known in Western culture.

LESSON TWO STUDY GUIDE

Objective Identification:
Michelangelo, Sistine Chapel, elevated prose, refrain, strophe

Subjective Expression:

1) Opinion: Do you tend to think of the Bible as a collection of art works, a list of rules, a record of history, a handbook for life, a phone call from God, or something else entirely? Explain your answer.

2) Recall: List and explain three distinctly poetic qualities of Genesis 1.

3) Deeper Analysis: Do a character study for God, our story's protagonist. Come up with three adjectives to describe his character, and refer to specific verses that back up your observations.

GENESIS 2:4 - 3   ADAM AND EVE

Genesis 2

⁴These are the generations of the heavens and of the earth when they were created, in the day that the LORD God made the earth and the heavens, ⁵And every plant of the field before it was in the earth, and every herb of the field before it grew: for the LORD God had not caused it to rain upon the earth, and there was not a man to till the ground. ⁶But there went up a mist from the earth, and watered the whole face of the ground. ⁷And the LORD God formed man of the dust of the ground, and breathed into his nostrils the breath of life; and man became a living soul.

⁸And the LORD God planted a garden eastward in Eden; and there he put the man whom he had formed. ⁹And out of the ground made the LORD God to grow every tree that is pleasant to the sight, and good for food; the tree of life also in the midst of the garden, and the tree of knowledge of good and evil. ¹⁰And a river went out of Eden to water the garden; and from thence it was parted, and became into four heads. ¹¹The name of the first is Pison: that is it which compasseth the whole land of Havilah, where there is gold; ¹²And the gold of that land is good: there is bdellium and the onyx stone. ¹³And the name of the second river is Gihon: the same is it that compasseth the whole land of Ethiopia. ¹⁴And the name of the third river is Hiddekel: that is it which goeth toward the east of Assyria. And the fourth river is Euphrates.

¹⁵And the LORD God took the man, and put him into the garden of Eden to dress it and to keep it. ¹⁶And the LORD God commanded the man, saying, "Of every tree of the garden thou mayest freely eat: ¹⁷But of the tree of the knowledge of good and evil, thou shalt not eat of it: for in the day that thou eatest thereof thou shalt surely die."

¹⁸And the LORD God said, "It is not good that the man should be alone; I will make him an help meet[h] for him." ¹⁹And out of the ground the LORD God formed every beast of the field, and every fowl of the air; and brought them unto Adam to see what he would call them: and whatsoever Adam called every living creature, that was the name thereof. ²⁰And Adam gave names to all cattle, and to the fowl of the air, and to every beast of the field; but for Adam there was not found an help meet for him.

²¹And the LORD God caused a deep sleep to fall upon Adam, and he slept: and he took one of his ribs, and closed up the flesh instead thereof; ²²And the rib, which the LORD God had taken from man, made he a woman, and brought her unto the man. ²³And Adam said,

> "This is now bone of my bones,
>   and flesh of my flesh:
> she shall be called Woman,
>   because she was taken out of Man."

²⁴Therefore shall a man leave his father and his mother, and shall cleave unto his wife: and they shall be one flesh. ²⁵And they were both naked, the man and his wife, and were not ashamed.

---

[h] Help meet = a mate designed to be his helper (FI)

Genesis 3

[1]Now the serpent was more subtil[i] than any beast of the field which the LORD God had made. And he said unto the woman, "Yea, hath God said, Ye shall not eat of every tree of the garden?" [2]And the woman said unto the serpent, "We may eat of the fruit of the trees of the garden: [3]But of the fruit of the tree which is in the midst of the garden, God hath said, 'Ye shall not eat of it, neither shall ye touch it, lest ye die.'" [4]And the serpent said unto the woman, "Ye shall not surely die: [5]For God doth know that in the day ye eat thereof, then your eyes shall be opened, and ye shall be as gods, knowing good and evil." [6]And when the woman saw that the tree was good for food, and that it was pleasant to the eyes, and a tree to be desired to make one wise, she took of the fruit thereof, and did eat, and gave also unto her husband with her; and he did eat. [7]And the eyes of them both were opened, and they knew that they were naked; and they sewed fig leaves together, and made themselves aprons.

[8]And they heard the voice of the LORD God walking in the garden in the cool of the day: and Adam and his wife hid themselves from the presence of the LORD God amongst the trees of the garden. [9]And the LORD God called unto Adam, and said unto him, "Where art thou?" [10]And he said, "I heard thy voice in the garden, and I was afraid, because I was naked; and I hid myself." [11]And he said, "Who told thee that thou wast naked? Hast thou eaten of the tree, whereof I commanded thee that thou shouldest not eat?" [12]And the man said, "The woman whom thou gavest to be with me, she gave me of the tree, and I did eat." [13]And the LORD God said unto the woman, "What is this that thou hast done?" And the woman said, "The serpent beguiled[j] me, and I did eat."

[14]And the LORD God said unto the serpent, "Because thou hast done this,

> Thou art cursed above all cattle,
>> and above every beast of the field;
> upon thy belly shalt thou go,
>> and dust shalt thou eat
>> all the days of thy life:
> [15]And I will put enmity
>> between thee and the woman,
>> and between thy seed and her seed;[k]
> it shall bruise thy head,
>> and thou shalt bruise his heel." [l]

---

[i] Subtil = subtle or sneaky (FI)
[j] Beguiled = enticed, charmed, tricked (FI)
[k] Enmity = hatred; the offspring of snakes and the offspring of women will forevermore hate each other. (FI)
[l] A descendant of Eve shall bruise the head of the Serpent, and the Serpent will bruise the heel of a descendant of Eve. The NIV Bible translates this verse to say that the human descendant shall "crush" the Serpent's head, and the Serpent will "bruise" the heel of the descendant. Most translations use the same verb in both parts of the sentence ("bruise" or "strike"). (BHL)

[16] Unto the woman he said,

> "I will greatly multiply thy sorrow and thy conception;
> > in sorrow thou shalt bring forth children;
> and thy desire shall be to thy husband,
> > and he shall rule over thee."

[17] And unto Adam he said, "Because thou hast hearkened unto the voice of thy wife, and hast eaten of the tree, of which I commanded thee, saying, 'Thou shalt not eat of it':

> Cursed is the ground for thy sake;
> > in sorrow shalt thou eat of it
> > all the days of thy life;
> [18] Thorns also and thistles shall it bring forth to thee;
> > and thou shalt eat the herb of the field;
> [19] In the sweat of thy face
> > shalt thou eat bread,
> till thou return unto the ground;
> > for out of it wast thou taken:
> for dust thou art,
> > and unto dust shalt thou return."

[20] And Adam called his wife's name Eve; because she was the mother of all living. [21] Unto Adam also and to his wife did the LORD God make coats of skins, and clothed them.

[22] And the LORD God said, "Behold, the man is become as one of us, to know good and evil: and now, lest he[m] put forth his hand, and take also of the tree of life, and eat, and live for ever": [23] Therefore the LORD God sent him forth from the garden of Eden, to till the ground from whence he was taken. [24] So he drove out the man; and he placed at the east of the garden of Eden Cherubims,[n] and a flaming sword which turned every way, to keep the way of the tree of life.

---

[m] Lest he = "He must not be allowed to…" (FI)
[n] Cherubim = a type of angel (FI)

LESSON THREE:
THE BIBLE AS LITERATURE

In this lesson we begin to outline some literary guidelines for exploring the Bible. What do I mean exactly with all this reference to the Bible "as literature" and talk of "exploring literary features" of the text? Well, there are many different ways of looking at and responding to the Bible, and a literary focus is just one of them. You could re-tell the story of Adam and Eve to children and teach them a lesson about temptation. You could read one of the Psalms at a funeral or wedding for the purpose of expressing a beautiful, hopeful sentiment. You could read the Bible like a theologian, for the purpose of discovering the nature of God and drawing a blueprint for Jewish or Christian spiritual growth. You could examine the Bible for its cultural insights into ancient history. You could read the Bible looking for a dramatic supernatural tale, for the purpose of entertainment. You could also read the Bible with a literary approach, simply because it is a great and enduring work of art.

LITERARY TERMS GLOSSARY

Protagonist
Antagonist
Conflict
Climax
Resolution
Theme
Symbol
Motif
Characterization
Narrative Persona
Irony
Archetype
Figurative Language
Imagery
Mood
Tone
Diction
Parallelism
Structure

ASSESSMENT OF LITERARY DEVICES

There are three components that contribute to a literary analysis of the Bible. The first is simple: apply the literary concepts you would normally use in a literature class. If you are reading a Bible story, identify the protagonist and the conflict. Judge the characters. See if you can find any metaphors, symbols, motifs, irony, or other literary devices. Draw out a theme. If you are reading a Bible poem, pay special attention to figurative language and imagery. Anything you might do when studying Poe or Twain or Shakespeare, do also with a biblical text.

HISTORICAL CRITICISM

> **Literary Criticism:** the art or practice of judging and commenting on the qualities and character of literary works (from the Oxford dictionary)
>
> **Historical Criticism:** literary criticism in the light of historical evidence or based on the context in which a work was written, including facts about the author's life and the historical and social circumstances of the time (from Encyclopaedia Britannica)

In the context of literature and film, "to criticize" does not mean "to make insults." Rather, it means to observe it closely and analyze its qualities and character (which could, of course, include insults). Among all the literary scholars in the world, there are differences of opinion about how to best critique literature, because there are always different angles from which you can begin your analysis: you might love a particular movie because it has important things to say about current social issues, whereas someone else might hate it because the dialogue was bland or the acting was weak. When it comes to criticism, there are always different angles of emphasis. Historical criticism requires (obviously) a historical angle.

A critic performing a historical analysis would research the author as well as issues of setting and culture relevant to the work's original composition and audience. For instance, if you were reading Shakespeare in your English class, a historical critique would require you to investigate the social and political climate of Shakespeare's culture as well as the types of people who may have attended his plays at The Globe. Regarding The Tempest, for example, a historical critic would discover that the play makes a political statement about the morality of colonization. A critic of Mark Twain's Huckleberry Finn would analyze its post-Civil War roots and the author's feelings about Southern culture and slavery. Historical criticism is a traditional and often an illuminating exercise in studying literature.

When reading the Bible, it is often helpful to do a historical assessment of the text, particularly since its 66 books were written over a span of more than 1000 years and in multiple historical settings. Such a reading might include an investigation of Jewish or Hellenistic culture and Hebrew or Greek language, or possibly the cultures of nearby civilizations in the ancient world. In the creation story of Genesis 1, for instance, one might research how other ancient Near East cultures viewed the physical earth (flat with a heavenly dome) and then decide if the Hebrew version of creation is similar or different, and if this has any bearing on our understanding of Genesis. Historical research and criticism can introduce you to new ideas or just open up some interesting comparisons and contrasts. It places the literature into an accurate cultural context rather than assuming 21st Century readers think exactly the same way as the biblical authors of 2000-3000 years ago did.º

As I write this section on historical analysis of the Bible, a copy of the <u>Archaeological Study Bible</u> sits on my desk. This NIV Bible includes introductions, footnotes, illustrations, and sidebars with information relevant to historical criticism of the text. For example, as I turn to the Book of Genesis, I find information on Moses' presumed authorship, creation myths from elsewhere in the ancient Near East, the geographical location of Eden, and the civilization of Sumer. In this textbook, we will look at similar ideas from similar sources.

GENRE TYPES

Apocalypse
Biography
Blogs
Criticism
Description
Drama
Epic Poetry
Epistles
Essays
Exposition
Fiction
History
Journalism
Law
Legend
Lyric Poetry
Myth
Narrative
Persuasion
Prophecy
Proverbs
Speeches

EVALUATION OF GENRE

Our third component for performing a literary analysis of the Bible is a bit more complex. First, we must acknowledge that human beings use words for many different purposes and in many different ways, and that a good literary analysis considers this fact. Language is symbolic and situational, and to really make sense of it, we have to figure out its context and form and intent. For example, if someone utters the sound "mat," he could mean a number of different things. If he is standing near a door, he might mean the door mat. If he is standing near a table, he could mean a placemat. Or, possibly, he could be speaking of a person named Matt, and if so, then you would have to figure out *which* Matt. This is a small example of why literary thinking requires awareness of *intent* in language. Genre is related to intent.

Once human beings start stringing together groups of words, the process of identifying intent becomes more complex. Say you are sitting on a park bench and find a scrap of paper with the following words handwritten on it: *bread, milk, butter, eggs, cherries, apples, chicken legs.*

º Do you ever use Spark Notes? The very first component of a Spark Note is a section on "Context." This section contains historical background and can contribute to a historical critique of the literature. Check out the "Context" section for <u>The Tempest</u> or <u>Huck Finn</u>.

You would likely interpret this text as a grocery list. The intent seems to be giving instructions for a shopping trip. But did you notice that the list has rhythm and rhyme, as well as alliteration? Try reading it aloud, like this:

> *Bread, milk,*
> *Butter, eggs,*
> *Cherries, apples,*
> *Chicken legs!*

Once you have noticed the musical features of the text, you might be more inclined to see it as a children's rhyme rather than a grocery list. So, was the intent of the text to help someone shop, or to get kids chanting and clapping rhythmically? All these observations are "literary" in nature.

Now, let's build up to something longer than a list or chant: a collection of sentences that lasts for several pages. With a longer text – a full work of literature – you must determine whether you are looking at a story, a speech, a poem, a personal letter, or some other type of written communication. If it is a story, then you still have to decide if it's more like a fairy tale or a biography, or something else altogether; after all, a fairy tale will merit a very different type of interpretation than a biography, since they have such different *intents*. In the 66 books of the Bible, there are many different types of texts, which correspond with many different intents of many different authors. When you are able to identify the genre of a Bible passage – which corresponds to its form and intent – you are better able to define your personal relationship with the text. Just as you will react differently to a grocery list versus a children's rhyme, or a fairy tale versus a biography, you will likewise react differently to Genesis depending on whether you see it as a history or a myth. As you identify a Bible book or passage's genre, you establish an interpretive position toward the text based on what you think the author intended.

Three Steps for a Literary Analysis of the Bible
1. Assessment of literary devices – Look for artistry
2. Historical criticism – Consider context and setting
3. Evaluation of genre – Determine your relationship to the text

PRODUCING YOUR OWN LITERARY ANALYSIS

Now, let's take an overall glance back at the three phases of literary analysis we've discussed in this lesson: assessing literary devices, considering historical context, and evaluating the genre (see chart on previous page). You can practice doing this three-step literary analysis of Bible passages by using the following **Biblical Literary Inventory**. This is simply a convenient checklist of literary concerns designed to help you focus your thoughts and remember the various literary devices you've learned in English classes, plus the historical and genre-related principles explained in this lesson. Throughout this textbook, you will find three versions of the **Inventory**: one for narrative, one for poetry, and one for expository prose. Often, we will culminate a lesson with a corresponding version of the **Inventory,** which may offer tips and reminders, provide a few sample answers, or leave you to analyze the text independently. Below, you will find a mostly-completed **Inventory for Narrative** that helps you to take a closer look at the Adam and Eve story. You will see that items 1-13 are part of the first step listed above, the assessment of literary devices such as conflict, theme, and characterization. Item 14 requires a historical angle of analysis, and item 15 asks you to determine genre and assess its significance. Blank versions of each type of **Inventory** are located in the Appendices.

BIBLICAL LITERARY INVENTORY: NARRATIVE

Narrative: The Story of Adam and Eve

I. Protagonist versus Antagonist – Adam versus the Serpent, or Adam versus curiosity... do you see any other possibilities? _Adam vs the wild_

II. Inciting Incident – Adam is given the Garden of Eden to tend, and he is forbidden from eating the fruit of one tree, called the Tree of the Knowledge of Good and Evil. Now we have a potential conflict.

III. Rising Action – God allows Adam to name all the animals, and he is given a mate, the first woman, Eve. The Serpent comes to Eve and convinces her to eat the fruit, which she does, and then she tempts Adam to do the same.

IV. Climax – Adam eats the forbidden fruit. Nothing will ever be the same again.

V. Falling Action – The Serpent and Eve receive punishments for their disobedience. The Serpent is cursed to crawl in the dust, be the target of hatred, and eventually have his head crushed by the foot of mankind. Eve is cursed in that her husband will be dominant over her, and her children will bring her pain in childbirth.

VI. Resolution – Adam, the protagonist, is punished. He is cursed with sorrow and with the difficulty of farming the land for his sustenance, rather than simply eating from the trees of the Garden. He is sentenced to an eventual death ("dust to dust") and an immediate expulsion from the paradise of Eden. It is also interesting to note that the Serpent (an antagonist) has been punished for his victory over Adam.

VII. Theme – The story of Adam and Eve asserts that disobedience to God has dire consequences. It also suggests that the consequences come about even if one is deceived – human beings have an obligation to keep God's commands. A theme of gender differences is also explored. What do you think the story reveals about the differences between men and women? _Women came from man, and God said that her desire was to his husband. God also said he would rule over her. Man has dominance over woman._

VIII. Symbolism – The Tree of the Knowledge of Good and Evil is a symbol, representing mankind's desire to know what God knows, to be like God. It also represents the line between <u>knowing</u> what's right and wrong and <u>NOT knowing</u>: the line between blissful naïveté and burdensome moral awareness. The crossing of this boundary is more than mere disobedience; it's a life changer. It is the end of innocence, the end of easy contentment, the end of simplicity, the beginning of ethical dilemmas and social conflict. It raises a variety of issues related to dangerous knowledge (think nuclear power, nuclear bombs, nuclear waste) and difficult moral debates (are nuclear bombs acceptable or evil?). Can you think of any other modern issues that somehow relate to the symbolism of "eating from the tree of the knowledge of good and evil" and then paying the consequences? _defense, gun, murder._

IX. Motif – One might note a motif of dominance that extends from Genesis 1 to 3. Mankind is given dominance over the animals. However, God maintains dominance over man by setting up the boundary of the Tree. When man defies God's dominance, God essentially puts mankind in his place – Adam loses his right to have easy food, and Eve loses the right to feel equal to her husband (the man becomes dominant over the woman). Even the Serpent loses the right to walk upright. An emerging theme is that although mankind enjoys a certain amount of dominance over the earth, he is not top dog and would be wise to keep his pride in check.

X. Character Development – Although not the protagonist, the character of God is important and interesting. He is generous in that he gives Adam everything he needs for comfort and companionship. He is mysterious in that he sets up a rather strange prohibition with the off-limits tree, and also when he seems to be unaware of where Adam and Eve are hiding. He is also firm and strict, perhaps unnecessarily harsh, when he lowers the death penalty for a single mouthful of forbidden fruit. God is a complex character who loves extravagantly and punishes severely.

XI. Narrative Persona – The Genesis narrator is clearly a religious persona, someone who is trying to convey the power of God and the proper role of mankind within the created world. For this reason, even if we think that God's response to Adam and Eve is a bit harsh, we must try to view the narrative through the eyes of the storyteller, who never provides any hint that he thinks God is being unfair. The point of the story is not God's harshness. The point of the story seems to be the culpability of mankind in getting himself into a situation of difficulty and death. The storyteller is trying to show you what's wrong with mankind, not what's wrong with God.

XII. Irony, Contrast, Foil and/or Reversals – This story includes a significant reversal in fortune for mankind. Adam goes from being the most privileged of all creatures to being an exile in a world of deception, difficulty, and death.

XIII. Additional Literary Devices – The Serpent in this tale is archetypal. Across many cultures and time periods, snakes have been used to represent evil. Like Nagini in <u>Harry Potter</u> or the pit of snakes in <u>Raiders of the Lost Ark</u>, snakes in art and literature often embody the very personification of darkness and death. This lends itself to the Christian interpretation of the passage, in that the Serpent is considered to be the devil in disguise. Along those lines, Genesis 3:15 is read as foreshadowing of Satan's defeat through Christ, which is explored throughout the New Testament.

XIV. Historical Criticism – There is no verifiable historical setting for the creation stories, nor any clearly-identifiable date of composition for Genesis. Therefore, it is difficult to pull any history-related analysis from the text. Some theologians have added up all the genealogies in the Old Testament and estimate a literal creation event as happening around 4000 B.C.E., a position called Young Earth Creationism. The scientific record estimates that the earth is 4.5 billion years old. Interestingly, the prevailing scientific description of the beginning of the universe, called the Big Bang (13 billion years ago), actually bears some fascinating similarities to Genesis 1:1 in that the hot and dense state of the newborn universe was "without form, and void." Furthermore, the explosive "Bang" would have released radiation that "created" the first light. The Big Bang theory was invented by a Catholic priest named Georges Lemaitre, who described it as "the Cosmic Egg exploding at the moment of the creation" and believed his theory complemented the Genesis account. Do you think it the Genesis 1 narrative is compatible with the Big Bang theory?

Yes, only if God created man much later after the event.

XV. Genre Awareness – To help you shape your final assessment of the text, select the genre that best fits the story. In the case of Genesis 1-11, most literary scholars choose *mythology*. Some theologians choose *history*. For a more complete discussion of the definition of mythology, proceed to Lesson Four. Additional definitions for other genres will be explored in future lessons throughout this textbook.

      ___ Mythology: Symbolically, what does the story reveal about human nature or God?
      ___ Legend / Epic: What themes of Judeo-Christian identity emerge?
      ___ History: What historical events have a practical bearing on the present and future?
      ___ Biography: Why is the subject of the biography worth special attention?
      ___ Drama: What aspects of the play a "hold a mirror up to nature"?
      ___ Short Story: What elements of intentional storytelling contribute to theme and unity?
      ___ Narrative Poetry: Why was the story told via elevated and/or figurative language?

Based on your selection, provide a response to the genre-related question provided above:

LESSON FOUR:
GENESIS AND MYTHOLOGY

Today we embark on a controversial topic – mentioning the Bible and "mythology" together in the same sentence might to some feel like a statement that equates the God of the Bible with Zeus. However, we are not setting out to label Genesis as a fairy tale. While in everyday conversation the word "myth" is often used to mean the same thing as "falsehood," this is a not a *literary* definition and therefore not appropriate to a literary analysis. There are many variations on the definition of "myth," from <u>Webster</u> to <u>Wikipedia</u>. One literature textbook might call it fictional, while another might employ more faith-friendly words like "religious" and "explanatory." Most literary scholars classify Genesis chapters 1-11 as mythology simply because these stories share many literary characteristics with the most ancient stories of other cultures, from the Africans to the Australians. The most notable characteristic of mythology is, in fact, a distinctly religious or philosophical intent.

This textbook will utilize a definition of mythology that comprises four of the most common elements of myth that you might find in a survey of various literary dictionaries and textbooks:

> *Myths are the world's oldest stories, passed down from generation to generation since ancient times; their content is unverifiable, usually supernatural or religious, and they attempt to explain life's mysteries or reveal deep truths about humanity.*

Throughout the rest of this lesson, we will take this definition apart, summarize it, analyze it, and see how well it applies to the tale of Pandora, whom the ancient Greeks knew as the world's first woman. If you are not familiar with Pandora, you can read a short version of her story at the end of this lesson. Let's get started thinking about mythology with a closer look at the first clause from the definition.

1) **Myths are the world's oldest stories, passed down from generation to generation.**
   Myths originated long before writing. They existed in an oral form for centuries before

their written forms became available to readers. The tale of Pandora, for instance, has been passed along for more than 3000 years, and no single definitive written source exists.

2) **Because they are so old, the settings of myths are generally pre-historic and unverifiable.** There are few-to-no historical certainties in myths, and certainly no eyewitness testimony like you would expect from a formal historical text. History generally requires a good primary or secondary source, and stories this old don't come with this kind of manuscript support. Obviously, no one observed Pandora opening her box and wrote it down for us with eyewitness authority. There are no concrete sources and no archeological evidence.

3) **Myths almost always concern the supernatural.** This makes sense because most (if not all) ancient cultures saw the world in religious terms. Myths are almost always religious in nature, whereas a legend or folk tale is often secular. Folk tales originated with the "folks" and myths originated with the divine. The story of Pandora is all about the powers of Zeus, making it more of a myth than a folk tale.

4) **Myths attempt to explain life's mysteries or reveal deep truths.** Some myths explain simple, physical mysteries like the passage of the sun across the sky. Some myths go deeper, explaining why people act the way they do – for instance, why women are so irresistible to men, as in the Pandora story. In this way, myths always reach for some type of truth. It might not be a concrete, factual sort of truth, but let us not confuse the word "truth" with the word "fact." For example, even though Pandora never literally existed and there is no _factual_ record of her magical box in history or archeology, it is still very _true_ that human beings are dangerously curious, and it is also true that the presence of evil in this world is almost always accompanied by hope, as we see in the story. Pandora was not a _real_ person, but the story is about the _reality_ of being human. Regardless of their physical factuality, myths are meant to be revelatory in some fashion regarding the mysteries and deeper truths of human life on earth.

Now let's summarize and shorten our definition of myth with a quick list of adjectives: ***Myths are ancient, unverifiable, supernatural, and revelatory.*** With this simplified approach, we can proceed into an analysis of Genesis 1-4.

First, the story of creation is as **ancient** as we can get, reaching back to the very beginning of time. Second, Adam and Eve, as characters in the Genesis narrative, are **unverifiable** – there is no archeological evidence or eyewitness report of Adam as a character who lived in Eden, named the animals, married Eve, and ate the forbidden fruit. This doesn't mean his existence is an impossibility – only that it is impossible to verify. Third, the story is clearly **supernatural and religious**. And, fourth, it is **explanatory and revelatory**, providing explanations for why people wear clothes, why snakes slither, and why childbirth is painful, and also revealing several profound truths about the human race. Some of those truths are universal, and some are religious, and it is therefore up to the readers which truths are to be embraced or believed. For instance, the Hebrew narrator clearly believes in God and asserts that God was the starting point for the earth and humanity. Humans are described as the custodians of life on earth, with God as the ultimate authority. Even if you do not believe in God at all, there is human truth here: indeed, mankind has largely dominated the earth, and yet we are still not the highest power on the planet. We can manage zoos, cure diseases, and build skyscrapers, but we are no match for the fierceness of wild animals, the invulnerability of certain bacteria, the vast force of a tsunami, or the long-term danger of global warming.

Indeed, the fourth part of our definition – that myths reveal truths about human life – is the most important part of studying mythology, so let's keep digging into the Eden story for a while. The richness of this myth in particular has long fascinated religious believers and nonbelievers alike, throughout the history of Western literature. The Eden story speaks to the ambition and pride of mankind, via the enduring symbolism we find in the Tree of the Knowledge of Good and Evil. The tree represents the temptation of ultimate knowledge, and how human beings will do anything to "be like God."

UNIVERSAL TRUTHS FROM EDEN

Humans are a dominant force upon the earth

Humans are not in ultimate control of the earth or their own fates

Humans are ambitious, curious, and prideful

Humans have a natural awareness of good and evil, unlike other creatures

The knowledge of humanity sometimes hurts humanity

Human culture tends to be patriarchal

Humans are naturally inclined to break rules, lie, and defy authority

Humans have a natural need for companionship

Human life is not paradise – there will be pain and hard work to stay alive

How true it is. Consider for a moment what we humans have done with our knowledge of the atom. We have unlocked the power within the very building blocks of matter, and the result is astounding. We can power entire cities with nuclear energy. We can also blow up entire cities with nuclear bombs. But what can we do with the aftermath of atom-splitting? We inevitably end up with nuclear waste, and we have not yet figured out how to dispose of it. We cannot make it go away. So far, all we know how to do is to lock it up, bury it, hope it stays there and does not irreparably pollute our planet. Is this not the story of Eden come alive in a modern sense? We have eaten the forbidden fruit of knowledge, tried to be like God, and the result is expulsion from Eden.

> **A CHRISTIAN READING OF THE EDEN STORY**
>
> The moment when Adam and Eve eat of the fruit is called the "**fall from grace**" in Christian theology, meaning that mankind is no longer suited for companionship with a holy God due to the sin that entered the world at that fateful moment. From this point onward, humans are said to have a "**sin nature.**"
>
> However, when God tells the serpent that a "seed" of Eve will "bruise" his head, he is foreshadowing the future birth of a human child – Jesus – who will one day deal a fatal blow to the serpent, who is Satan. So when God bars Adam from returning to Eden, he does so in order to prevent him from eating of the Tree of Life and therefore making his fallen state eternal.

Some readers think that the story of Eden is a larger symbol of human evolution. In this case, Genesis 1:1 would coincide with the Big Bang, and the days of creation would represent eons of earth's evolution. Day six, the climax of the creation story, would describe in narrative form how human beings came about as the most highly developed form of life, and therefore most like "God." They are given dominion over the other animals, further reflecting human dominance in the animal kingdom. The second part of the creation story, set in Eden, explains how early man formed patriarchal family units and learned to farm. The prohibition of eating from the tree might signify the development of social codes and laws, and the results of eating from the tree represent the emergence of a moral code of right and wrong. From this point on, the story moves into the more philosophical contemplations of human relationships with each other and with God. In this fashion, many religious thinkers are able to find truth in Genesis alongside evolutionary science.

The social and metaphysical subject matter in Genesis is thought-provoking and enduring. The nature of its message has profound symbolic meaning, which is the defining quality of mythical truth. As the primary mythology of Western culture, Genesis still speaks to the heart of a modern world-view.

PANDORA'S BOX

According to the Greeks, the first human woman was named Pandora. Zeus, the king of the gods, oversaw her creation. He had Hephaestus build her out of water and clay. He had Aphrodite teach her the ways of love and beauty, Athena the secrets of wisdom, and Apollo the art of music. In fact, the name Pandora means "all-gifted."

Pandora was a gift for mankind, but not a very sincere gift. Zeus was angry with Prometheus for having stolen fire from Mount Olympus and given it to humanity. Zeus did not want humans to enjoy the powers of the gods, so he reciprocated with a scheme. Pandora was presented to Prometheus' brother as a bride. The happy couple also received a wedding present from Zeus – a box that they were never supposed to open under any circumstance. But Pandora's curiosity got the best of her, and she opened it. As soon as the seal was cracked, every Evil now known to man escaped from the box and spread quickly over the earth. She tried to close the lid, but it was too late. Only one thing remained at the bottom of the box, and it was called Hope.

"The Temptation of Eve"
by John Roddam Spencer-Stanhope

"Pandora"
by Jules Joseph Lefebvre (1882)

LESSONS THREE & FOUR STUDY GUIDE

Objective Identification: Mythology, fiction, metaphysical, revelation/revelatory, Pandora

Subjective Expression:

1) Comparison: Compare and contrast the Hebrew story of Eve to the Greek story of Pandora's Box. You may also wish to compare and contrast the Victorian era paintings (from the previous page) of the two women.

2) Culture Connection: Apply the four-part definition of mythology as presented here to another creation myth from a culture of your choice – perhaps from your family's cultural heritage.

3) Research: You may have noticed that the Genesis account does not identify the Tree of the Knowledge of Good and Evil as an apple tree. Find out where this common assumption started.

4) Deeper Analysis: Interpret the gender-related theme behind Adam and Eve's curses: how does the Genesis storyteller view the differences between men and women? If you wish, ask a Jewish or Christian authority figure to assist you (or find one on-line).

5) Opinion: Did this lesson change your concept of "myth" in any way? Explain.

6) Research: Look for information about "Mitochondrial Eve" and "Y-Chromosomal Adam." Find out if the Adam and Eve characters are currently scientifically verifiable.

QUOTABLE QUOTES

> HISTORY can tell you facts about a people, but MYTH shows you their personality, their beliefs, fears, and hopes. Relying only on HISTORY to tell you about a people is like reading someone's driver's license instead of meeting him or her face-to-face.

Zachary Hamby
"Why Study Mythology"
Teacherweb.com

Scott

Now there you go doing exactly what I expected from the beginning, reducing the importance of Genesis to mere mythology! My family, church, and I take offense at that label, which basically says that the Bible is not historical or factual. I think there is plenty of evidence for Genesis being historical and factual!

Dear Scott,

Your assessment of Genesis as history is not uncommon or unfounded. However, one of the primary goals of this text is to show you how literary scholars approach the Bible… and now you know. And, you know *why*. So if you care to disagree, you are now better equipped for the debate.

That issue notwithstanding, here is a fact that may help your historical argument. There is indeed a significant difference between the Hebrew myths and those from many other cultures worldwide: Genesis contains several very specific genealogical lists, and that is unique. Check out the genealogies found in chapters 4, 10 and 11 (they are not reproduced in this textbook because they are not narrative, but you can find them in any actual Bible). Genesis records a name-specific patriarchal lineage from Adam to Abraham. Some theologians have found this sufficient evidence to justify calling Genesis history; it may also suggest a historical intent. Secular scholars, however, do not apply the *history* label because Genesis lacks primary or secondary source support and has few concrete details (unlike the Moses narrative, which does fit a *history* definition; Lesson 10 will explore this further).

I would encourage you to explore these ideas further outside of class. There are many good books available on the topic of how to read Genesis and how to think about Genesis in the context of history and science (see page 277 for book recommendations). The next lesson in this book will outline more of those ideas for you.

LESSON FIVE: GENESIS AND SCIENCE

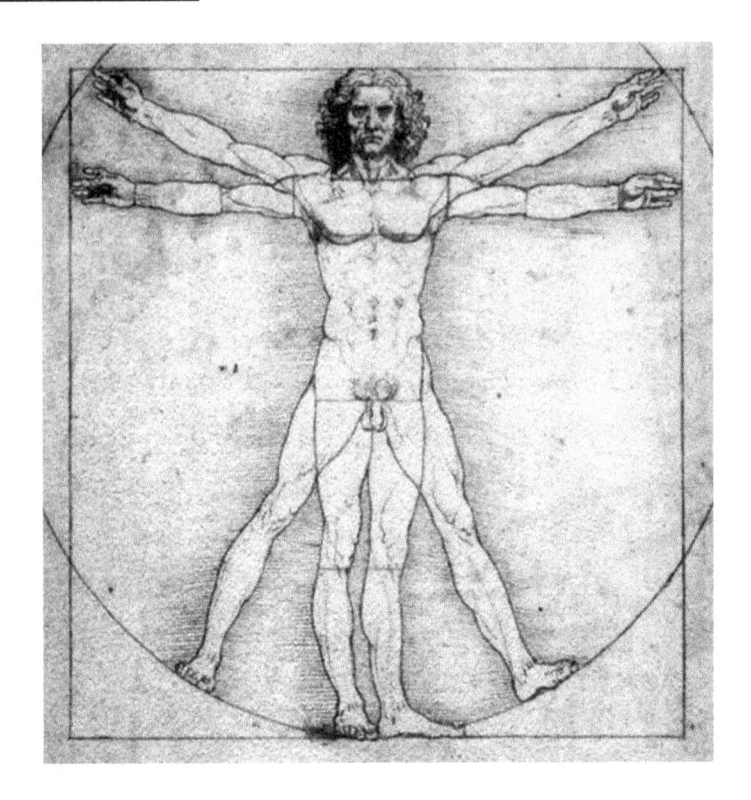

"Vitruvian Man" by Leonardo da Vinci (1490)

In the United States, the debates between creationists and evolutionists have raged for nearly 100 years. Persons of faith who believe in creation often argue that Genesis should be read as a supplement to the scientific study of evolution. They say it is only fair that the popular scientific "theory" be taught alongside the religious "theory." Science teachers, however, assert that religious studies have no place in a science classroom.

It should be noted that English and social studies teachers work in a different realm from their science colleagues. In particular, the study of Genesis has an important place in a literature classroom. As students of literature, we come to the text of Genesis 1-11 with an interest in narrative and poetry, with science set aside. So why have a lesson on Genesis and science? Our purpose is to acknowledge the creation-evolution controversy in its relationship to the Genesis text and the interpretive options the text presents. We will explore some basic terminology with which you may continue your own investigation of the creation-evolution debate outside the classroom. Where do you find yourself among the field of participants?

YOUNG EARTH CREATIONISTS

Genesis as history: From a "YEC" point of view, Genesis 1-11 is read as literal, accurate history, and the world is believed to have been created in six 24-hour days about 6,000 years ago. A YEC would also believe that Noah's flood literally covered the entire earth, killing all people and animals on the planet except for Noah and his family, as described in the biblical text.

Literary perspective on young earth creationism: A purely historical/literal reading raises some natural questions: How can the earth receive light on day one, when the sun isn't created until day four? How can one man actually name all the animals of the earth? How is it that the Genesis 1 account says animals were created before men, and Genesis 2 says Adam was created before the animals?

Theologians and "creation scientists" have posed various answers to these questions, for instance that the light of the Spirit of God illuminated the universe prior to the sun's formation. Regarding Adam and the animals, YEC's point out that he only named the "beasts of the field," the "fowl of the air," and the "cattle" (no insects or fish), and furthermore that he may have only assigned names to each *genus* or *family* rather than the much longer list of individual *species* (with *genus* or *family* being parallel to the "kinds" of animals mentioned in 1:24). Answers in Genesis.org, the website run by Ken Ham's Creation Museum, estimates that the task of naming 2,500 *genera* would have required less than four hours with an hourly five-minute break.[p] This website presents numerous arguments in holding with a literal interpretation of the Bible.

OLD EARTH CREATIONISTS

Genesis as history that is open to interpretation: OEC's believe in creation (that God put mankind fully formed onto the planet with no process of evolution) but they are more open to mainline claims of physical science, for instance that the earth is 4.5 billion years old – thus the "old earth" moniker. Persons who hold this point of view are sometimes called progressive creationists.

Literary perspective on old earth creationism: Although Old Earth Creationists believe that Genesis should be identified as history, they are generally more open than YEC's to some non-

---

[p] Kulikovsky, Andrew. "How Could Adam Have Named All the Animals in a Single Day?" Answers in Genesis.org. 1 June 2005. Web.

traditional interpretations of the text, for instance in the areas of word translation and storyteller point of view.

Most significantly, an OEC would likely be aware of the meaning of the Hebrew word *yom* in Genesis 1, where the seven days of creation are explained. This word is translated as "day," but some language scholars explain that, in other places in the Bible, *yom* can mean something like "period of time." In Genesis 2:4, the word *yom/day* refers backward to the completed six-day period of creation: "These are the generations of the heavens and of the earth when they were created, in the day that the Lord God made the earth and the heavens." This usage illustrates how the word *yom/day* can vary in meaning depending on its context. Keeping this in mind, one might interpret the days of Genesis 1 to be unspecified eras of time rather than literal 24-hour periods.

Furthermore, an OEC might be open to the idea of Genesis 1 as a symbolic poem, given its poetic nature. Since the original author recorded his thoughts poetically, an OEC might be open to a poetic/metaphorical reading of the text. Thus, Genesis 1 may be read as divinely-inspired poetry wherein the days of creation figuratively represent eras. It should be noted, however, that in chapter 2, when the storyteller ceases to use poetic language, a shift to literal history would occur.

Another example of non-traditional interpretation would involve the reading of Genesis 6-9, where we find the story of Noah's flood. This tale can be read with an interpretive sensitivity to its ancient Middle Eastern point of view – that the original storyteller likely *experienced* the "great flood" such that it *seemed* to cover the entire world and was of course reported this way, when in reality it may have only covered the Middle Eastern or Mediterranean region.

In summary, an OEC reader trusts the Genesis narratives as divinely inspired and spiritually authoritative, but recognizes that the subtleties of the text might invite new angles of translation and interpretation. It is a slightly less rigid view of creationism.

THEISTIC EVOLUTIONISTS

Genesis as myth (perhaps an inspired myth): From a TE point of view, Genesis 1-11 would be read as a work of mythology, having no relevance to scientific thought and little to nothing in common with the genre of historical literature. Darwinian evolution would be fully accepted alongside faith in God and in God's authorship of the evolutionary process. Genesis is seen by many TE's as fully useful for spiritual instruction but not for scientific details of any sort. The creation stories would be viewed as symbolic. A Christian or Jewish TE might very well believe that the Hebrew myths were inspired by God and superior to other world mythologies, and that perhaps other cultures' mythologies descended from the Genesis stories, but they would not look upon Adam or Noah as historical.

Literary perspective on theistic evolution: TE's would likely believe that different types of writing call for different types of reading, i.e. that mythology should be read for symbolic and spiritual messages, poetry should be read for emotional and sensory impact, and science should be read with an eye for concrete observation and logical conclusion. Judeo-Christian TE's go to Genesis to learn about mankind's moral nature and relationship to God, and they go to scientists to learn about mankind's biological past and present.

Opponents of theistic evolution say that to "reduce" Genesis to mythology invalidates all other spiritual and historical claims of the remaining books of the Bible, a position held by many conservative readers. TE's are not bothered by this objection, arguing that the different books of the Bible came to us in different genres and therefore require different types of thinking. Genesis 1-11, because it looks like mythology, asks for a symbolic reading; in the same way, the gospels, because they look like biography, may ask for a more literal reading.

ATHEISTS / EVOLUTIONISTS

Genesis as mythology and fiction: An atheist would consider Genesis not only myth but fiction. It may be read for cultural or humanistic insight or as entertainment.

Literary perspective on evolution: An interest in Genesis might be archetypal, cultural, or artistic – no different from an interest in novels, fairy tales, or movies. God is a pretty fascinating character: hiding himself, revealing himself, loving people, cursing people, and generally overseeing a wild, sexy course of events. The themes are largely universal and worthy of lively philosophical debates. So even if you classify yourself among this final category of skeptical Genesis readers, you should find plenty of human interest here. Genesis certainly holds up as an excellent source of narrative, compelling enough in its drama to captivate audiences for around 3000 years.

LESSON FIVE STUDY GUIDE

Objective Identification:

Old Earth Creation, Young Earth Creation, evolution, Darwin, theistic evolution

Subjective Expression:

1) Recall: Summarize the point of view that you find most believable. Explain why it makes sense to you.

2) Opinion: Which position is least appealing to you? What one aspect of this position might you deem reasonable or at least sympathetic?

3) Further Research: Look up the "Scopes Monkey Trials" and learn about the court case that first challenged the teaching of evolution in public schools.

QUOTABLE QUOTES

> If…we believe that we are living souls, God's dust and God's breath, acting our parts among other creatures all made of the same dust and breath as ourselves; and if we understand that we are free, within the obvious limits of moral human life, to do evil or good to ourselves and to the other creatures – then all our acts have a supreme significance. If it is true that we are living souls and morally free, then all of us are artists. All of us are makers, within mortal terms and limits, of our lives, of one another's lives, of things we need and use...

Wendell Berry
The Art of the Commonplace: The Agrarian Essays

GENESIS 4 — CAIN AND ABEL

¹And Adam knew Eve his wife; and she conceived, and bare Cain, and said, "I have gotten a man from the LORD." ²And she again bare his brother Abel. And Abel was a keeper of sheep, but Cain was a tiller of the ground.

³And in process of time it came to pass, that Cain brought of the fruit of the ground an offering unto the LORD. ⁴And Abel, he also brought of the firstlings of his flock and of the fat thereof. And the LORD had respect unto Abel and to his offering: ⁵But unto Cain and to his offering he had not respect. And Cain was very wroth, and his countenance fell.[q] ⁶And the LORD said unto Cain, "Why art thou wroth? and why is thy countenance fallen? ⁷If thou doest well, shalt thou not be accepted? and if thou doest not well, sin lieth at the door. And unto thee shall be his desire, and thou shalt rule over him."

⁸And Cain talked with Abel his brother: and it came to pass, when they were in the field, that Cain rose up against Abel his brother, and slew him.

⁹And the LORD said unto Cain, "Where is Abel thy brother?" And he said, "I know not: Am I my brother's keeper?" ¹⁰And he said, "What hast thou done? the voice of thy brother's blood crieth unto me from the ground. ¹¹And now art thou cursed from the earth, which hath opened her mouth to receive thy brother's blood from thy hand; ¹²When thou tillest the ground, it shall not henceforth yield unto thee her strength; a fugitive and a vagabond[r] shalt thou be in the earth." ¹³And Cain said unto the LORD, "My punishment is greater than I can bear. ¹⁴Behold, thou hast driven me out this day from the face of the earth; and from thy face shall I be hid; and I shall be a fugitive and a vagabond in the earth; and it shall come to pass, that every one that findeth me shall slay me."

¹⁵And the LORD said unto him, "Therefore whosoever slayeth Cain, vengeance shall be taken on him sevenfold." And the LORD set a mark upon Cain, lest any finding him should kill him. ¹⁶And Cain went out from the presence of the LORD, and dwelt in the land of Nod, on the east of Eden.

¹⁷And Cain knew his wife; and she conceived, and bare Enoch: and he builded a city, and called the name of the city, after the name of his son, Enoch. ¹⁸And unto Enoch was born Irad: and Irad begat Mehujael: and Mehujael begat Methusael: and Methusael begat Lamech. ¹⁹And Lamech took unto him two wives: the name of the one was Adah, and the name of the other Zillah. ²⁰And Adah bare Jabal: he was the father of such as dwell in tents, and of such as have cattle. ²¹And his brother's name was Jubal: he was the father of all such as handle the harp and organ. ²²And Zillah, she also bare Tubalcain, an instructer of every artificer in brass and iron: and the sister of Tubalcain was Naamah. ²³And Lamech said unto his wives, Adah and Zillah, "Hear my voice; ye wives of Lamech, hearken unto my speech: for I have slain a man to my wounding, and a young man to my hurt. ²⁴If Cain shall be avenged sevenfold, truly Lamech seventy and sevenfold."

---

[q] Wroth = angry (full of wrath); countenance = facial expression. (FI)
[r] Fugitive = someone who is running away from the law; vagabond = someone who wanders without a home (FI)

²⁵And Adam knew his wife again; and she bare a son, and called his name Seth: "For God," said she, "hath appointed me another seed instead of Abel, whom Cain slew." ²⁶And to Seth, to him also there was born a son; and he called his name Enos: then began men to call upon the name of the LORD.

Genesis 5 (Genealogy)

GENESIS 6-11   NOAH AND THE ARK

Genesis 6

¹And it came to pass, when men began to multiply on the face of the earth, and daughters were born unto them, ²That the sons of God saw the daughters of men that they were fair; and they took them wives of all which they chose. ³And the LORD said, "My spirit shall not always strive with man, for that he also is flesh: yet his days shall be an hundred and twenty years."[s] ⁴There were giants in the earth in those days; and also after that, when the sons of God came in unto the daughters of men, and they bare children to them, the same became mighty men which were of old, men of renown. ⁵And God saw that the wickedness of man was great in the earth, and that every imagination of the thoughts of his heart was only evil continually.

⁶And it repented the LORD that he had made man on the earth, and it grieved him at his heart. ⁷And the LORD said, "I will destroy man whom I have created from the face of the earth; both man, and beast, and the creeping thing, and the fowls of the air; for it repenteth me that I have made them." ⁸But Noah found grace in the eyes of the LORD. ⁹These are the generations of Noah: Noah was a just man and perfect in his generations, and Noah walked with God. ¹⁰And Noah begat three sons, Shem, Ham, and Japheth. ¹¹The earth also was corrupt before God, and the earth was filled with violence. ¹²And God looked upon the earth, and, behold, it was corrupt; for all flesh had corrupted his way upon the earth.

¹³And God said unto Noah, "The end of all flesh is come before me; for the earth is filled with violence through them; and, behold, I will destroy them with the earth. ¹⁴Make thee an ark of gopher wood; rooms shalt thou make in the ark, and shalt pitch it within and without with pitch.[t] ¹⁵And this is the fashion which thou shalt make it of: The length of the ark shall be three hundred cubits, the breadth of it fifty cubits, and the height of it thirty cubits.[u] ¹⁶A window shalt thou make to the ark, and in a cubit shalt thou finish it above; and the door of the ark shalt thou set in the side thereof; with lower, second, and third stories shalt thou make it. ¹⁷And, behold, I, even I, do bring a flood of waters upon the earth, to destroy all flesh, wherein is the breath of life, from under heaven; and every thing that is in the earth shall die."

---

[s] "I will not always be willing to put up with mankind; after all, he is only mortal, not eternal like me. I will limit his lifespan to 120 years." In the early books of the Bible, the lifespans of humans are described as much longer than what we would recognize as a normal lifespan today. (EP)

[t] Pitch = tar, which would be used for waterproofing (FI)

[u] Cubit = this is the oldest unit of measurement on record. One cubit was measured using a man's forearm, from his elbow to his fingertip. It was probably about 18 inches long. (FI)

[18] "But with thee will I establish my covenant;[v] and thou shalt come into the ark, thou, and thy sons, and thy wife, and thy sons' wives with thee. [19] And of every living thing of all flesh, two of every sort shalt thou bring into the ark, to keep them alive with thee; they shall be male and female. [20] Of fowls after their kind, and of cattle after their kind, of every creeping thing of the earth after his kind, two of every sort shall come unto thee, to keep them alive. [21] And take thou unto thee of all food that is eaten, and thou shalt gather it to thee; and it shall be for food for thee, and for them." [22] Thus did Noah; according to all that God commanded him, so did he.

Genesis 7

[1] And the LORD said unto Noah, "Come thou and all thy house into the ark; for thee have I seen righteous before me in this generation. [2] Of every clean beast thou shalt take to thee by sevens, the male and his female: and of beasts that are not clean by two, the male and his female.[w] [3] Of fowls also of the air by sevens, the male and the female; to keep seed alive upon the face of all the earth. [4] For yet seven days, and I will cause it to rain upon the earth forty days and forty nights; and every living substance that I have made will I destroy from off the face of the earth." [5] And Noah did according unto all that the LORD commanded him. [6] And Noah was six hundred years old when the flood of waters was upon the earth.

[7] And Noah went in, and his sons, and his wife, and his sons' wives with him, into the ark, because of the waters of the flood. [8] Of clean beasts, and of beasts that are not clean, and of fowls, and of every thing that creepeth upon the earth, [9] There went in two and two unto Noah into the ark, the male and the female, as God had commanded Noah. [10] And it came to pass after seven days, that the waters of the flood were upon the earth. [11] In the six hundredth year of Noah's life, in the second month, the seventeenth day of the month, the same day were all the fountains of the great deep broken up, and the windows of heaven were opened. [12] And the rain was upon the earth forty days and forty nights.

[13] In the selfsame day entered Noah, and Shem, and Ham, and Japheth, the sons of Noah, and Noah's wife, and the three wives of his sons with them, into the ark; [14] They, and every beast after his kind, and all the cattle after their kind, and every creeping thing that creepeth upon the earth after his kind, and every fowl after his kind, every bird of every sort. [15] And they went in unto Noah into the ark, two and two of all flesh, wherein is the breath of life. [16] And they that went in, went in male and female of all flesh, as God had commanded him: and the LORD shut him in.

[17] And the flood was forty days upon the earth; and the waters increased, and bare up the ark, and it was lifted up above the earth. [18] And the waters prevailed, and were increased greatly upon the earth; and the ark went upon the face of the waters. [19] And the waters prevailed exceedingly upon the earth; and all the high hills, that were under the whole heaven, were covered. [20] Fifteen cubits upward did the waters prevail; and the mountains were covered. [21] And all flesh died that moved upon the earth, both of fowl, and of cattle, and of beast, and of every creeping thing that creepeth

---

[v] Covenant = promise or contract (FI)
[w] Clean beast = an animal considered to be "clean enough" for eating and for sacrificing. More clean beasts would have been needed for these purposes. Interestingly, the Jewish laws regarding clean and unclean beasts are not established in the biblical text until the third book of the Bible, after Moses provides the Ten Commandments.

upon the earth, and every man: ²²All in whose nostrils was the breath of life, of all that was in the dry land, died. ²³And every living substance was destroyed which was upon the face of the ground, both man, and cattle, and the creeping things, and the fowl of the heaven; and they were destroyed from the earth: and Noah only remained alive, and they that were with him in the ark. ²⁴And the waters prevailed upon the earth an hundred and fifty days.

Genesis 8

¹And God remembered Noah, and every living thing, and all the cattle that was with him in the ark: and God made a wind to pass over the earth, and the waters assuaged; ²The fountains also of the deep and the windows of heaven were stopped, and the rain from heaven was restrained; ³And the waters returned from off the earth continually: and after the end of the hundred and fifty days the waters were abated. ⁴And the ark rested in the seventh month, on the seventeenth day of the month, upon the mountains of Ararat. ⁵And the waters decreased continually until the tenth month: in the tenth month, on the first day of the month, were the tops of the mountains seen.

⁶And it came to pass at the end of forty days, that Noah opened the window of the ark which he had made: ⁷And he sent forth a raven, which went forth to and fro, until the waters were dried up from off the earth. ⁸Also he sent forth a dove from him, to see if the waters were abated from off the face of the ground; ⁹But the dove found no rest for the sole of her foot, and she returned unto him into the ark, for the waters were on the face of the whole earth: then he put forth his hand, and took her, and pulled her in unto him into the ark. ¹⁰And he stayed yet other seven days; and again he sent forth the dove out of the ark; ¹¹And the dove came in to him in the evening; and, lo, in her mouth was an olive leaf pluckt off: so Noah knew that the waters were abated from off the earth. ¹²And he stayed yet other seven days; and sent forth the dove; which returned not again unto him any more.

¹³And it came to pass in the six hundredth and first year, in the first month, the first day of the month, the waters were dried up from off the earth: and Noah removed the covering of the ark, and looked, and, behold, the face of the ground was dry. ¹⁴And in the second month, on the seven and twentieth day of the month, was the earth dried. ¹⁵And God spake unto Noah, saying, ¹⁶"Go forth of the ark, thou, and thy wife, and thy sons, and thy sons' wives with thee. ¹⁷Bring forth with thee every living thing that is with thee, of all flesh, both of fowl, and of cattle, and of every creeping thing that creepeth upon the earth; that they may breed abundantly in the earth, and be fruitful, and multiply upon the earth."

¹⁸And Noah went forth, and his sons, and his wife, and his sons' wives with him: ¹⁹Every beast, every creeping thing, and every fowl, and whatsoever creepeth upon the earth, after their kinds, went forth out of the ark. ²⁰And Noah builded an altar unto the LORD; and took of every clean beast, and of every clean fowl, and offered burnt offerings on the altar. ²¹And the LORD smelled a sweet savour; and the LORD said in his heart, "I will not again curse the ground any more for man's sake; for the imagination of man's heart is evil from his youth; neither will I again smite any more every thing living, as I have done. ²²While the earth remaineth, seedtime and harvest, and cold and heat, and summer and winter, and day and night shall not cease."

Genesis 9

¹And God blessed Noah and his sons, and said unto them, "Be fruitful, and multiply, and replenish the earth. ²And the fear of you and the dread of you shall be upon every beast of the earth, and upon every fowl of the air, upon all that moveth upon the earth, and upon all the fishes of the sea; into your hand are they delivered. ³Every moving thing that liveth shall be meat for you; even as the green herb have I given you all things. ⁴But flesh with the life thereof, which is the blood thereof, shall ye not eat. ⁵And surely your blood of your lives will I require; at the hand of every beast will I require it, and at the hand of man; at the hand of every man's brother will I require the life of man. ⁶Whoso sheddeth man's blood, by man shall his blood be shed: for in the image of God made he man. ⁷And you, be ye fruitful, and multiply; bring forth abundantly in the earth, and multiply therein."

⁸And God spake unto Noah, and to his sons with him, saying, ⁹"And I, behold, I establish my covenant with you, and with your seed after you; ¹⁰And with every living creature that is with you, of the fowl, of the cattle, and of every beast of the earth with you; from all that go out of the ark, to every beast of the earth. ¹¹And I will establish my covenant with you, neither shall all flesh be cut off any more by the waters of a flood; neither shall there any more be a flood to destroy the earth."

¹²And God said, "This is the token of the covenant which I make between me and you and every living creature that is with you, for perpetual generations: ¹³I do set my bow[x] in the cloud, and it shall be for a token of a covenant between me and the earth. ¹⁴And it shall come to pass, when I bring a cloud over the earth, that the bow shall be seen in the cloud: ¹⁵And I will remember my covenant, which is between me and you and every living creature of all flesh; and the waters shall no more become a flood to destroy all flesh. ¹⁶And the bow shall be in the cloud; and I will look upon it, that I may remember the everlasting covenant between God and every living creature of all flesh that is upon the earth." ¹⁷And God said unto Noah, "This is the token of the covenant, which I have established between me and all flesh that is upon the earth."

¹⁸And the sons of Noah, that went forth of the ark, were Shem, and Ham, and Japheth: and Ham is the father of Canaan. ¹⁹These are the three sons of Noah: and of them was the whole earth overspread. ²⁰And Noah began to be an husbandman, and he planted a vineyard: ²¹And he drank of the wine, and was drunken; and he was uncovered within his tent. ²²And Ham, the father of Canaan, saw the nakedness of his father, and told his two brethren without. ²³And Shem and Japheth took a garment, and laid it upon both their shoulders, and went backward, and covered the nakedness of their father; and their faces were backward, and they saw not their father's nakedness. ²⁴And Noah awoke from his wine, and knew what his younger son had done unto him. ²⁵And he said, "Cursed be Canaan; a servant of servants shall he be unto his brethren." ²⁶And he said, "Blessed be the LORD God of Shem; and Canaan shall be his servant. ²⁷God shall enlarge Japheth, and he shall dwell in the tents of Shem; and Canaan shall be his servant." ²⁸And Noah lived after the flood three hundred and fifty years. ²⁹And all the days of Noah were nine hundred and fifty years: and he died.

Genesis 10 (Genealogy)

---

[x] Bow = rainbow

GENESIS 11:1-9　　　TOWER OF BABEL

Genesis 11

¹And the whole earth was of one language, and of one speech. ²And it came to pass, as they journeyed from the east, that they found a plain in the land of Shinar; and they dwelt there.

³And they said one to another, "Go to, let us make brick, and burn them thoroughly. And they had brick for stone, and slime had they for mortar. ⁴And they said, "Go to, let us build us a city and a tower, whose top may reach unto heaven; and let us make us a name, lest we be scattered abroad upon the face of the whole earth."

⁵And the LORD came down to see the city and the tower, which the children of men builded. ⁶And the LORD said, "Behold, the people is one, and they have all one language; and this they begin to do: and now nothing will be restrained from them, which they have imagined to do. ⁷Go to, let us go down, and there confound their language, that they may not understand one another's speech." ⁸So the LORD scattered them abroad from thence upon the face of all the earth: and they left off to build the city.

⁹Therefore is the name of it called Babel; because the LORD did there confound the language of all the earth:[y] and from thence did the LORD scatter them abroad upon the face of all the earth.

Genesis 11:10-32 (Genealogy)

---

[y] Based on the wording of this verse, it sounds as if God named the tower "Babel" in reference to the English word *babble*, but of course there was no such thing as English when this story was written! Actually, what we have here is a pun – and who says God has no sense of humor? *Babel* was the Hebrew name for Babylon, a Mesopotamian city-state (which eventually became a great empire). *Babel* literally means "gate of god," referring to the religious purpose of a ziggurat, and the Tower of Babel certainly appears to be a ziggurat. The pun comes about because Babel sounds a lot like another Hebrew word, *balal* (baw-lal), which means "to mix up or confuse." Chances are that Babel already had the name Babylon, and the writer of Genesis employed a clever play on Hebrew words, possibly as a way of ridiculing the Babylonians. Fast forward about three thousand years, and we find that the English word *babble* evolved from other European words with similar sounds and meanings, but linguists have not been able to formally trace the word back to the notorious tower of Genesis 11. Divine coincidence, perhaps?!

LESSON SIX:
A HISTORY IN SYMBOLS

"The Tower of Babel" by Pieter Bruegel the Elder (1563)

If the story of Adam and Eve is about humanity coming into an awareness of good and evil, then the story of Cain is about humanity developing a justice system, the flood story is about the collective crimes of humanity, and the tale of Babel is an account of urban civilization and human progress. All of these stories are religious lessons, first and foremost, but they also contain humanistic truth and anthropological interest. The stories of Adam, Cain, Noah, and Babel can be studied as a symbolic timeline of early mankind's moral and social development.

We see in Genesis 2 that God first establishes a code of conduct for humanity when he issues the tree edict. When Adam and Eve eat the fruit of "knowledge of good and evil," they cross the line from innocent creatures into full moral awareness. At this moment, they know the difference between right and wrong not only because they have disobeyed, but because the tree supernaturally opens their eyes to a moral reality. Human life will never be the same.

In Genesis 4, the evils of mankind grow to include murder, arguably the worst crime of all. It is interesting to note that in this story, however, it is not God who levies the punishment –

it is the earth! The spilled blood of Cain cries out to God, convicting Cain of his crime. Next, *the earth* curses Cain for his wrongdoing; God simply upholds the earth's right to punish him, and the earth henceforth refuses to bear Cain any more crops (remember, Cain was a farmer). Because of this, Cain must become a nomad; in this way, the story helps explain the nomadic culture of ancient Jews. It also explains the core of humanity's natural moral code, that it is innately wrong to kill another person in cold blood. Even the blood itself objects!

Eventually, human society grows to a size and complexity that requires the codification of morals, and the earliest archeological record of this is known as Hammurabi's Code, which was the law of the land in ancient Babylon. The code is famous for the edict "an eye for an eye, a tooth for a tooth," a phrase which appears in the Bible as part of God's law for the Israelites (Exodus 21:24). The principle is one of lawful retaliation: not so much the *right* of retaliation, but the *limitation* of retaliation. It was a mark of a civilized society, that revenge should not flourish ungoverned; rather, the law *limited* the penalty to one befitting the severity of the crime, and no worse. Hammurabi's Code reflects the moral issue inherent in the Cain and Abel story. The story suggests that there is a Natural Law in place, something akin to Mother Nature: a code of earthly justice that requires lawbreakers to pay a fair and even penalty for their crimes. The discussion between God and Cain suggests that an "eye for an eye" principle is inherent to Cain's thinking, because Cain knows that he deserves to be murdered as a result of having committed murder.

As we approach the flood story, we find out that in the space of eight generations the wickedness of mankind has grown to mammoth proportions, and Cain's legacy is apparent: "The earth was also corrupt before God, and the earth was filled with violence" (6:11). Cain got off easy with a sentence of homelessness and hunger, but the people of Noah's day have gotten so bad that simple mercy is not an option. However, the *story isn't really about all the people who drown*, because all of our attention is placed on the protagonist, Noah, who gets saved. His good fortune comes because of God's mercy, and he is required to suffer a pretty terrible ordeal before getting the chance to start a fresh life on a "cleansed" planet. Within the scope of our symbolic history lesson, the Noah story indicates that humanity is in constant violation of Natural Law, and that our inherent evil cannot be ignored, but hard-won redemption is always available. Human morals simply don't develop on a linear path – we don't just get better and better. Everything is cyclical, and the cycle requires suffering, cleansing, lessons learned, and renewal.

By the time we get to Babel, civilization is flourishing. Humanity has gained the knowledge and experience to build a city. The Babylonians have come a long way from living naked in a garden: this is a fully-developed urban community, complete with art, architecture, and civil projects. The Tower of Babel is probably a ziggurat, a large Mesopotamian temple built in tiers in order that the local god can walk down the "steps" and receive worship and sacrifices from his people. The Hebrew God, however, is not pleased with this idea! In the story, we are told that the people are interested not in God coming down to them, but in their going up to God – not to offer a sacrifice and thus invite God's presence, but to force their way up to heaven with arrogance rather than humility. The text even says that the builders want to "make a name for themselves," which implies a desire for fame and, thus, pride. God is not content to let mankind's pride get out of hand, nor is he willing to let them make their own way to heaven. Some readers see this as proof of God's selfishness and tyranny and a refusal to share heaven with mortals, while others see God's actions as just and protective: his nonviolent prevention of a foolish venture doomed to fail from the beginning. From a secular and symbolic point of view, the story reveals the powerful results of human ingenuity coupled with the dangers of pride. Indeed, not all of mankind's vices are violent, as with Cain and the flood narrative. Sometimes man's greatest enemy is his own demand for progress, dominion, and power.

> **A TIMELINE OF MORALITY AND LAW**
>
> **Adam:** Moral awareness of right and wrong; the justness of punishment for wrongdoing.
>
> **Cain:** Recognition of universal moral code; connection to early legal codes (Hammurabi) and civilized limits to retaliation.
>
> **Noah:** Philosophical awareness of humanity as a sinful species, in need of meaningful penance and second chances.
>
> **Babel:** Fully-developed social and legal structures... but is humanity a danger to itself?

This final biblical myth still speaks to the condition of modern civilization. Given the role of communication and technology inherent in the story's details, we can see ourselves in Babel. Here's a perfect example: the World Wide Web. People have worked together successfully, like the Babylonians, to create this immeasurable structure of information and commerce as we "reach for the stars." But what problems lie on the horizon? Once we become too dependent upon our own creation, we will become subject to the disasters of human limitation. For instance, a long term electricity outage would cripple us. It has already become possible to steal another person's very identity on the Internet. It has become easier to lie on a massive scale, and easier to mobilize large groups of people toward either good or evil enterprises. The story of the Tower may serve as a cautionary tale on the theme of progress – humanity has come a long way since his "caveman days," but perhaps progress and ambition are not all they're cracked up to be. Large scale success, in the light of ever-present human wickedness, often paves the way for large scale catastrophe. The inherent evil in mankind cannot always be restrained with a good legal code. Ultimately, only God or fate will prevail.

Indeed, the themes of law and social order in these stories cannot be stripped away from their central character, the God who created the world with order and gave mankind dominion over the earth – but not over heaven and not over morality. God wakes up Adam and Eve to the reality of good and evil, and he establishes the principle of punishment for wrongdoing. He is strict about this, and yet somewhat merciful: he does not strike Adam dead on the day of his disobedience, as he had threatened, but there are long-term penalties. With Cain, he supports the natural consequences of violating Natural Law, but in the end he offers Cain protection. However, God has his limits, and he will not allow free reign of unanswered violence. The story of Noah is about God's willingness to forgive and restore, but it also illustrates the difficult path of penance and (although it is not the focus of the story) it clarifies a severe condemnation of violent wickedness. Finally, God will not stand for the pride of the Babylonians, either. They have not committed a crime *per se*, but they are audacious enough to think that they have the power to control heaven. God does not let humans suffer under the misapprehension that they are little gods. The Hebrew God is one of justice *and mercy* – a paradox of legal standards that the Bible will explore from beginning to end.

A "YOUNG-EARTH" TIMELINE OF BIBLICAL HISTORY

Creation: around 4000 B.C.

Adam: lives 930 years and has three recorded sons: Cain, Abel, and Seth

Cain: second generation

Noah: ninth generation, coinciding with approximately 3000 B.C.

Babylon: founded by Nimrod, the third generation after the flood, (Gen. 10) perhaps around 2300 B.C. According to extra-biblical sources, Babel was part of the multilingual Akkadian empire.

Peleg: fifth generation after the flood (Gen. 10) and often associated with the tower at Babel

Hammurabi: 1792-1750 B.C.

Moses: writes Genesis (through Deuteronomy) around 1300 B.C.

BIBLICAL LITERARY INVENTORY — NARRATIVE

Narrative: The Story of Cain and Abel   **Passage:** Genesis 4

I. Protagonist and Antagonist – Cain is the protagonist. Interestingly, he is the "bad" one. His antagonist seems internal – his jealousy and anger.

II. Inciting Incident – God rejects Cain's offering.

III. Rising Action – God warns Cain that he should be careful with his anger, that sin is sitting outside his door waiting to attack, but that Cain is capable of ruling over sin.

IV. Climax – Cain kills Abel.

V. Falling Action – God asks Cain where his brother is, and Cain evades the question. The truth is confirmed when the earth literally calls out against Cain for having spilt Abel's blood upon the ground. The earth curses Cain for his act of murder. Cain is terrified that this curse will result in someone else killing him in revenge.

VI. Resolution – God puts a mark on Cain that protects him from revenge.

VII. Theme – Because the earth cries out against Cain, and it is the earth that curses him, the theme of the story seems to be the unnaturalness of murder – when a living soul kills another living soul, the very laws of nature are upset. The story suggests that the lawlessness of murder is not just a sin against society but against the earth, that there is a Natural Law which forbids it. Some readers see a sort of "karma" in the story as well: what goes around comes around and you can stop yourself from sending it around any further!

VIII. Symbolism – The mark of Cain is a well-known biblical symbol. The mark represents the protection and mercy of God. This suggests yet another theme, that God's mercy surpasses his vengeance.

IX. Motif – Not applicable.

X. Character Development – God seems arbitrary and petty at the beginning of the story when he rejects Cain's sacrifice for no apparent reason. However, he is very gentle with Cain when Cain gets angry, and he even warns Cain to be careful. Finally, God is merciful and protective even after Cain commits murder.

XI. Narrative Persona – We are still dealing with the same narrator from chapters 1-3. His central concern seems to be the exploration of God's nature and his ongoing relationship with mankind.

XII. Irony, Contrast, Foil and/or Reversals – After reading about God's firm hand with Adam and Eve, you might expect an "eye for an eye" approach with Cain, but in fact God responds with protection instead of punishment. It is the earth, not God, who levies the punishment. God puts a mark on Cain preventing people from killing him in revenge.

XIII. Additional Literary Devices – This story uses a lot of personification. First, sin is personified as sitting at the door trying to get in. Second, Abel's blood cries out and the earth comes alive as an angry Mother Earth figure, dead set on vengeance for Cain's violation of natural law. The personification of sin and earth complements the mythological nature of the story, in that sin literally tempts Cain and the earth literally objects. It is clearly an instructive story.

XIV. Historical Criticism – From a modern reader's perspective, God might seem harsh and arbitrary for rejecting Cain's offering of vegetables while accepting his brother's offering of animal "firstlings and the fat thereof." It is important to note that animal sacrifice was a ritual that figured prominently in most ancient cultures. Some cultures believed they were feeding the gods. Some cultures may have been demonstrating penance. Looking at the story from an appropriate cultural perspective, why might the God of Genesis have rejected Cain's sacrifice?

_____

_____

XV. Genre Awareness (select one) – Select the genre that best fits the story to help you shape your final assessment of the text.

    ___ Mythology: Symbolically, what does the story reveal about human nature or God?

    ___ Legend / Epic: What themes of Judeo-Christian identity emerge?

    ___ History: What historical events have a practical bearing on the present and future?

    ___ Biography: Why is the subject of the biography worth special attention?

    ___ Drama: What aspects of the play a "hold a mirror up to nature"?

    ___ Short Story: What elements of intentional storytelling contribute to theme and unity?

Based on your selection, provide a response to the genre-related question provided above:

_____

_____

_____

BIBLICAL LITERARY INVENTORY — NARRATIVE

Narrative: The Story of the Tower of Babel   **Passage:** Genesis 11:1-9

I. Protagonist and Antagonist – The builders of the tower are the protagonists. Who or what is the antagonist? _____

II. Inciting Incident – All the people of the earth (who, by the way, all speak a single language) move onto a single plain together and prepare to build a city there.

III. Rising Action – _____
_____

IV. Climax – God confounds their single language – they can no longer communicate.

V. Falling Action – The building of the tower and the city is effectively halted.

VI. Resolution –_____
_____

VII. Theme – God will not let people build their way to heaven, literally or figuratively. Perhaps this suggests that the way to heaven is not through man's effort. There is also a theme of communication, that it is essential to community and productivity. Anything else?
_____
_____

VIII. Symbolism – The tower itself might be seen as a symbol of mankind's ingenuity. Or, from a negative perspective, it could be a symbol of mankind's pride. Perhaps the real antagonist in the story is the pride of humanity. What answer did you provide in item I?

IX. Motif – There is a very interesting motif in this story that extends back through the Noah story – the words "imagination" and "imagine." Each time these words are used, it involves a description of why God is punishing mankind. Here are the three verses:

> *And God saw that the wickedness of man was great upon the earth, and that every imagination of the thoughts of his heart was only evil continually (6:5-6)*

> *I will not again curse the ground any more for man's sake; for the imagination of man's heart is evil from his youth (8:21).*

> *Behold, the people is one, and they have all one language; and this they begin to do: and now nothing will be restrained from them, which they have imagined to do (11:6-7).*

This "imagination" pattern seems to reveal that there is deep-seated wickedness lurking in the heart of humanity, and that if God lets men do whatever they want, whatever they imagine, then evil will surely prevail. Recognition of this motif suggests that God puts an end to the Babel enterprise in order to protect the people from their own inherent wickedness. Aside from the Internet issue discussed in Lesson 6, can you think of a modern example of mankind's dark side emerging through his imagination? _____

_____

X. Character Development – God might be seen as selfish, refusing to share heaven with humanity. Then again, he might just have a bigger picture in mind, whereby human beings should not or could not build their own way to heaven. God could also be seen as mysteriously merciful, punishing them with confusion but simultaneously saving them from their own evil imaginations. What do you think? _____

_____

_____

XI. Narrative Persona – We are still dealing with the same narrator from chapters 1-3, so there's nothing new to add to former lessons.

XII. Irony, Contrast, Foil and/or Reversals – None apparent.

XIII. Additional Literary Devices – None apparent.

XIV. Historical Criticism – The time frame of ziggurats and the founding of Babylon agree historically with the setting and composition of the Babel story, as does the record of the Akkadian empire being multilingual. However, the preceding chapter (10) tells us that Noah's grandson Nimrod is associated with the founding of Babylon: "And the beginning of his kingdom was Babel…in the land of Shinar" (10:10). It also describes his great-great-great-grandson, Peleg, as a man in whose lifetime "the earth divided" (10:25) which is sometimes interpreted as a reference to the building of the Tower. It is difficult to imagine that a post-flood second generation (lead by Nimrod) could have been numerous enough to build a ziggurat or found a city. What about a post-flood fifth generation, associated with Peleg? Do you find the Genesis account to be historically viable or not? Why? _____

_____

_____
_____
_____

XV. Genre Awareness (select one) –

___ Mythology: Symbolically, what does the story reveal about human nature or God?

___ Legend / Epic: What themes of Judeo-Christian identity emerge?

___ History: What historical events have a practical bearing on the present and future?

Based on your selection, provide a response to the genre-related question provided above:

_____
_____
_____

LESSON SIX STUDY GUIDE

Objective Identification: Cain, Abel, Noah, Babel, Babylon, Hammurabi's Code, ziggurat

Subjective Expression:

1) Recall: What does Cain say, specifically, when he claims to be unaware of where his brother is? This is a very famous line from the text, and you will come across allusions to it from time to time, for instance the 2014 initiative by President Barack Obama that was designed to help young men of color work toward better education and stronger families.

2) Creative Response: What was the "mark" of Cain? This is another common biblical allusion you will find in literature. How would you draw a picture of Cain with such a mark upon him? The text doesn't give us an image, only the term.

3) Further Research: Explore the founding of the city of Babylon and the growth of the Babylonian empire. Be sure to include the following, in chronological order: Hammurabi, the triumph of the Assyrian empire, the neo-Babylonian empire and its deportment of Jews during the Babylonian exile, and the final triumph of the Persian empire through Cyrus the Great.

THE STORY OF UTNAPISHTIM
FROM THE EPIC OF GILGAMESH

The Sumerian gods were angry, and they had conspired a secret plot to destroy all mankind with a flood. Rumor had it that the gods were tired of the constant noise of the human race, and they were full of regret for having created them to begin with. One god, however, had a favorite among the humans, and he decided to warn this man – Utnapishtim – of the impending flood. He whispered to him through the reeds of his house and told him to tear down the house and build a boat instead.

Utnapishtim was given very specific guidelines for his boat. It would be a square of 120 cubits with six decks divided into seven and nine compartments. The boat was launched into the water, and Utnapishtim loaded his gold, himself, and an assortment of living creatures onto the boat. Then he sealed the entrance and went to bed. The next morning, a black cloud covered the sky and a storm broke loose.

The thunder god filled the air with noise, and the lightning gods flashed their anger across the land, which shattered. Everything turned black, and all the people were terrified. In fact, even the gods themselves were afraid. They retreated from earth to heaven and cried with regret and fear for having brought on the terrible flood. But it was too late. The flood continued six days and seven nights until finally the whirlwind stopped and the waters receded. The humans had all turned to clay. Utnapishtim, however, had survived the storm in his hearty boat.

The boat had lodged itself at the top of a mountain, where it rested for six days, and on the seventh day, Utnapishtim released a dove. The dove, finding no dry land on which to perch, returned to him. He then released a swallow, which also returned. Finally, he sent out a raven, but the raven did not come back. Utnapishtim then knew that the land was dry enough for life to renew itself, and so he released all his livestock. He himself left the boat and offered a sacrifice to the gods, particularly the one kind god who had warned him about the flood.

When the gods smelled the sweet aroma of the sacrifice, they gathered once more on earth to eat, for they had become very hungry and thirsty up in the heavens. There was a great fight among the gods over the disastrous flood, with blame being flung in all directions, and finally all the gods agreed to grant Utnapishtim and his wife immortality. They once again board the boat and are transported far away, past the underworld and into the eternal garden where they now reside for eternity, among the gods themselves.

LESSON SEVEN:
NOAH LIKE YOU'VE NEVER SEEN HIM BEFORE

"The Dove Sent Forth from the Ark" by Gustave Dore (1866)

The story of Noah and his ark is more than famous – it's iconic. In fact, you may be so familiar with the children's version of the tale that the original text may hold a few surprises. This lesson focuses on the unexpected elements, both inside the text and beyond. We will take a mature look at the story and try to see beyond the cute images of animal couples sailing happily on an open boat. The two images appearing here represent two polar opposites in the interpretation of the Noah story – is "Noah's Ark" a cute and child-friendly bedtime story, or is it a dark, disturbing tale of destruction?

NEPHILIM

We will begin at the beginning, with the first four verses of chapter six. What do you make of this unusual prologue? Seemingly unrelated to the story of the ark, we find something that sounds more like Greek myth than what we expect from the Bible. It raises more questions than it asks: "Who were these giants?" "What is meant by the *sons of God*?" "Why are the sons of God impregnating human women?" The Hebrew word translated to mean "giants" is *nephilim*, and linguists sometimes argue that it means "those that cause others to fall down" or "fallen ones," thereby associating them with fallen angels or demons. Indeed, the "sons of God" may be angels. The offspring of the nephilim are described as "mighty" and famous, perhaps linking them with ancient heroic characters like the Titans of Greece. In any case, these expository details set the stage for a world in which human beings have been infiltrated and corrupted, and are behaving wickedly and violently, perhaps under the influence of evil spirits. Even if you manage to make sense of it, this is an odd story!

PITCH AND CUBITS

Next – were you surprised by the description of the ark itself? Far from the nursery school illustrations you may be familiar with, the actual ark is made of gopher wood (a detail presented with humor in the movie Evan Almighty) and coated inside and out with pitch, which is a black tree gum. So much for the image of a brown, wood-hewn ark – it was actually painted black. And exactly how big was it? The precise dimensions of the ark are described in cubits, which is one of the oldest measurement units known to man. A cubit was measured from the tip of the finger to the elbow; the modern equivalent is something like 18 inches. Thus, Noah's ark was 300 cubits long (450 feet, or one and a half football fields) by 50 cubits wide (75 feet wide, or the length of a tennis court) by 30 cubits (45 feet tall). The ark had three stories in it, which would make each story 15 feet high (standard ceiling height in residential homes is 8 feet). Are you getting the picture? This is a giant box, not a rounded "boat" shape with a cute little roof on top. Furthermore, there is only one small window, set into the top level of the ark at about one cubit down. How are we doing with the surprises so far?

FOUNTAINS OF THE DEEP

The description of the rain and flooding are also interesting, for both scientific and historical reasons. In the ancient world (prior to the Golden Age of Greece) people in the Mesopotamian and Mediterranean regions held to a view of the cosmos commonly referred to as the "Three Story Universe." Unlike our scientifically-accurate image of a round planet in a solar system, ancient people imagined a world with a dome that covered a flat earth and separated it from the heavens, with a layer of water in between sometimes called "the ocean of heaven." The underworld or abyss – the opposite of heaven – lay just beneath the ground, intermingled with the "primeval ocean" (the chaotic ocean from which the earth emerged, possibly described in Genesis 1:1 when the Spirit of God hovers over the deep). The flat earth was thought to be held up by pillars, called the Pillars of the Earth, a phrase which is still common in modern language, and you may have heard it in relation to a popular novel and miniseries by Ken Follett. Even the Book of Job in the Bible mentions these pillars, when it says that God moves the mountains and "shaketh the earth out of her place, and the pillars thereof tremble" (9:6). In fact, the details of the Genesis creation story overlap significantly with this ancient point of view, as illustrated in the diagram below. In the Noah story, we see in Genesis 7:11 that waters poured from the

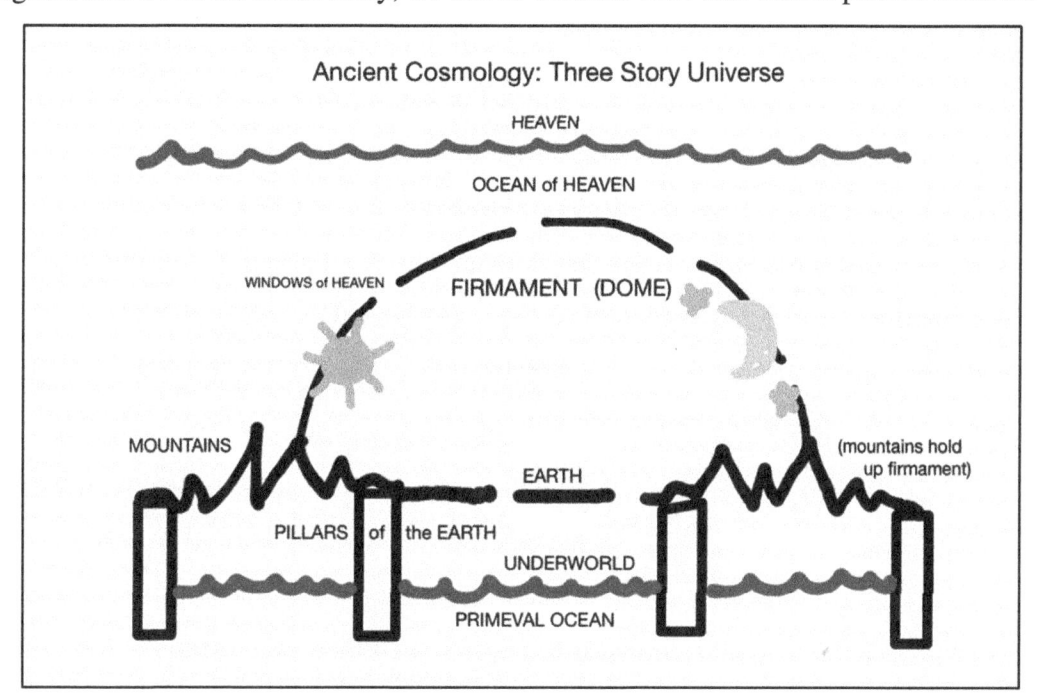

Ancient Cosmology: Three Story Universe

heavens and they also sprang up from the deep: "all the fountains of the great deep [were] broken up, and the windows of heaven were opened." The flood ends in a parallel manner: "The fountains also of the deep and the windows of heaven were stopped, and the rain from heaven was restrained" (8:2). These descriptions might correlate to the cosmological description shared by many ancient people, from the Babylonians and Sumerians to the Egyptians – and perhaps the Hebrews as well.

TWO BY TWO

Now let's take a closer look at the animals who entered the ark. Two of every "sort" of animal are taken in, a phrase that could mean "species" or something slightly more broad, like one representative of each animal "family." Calculations of how many animals would have been on the ark vary widely, and we will leave the counting for another day. One surprise we find in the wording of the text, however, is that more than two of some animals were taken in – in fact, seven pairs of the "clean" animals. This is quite a bit more than most people imagine when they picture Noah's animals lined up to board the boat two-by-two. These clean animals would have been used for sacrifices and for food. Literary scholars and liberal theologians, however, dispense of the entire question. If one reads the story of Noah as a myth, then the literal numbers do not matter.

GILGAMESH

While we're on the topic of myths, were you surprised when you read the story of Utnapishtim? This tale, paraphrased before this lesson, is a myth that survives from the ancient Sumerian Epic of Gilgamesh, one of the world's oldest heroic sagas. Gilgamesh has the good fortune to meet Utnapishtim, known as the only human to ever be granted immortality by the gods. In the Sumerian story of a great flood, we see many interesting parallels to Noah. With your classmates, compile a list of similarities and differences. Why do you think the stories are so remarkably alike? Both tales refer to heroes living in the same area of the globe (what we call the Middle East) at roughly the same era of ancient history. One might conclude that these two stories are overlapping versions of the same legend, passed along by word of mouth for many centuries until two different cultures had personalized the ancient memories of a regional flood into myths that reflected their own religious points of view. If there was indeed a flood such as these stories dscribe, perhaps one of these is the original story and one is a rumor… with this question, we cross into the realm of faith. But the existence of a Sumerian sister-story to Genesis is, nevertheless, a fascinating discovery. It might interest you further to find that nearly every culture around the globe, from Africa to Australia, has some sort of flood story in its mythical tradition – but the Sumerian and Hebrew stories have more amazing parallel details between them than others.

ARCHETYPE

The flood motif in world literature is so common that we can even call it *archetypal*. An archetype is a "prototype" in literature, either a recurrent story element or a universal symbol. The flood archetype is both. It is most certainly recurrent, found in dozens of myths and legends around the world, and it can also function in a universally symbolic way. This archetypal symbolism is related to water. Water is a substance that nourishes and cleans us, and storytellers frequently use water images – particularly images of floods or people being submerged in water and then coming back up again – to represent an act of spiritual cleansing, like we find in the ritual of baptism. Floods can symbolize cleansing on a large scale. In the Noah story, the flood is used to cleanse humanity of its extreme wickedness and violence, which may have been precipitated by a demonic attack as suggested earlier in our lesson.

The archetypal number seven appears frequently in the story as well: seven pairs of clean animals, seven pairs of birds, seven days of warning before the flood starts, a retreat of the waters on the seventeenth day of the seventh month, seven days of waiting before sending out the second dove, and seven more days of waiting before sending out the dove one last time. The number seven is often related to the concept of completion and/or perfection whenever you find it purposefully used in literature. Think back to the beginning of Genesis itself… seven days to complete the creation of the earth, and seven days in our modern

> **UNIVERSAL ARCHETYPES FOUND IN THE BIBLE**
>
> **Water / Flood:** cleansing and/or nourishing
>
> **Light / Dark:** good and evil
>
> **Snakes:** evil (poisonous)
>
> **Birds:** messengers from heaven
>
> **Seven:** completion, perfection, and sometimes divinity
>
> **Six:** humanity, which is incomplete, and created on day six
>
> **Three:** conceptual or spiritual unity, body-mind-spirit
>
> **Four:** the earth (four seasons, four directions, four elements, four corners)
>
> **Hero Cycle:** a hero who is called, proceeds into an unfamiliar realm of challenge and danger, goes through "hell," eventually becomes a true hero, and goes home victorious and legendary

week. Humans have used the number seven in this fashion for many thousands of years – Seven Wonders of the World, the seven Chakras from India, seven dwarves, seven years (and seven books) at Hogwarts School of Witchcraft and Wizardry. The significance of this number runs deep into history and across cultures. Some say it reflects an ancient spiritual equation, 3+4=7, whereby the three is a male number and four is a female number, or whereby three is a spiritual number (body-mind-spirit, holy trinity) and four is an earthy, physical number (four seasons, four directions, four elements, four corners of the earth). Seven represents a complete total and is often associated with God. The recurrence of the number seven in Noah's story suggests perfection within the details of the plan for saving mankind from destruction.

NEW CREATION

The number seven is only part of the bigger meaning of the story, of course. Christian theologians say it is about God's plan to save the righteous and faithful from destruction, with the ark being a symbol for the church and the rainbow being a symbol of hope for eternal salvation. On a more universal and mythical level, the story illustrates the triumph of goodness, wisdom, and perseverance over evil, as well as the triumph of the human spirit to preserve life in all its varieties, from human, to animal and physical, to spiritual. From either angle, it's a story about renewal and second chances. In fact, the language of the story reinforces the theme of a "second creation" as the storyteller frequently borrows familiar words from Genesis 1. God tells Noah and his sons to "be fruitful and increase in number." Phrases like "birds of the sky," the "breath of life," and "every creature that moves along the ground" tie the Noah story to the creation story. Furthermore, God reminds Noah that he is made "in the image of God" and that mankind is to be ruler over the animals. These allusions back to Genesis 1 clearly establish the story of the flood as a new beginning for mankind.

> **LITERARY SOURCES FOR THE FLOOD STORY**
>
> Many modern scholars believe that the Noah narrative was composed using two older accounts. The theory states that the Hebrew author took two different documents, which are referred to as "J" and "P," and merged them into a unified whole. You may have noticed some unnecessary repetitiveness while you were reading. For instance, in 6:5-8 God proclaims humans to be evil and announces their destruction. Then he says all these things again in 6:11-13. In fact, a different Hebrew word for "God" is used in the two sets of verses. These clues, among others, prompted scholars to propose the two-source theory.

We have discussed so many unexpected elements in the Noah story during this lesson that perhaps a quick review is in order before we conclude. First, we have the odd, mythical tale of giants and perhaps fallen angels invading the world, which causes mankind to be corrupted. God's answer is to flood the world and wipe out humanity, but he will mercifully save one man and his family. The boat Noah builds is quite unlike any of the childhood images that cover the walls of American kindergartens. The story is, in fact, full of surprises. Mythically speaking, the story is about the salvation of righteous, wise, and courageous people in the face of evil (a story remarkably similar to other flood myths around the world). Archetypally, it is the story of human beings in need of cleansing and repentance. Universally, it is a story of hope, of new beginnings. And religiously, it is the story of God's intent to punish evil and reward goodness. It is a powerful tale full of adventure, death, salvation, symbols, numbers, history, wisdom, hope, and mystery.

LESSON SEVEN STUDY GUIDE

Objective Identification:
nephilim, cubit, pillars of the earth (cosmology), Gilgamesh, archetype

Subjective Expression:

1) Opinion: What, if anything, surprised you about this close study of the Noah story? Do you look at it any differently than you used to?

2) Recall: Summarize the elements of the ancient "three story universe."

3) Comparison: Compare and contrast the stories of Noah and Utnipishtim.

4) Further Research: See how many other "great flood" narratives you can find in other cultures' myths and legends. How similar are they to the biblical story?

5) Opinion: Of the various interpretations offered in this lesson, which do you prefer? In one sentence, summarize what you believe to be the meaning of the Noah story.

BIBLICAL LITERARY INVENTORY — NARRATIVE

Narrative – Noah and the Ark   **Passage** – Genesis 6-9

I. Protagonist and Antagonist – Is the protagonist God or Noah? Who or what is the antagonist? _____

II. Inciting Incident – What event actually causes the problem to emerge?

_____

III. Rising Action – _____

_____

IV. Climax – _____

_____

V. Falling Action – _____

_____

VI. Resolution – _____

_____

VII. Theme – (think about item IX before responding)_____

_____

_____

_____

VIII. Symbolism – _____

_____

_____

IX. Motif – _____

_____

_____

X. Character Development – Analyze Noah all the way through the end of Chapter 9:

_____

_____

_____

_____

XI. Narrative Persona – The point of view of the speaker is third person limited; the storyteller is not very concerned with the stories of the people who get punished and die. Those who drown in this tale are background characters. The focus of the story is "limited" to the journey of Noah and his family. Therefore, its core message (as intended by the original narrator) concerns Noah's experience of the flood. This literary angle may enhance your interpretation of the story's theme.

XII. Irony, Contrast, Foil and/or Reversals – _____
_____
_____

XIII. Additional Literary Devices – _____
_____
_____

XIV. Historical Criticism – You have read about the ancient cosmology model known as the "Three Story Universe," which scholars believe to have been common throughout the ancient Mediterranean and Mesopotamian region. Do you think the Genesis description of the "fountains of the deep" and "windows of heaven" coincides with this model, or is it simply a figurative way of explaining heavy rain and rising floodwaters? _____
_____
_____

XV. Genre Awareness (select one) –
    ___ Mythology: Symbolically, what does the story reveal about human nature or God?
    ___ Legend / Epic: What themes of Judeo-Christian identity emerge?
    ___ History: What historical events have a practical bearing on the present and future?
    ___ Biography: Why is the subject of the biography worth special attention?
    ___ Drama: What aspects of the play a "hold a mirror up to nature"?
    ___ Short Story: What elements of intentional storytelling contribute to theme and unity?
    ___ Narrative Poetry: Why was the story told via elevated and/or figurative language?
Based on your selection, provide a response to the genre-related question provided above:
_____
_____
_____

HERO STORIES

And I will...make thy name great

GENESIS 12-25 — ABRAHAM

Genesis 10:27-32 (Ninth Generation after Babel)

Now these are the generations of Terah: Terah begat Abram, Nahor, and Haran; and Haran begat Lot. ^{28} And Haran died before his father Terah in the land of his nativity, in Ur of the Chaldees.

^{29} And Abram and Nahor took them wives: the name of Abram's wife was Sarai; and the name of Nahor's wife, Milcah, the daughter of Haran, the father of Milcah, and the father of Iscah. ^{30} But Sarai was barren; she had no child.

^{31} And Terah took Abram his son, and Lot the son of Haran his son's son, and Sarai his daughter in law, his son Abram's wife; and they went forth with them from Ur of the Chaldees, to go into the land of Canaan; and they came unto Haran, and dwelt there. ^{32} And the days of Terah were two hundred and five years: and Terah died in Haran.

Genesis 12 (Abram is Called and Goes to Egypt)

^{1}Now the LORD had said unto Abram, "Get thee out of thy country, and from thy kindred, and from thy father's house, unto a land that I will shew thee: ^{2}And I will make of thee a great nation, and I will bless thee, and make thy name great; and thou shalt be a blessing: ^{3}And I will bless them that bless thee, and curse him that curseth thee: and in thee shall all families of the earth be blessed."

^{4}So Abram departed, as the LORD had spoken unto him; and Lot went with him: and Abram was seventy and five years old when he departed out of Haran. ^{5}And Abram took Sarai his wife, and Lot his brother's son, and all their substance that they had gathered, and the souls that they had gotten in Haran; and they went forth to go into the land of Canaan; and into the land of Canaan they came. ^{6}And Abram passed through the land unto the place of Sichem, unto the plain of Moreh. And the Canaanite was then in the land. ^{7}And the LORD appeared unto Abram, and said, "Unto thy seed will I give this land": and there builded he an altar unto the LORD, who appeared unto him. ^{8}And he removed from thence unto a mountain on the east of Bethel, and pitched his tent, having Bethel on the west, and Hai on the east: and there he builded an altar unto the LORD, and called upon the name of the LORD.

^{9}And Abram journeyed, going on still toward the south. ^{10}And there was a famine in the land: and Abram went down into Egypt to sojourn there; for the famine was grievous in the land. ^{11}And it came to pass, when he was come near to enter into Egypt, that he said unto Sarai his wife, "Behold now, I know that thou art a fair woman to look upon: ^{12}Therefore it shall come to pass, when the Egyptians shall see thee, that they shall say, 'This is his wife': and they will kill me, but they will save thee alive. ^{13}Say, I pray thee, thou art my sister: that it may be well with me for thy sake; and my soul shall live because of thee."

[14]And it came to pass, that, when Abram was come into Egypt, the Egyptians beheld the woman that she was very fair. [15]The princes also of Pharaoh saw her, and commended her before Pharaoh: and the woman was taken into Pharaoh's house. [16]And he entreated Abram well for her sake: and he had sheep, and oxen, and he asses, and menservants, and maidservants, and she asses, and camels. [17]And the LORD plagued Pharaoh and his house with great plagues because of Sarai Abram's wife. [18]And Pharaoh called Abram and said, "What is this that thou hast done unto me? why didst thou not tell me that she was thy wife? [19]Why saidst thou, 'She is my sister'? so I might have taken her to me to wife: now therefore behold thy wife, take her, and go thy way." [20]And Pharaoh commanded his men concerning him: and they sent him away, and his wife, and all that he had.

Genesis 13 (Lot and the Promised Land)

[1]And Abram went up out of Egypt, he, and his wife, and all that he had, and Lot with him, into the south. [2]And Abram was very rich in cattle, in silver, and in gold. [3]And he went on his journeys from the south even to Bethel, unto the place where his tent had been at the beginning, between Bethel and Hai; [4]Unto the place of the altar, which he had make there at the first: and there Abram called on the name of the LORD. [5]And Lot also, which went with Abram, had flocks, and herds, and tents. [6]And the land was not able to bear them, that they might dwell together: for their substance was great, so that they could not dwell together. [7]And there was a strife between the herdmen of Abram's cattle and the herdmen of Lot's cattle: and the Canaanite and the Perizzite dwelled then in the land.

[8]And Abram said unto Lot, "Let there be no strife, I pray thee, between me and thee, and between my herdmen and thy herdmen; for we be brethren. [9]Is not the whole land before thee? separate thyself, I pray thee, from me: if thou wilt take the left hand, then I will go to the right; or if thou depart to the right hand, then I will go to the left." [10]And Lot lifted up his eyes, and beheld all the plain of Jordan, that it was well watered every where, before the LORD destroyed Sodom and Gomorrah, even as the garden of the LORD, like the land of Egypt, as thou comest unto Zoar. [11]Then Lot chose him all the plain of Jordan; and Lot journeyed east: and they separated themselves the one from the other.

[12]Abram dwelled in the land of Canaan, and Lot dwelled in the cities of the plain, and pitched his tent toward Sodom. [13]But the men of Sodom were wicked and sinners before the LORD exceedingly. [14]And the LORD said unto Abram, after that Lot was separated from him, "Lift up now thine eyes, and look from the place where thou art northward, and southward, and eastward, and westward: [15]For all the land which thou seest, to thee will I give it, and to thy seed for ever. [16]And I will make thy seed as the dust of the earth: so that if a man can number the dust of the earth, then shall thy seed also be numbered. [17]Arise, walk through the land in the length of it and in the breadth of it; for I will give it unto thee." [18]Then Abram removed his tent, and came and dwelt in the plain of Mamre, which is in Hebron, and built there an altar unto the LORD.

Genesis 14 (Abram's Forces Smite his Enemies)

Genesis 15 (The Covenant)

¹After these things the word of the LORD came unto Abram in a vision, saying, "Fear not, Abram: I am thy shield, and thy exceeding great reward." ²And Abram said, "LORD God, what wilt thou give me, seeing I go childless, and the steward of my house is this Eliezer of Damascus?"[z] ³And Abram said, "Behold, to me thou hast given no seed: and, lo, one born in my house is mine heir." ⁴And, behold, the word of the LORD came unto him, saying, "This shall not be thine heir; but he that shall come forth out of thine own bowels shall be thine heir."[aa] ⁵And he brought him forth abroad, and said, "Look now toward heaven, and tell the stars, if thou be able to number them": and he said unto him, "So shall thy seed be." ⁶And he believed in the LORD; and he counted it to him for righteousness.

⁷And he said unto him, "I am the LORD that brought thee out of Ur of the Chaldees, to give thee this land to inherit it". ⁸And he said, "LORD God, whereby shall I know that I shall inherit it?" ⁹And he said unto him, "Take me an heifer of three years old, and a she goat of three years old, and a ram of three years old, and a turtledove, and a young pigeon." ¹⁰And he took unto him all these, and divided them in the midst, and laid each piece one against another: but the birds divided he not. ¹¹And when the fowls came down upon the carcasses, Abram drove them away.[bb]

¹²And when the sun was going down, a deep sleep fell upon Abram; and, lo, an horror of great darkness fell upon him. ¹³And he said unto Abram, "Know of a surety that thy seed shall be a stranger in a land that is not theirs, and shall serve them; and they shall afflict them four hundred years; ¹⁴And also that nation, whom they shall serve, will I judge: and afterward shall they come out with great substance. ¹⁵And thou shalt go to thy fathers in peace; thou shalt be buried in a good old age. ¹⁶But in the fourth generation they shall come hither again: for the iniquity of the Amorites is not yet full."[cc]

¹⁷And it came to pass, that, when the sun went down, and it was dark, behold a smoking furnace, and a burning lamp that passed between those pieces. ¹⁸In the same day the LORD made a covenant with Abram, saying, "Unto thy seed have I given this land, from the river of Egypt unto the great river, the river Euphrates: ¹⁹The Kenites, and the Kenizzites, and the Kadmonites, ²⁰And the Hittites, and the Perizzites, and the Rephaims, ²¹And the Amorites, and the Canaanites, and the Girgashites, and the Jebusites."

---

[z] Steward of my house = my servant, who shall serve as my heir if I have no children. (FI)
[aa] One who comes out of Abram's bowels means one who is actually born from Abram's semen (FI)
[bb] This passage describes a ritual of animal sacrifice. It will be discussed in detail in the next lesson.
[cc] This passage describes a prophecy of what will happen to Abram's future offspring – what will become the nation of Israel. (FI)

Genesis 16 (Hagar and Ishmael)

¹Now Sarai Abram's wife bare him no children: and she had an handmaid, an Egyptian, whose name was Hagar. ²And Sarai said unto Abram, "Behold now, the LORD hath restrained me from bearing: I pray thee, go in unto my maid; it may be that I may obtain children by her."[dd] And Abram hearkened to the voice of Sarai. ³And Sarai Abram's wife took Hagar her maid the Egyptian, after Abram had dwelt ten years in the land of Canaan, and gave her to her husband Abram to be his wife. ⁴And he went in unto Hagar, and she conceived: and when she saw that she had conceived, her mistress was despised in her eyes.[ee]

⁵And Sarai said unto Abram, "My wrong be upon thee: I have given my maid into thy bosom; and when she saw that she had conceived, I was despised in her eyes: the LORD judge between me and thee." ⁶But Abram said unto Sarai, "Behold, thy maid is in thine hand; do to her as it pleaseth thee." And when Sarai dealt hardly with her, she fled from her face.

⁷And the angel of the LORD found her by a fountain of water in the wilderness, by the fountain in the way to Shur. ⁸And he said, "Hagar, Sarai's maid, whence camest thou? and whither wilt thou go?" And she said, "I flee from the face of my mistress Sarai." ⁹And the angel of the LORD said unto her, "Return to thy mistress, and submit thyself under her hands." ¹⁰And the angel of the LORD said unto her, "I will multiply thy seed exceedingly, that it shall not be numbered for multitude." ¹¹And the angel of the LORD said unto her, "Behold, thou art with child and shalt bear a son, and shalt call his name Ishmael; because the LORD hath heard thy affliction. ¹²And he will be a wild man; his hand will be against every man, and every man's hand against him; and he shall dwell in the presence of all his brethren." ¹³And she called the name of the LORD that spake unto her, "Thou God seest me": for she said, "Have I also here looked after him that seeth me?" ¹⁴Wherefore the well was called Beerlahairoi;[ff] behold, it is between Kadesh and Bered. ¹⁵And Hagar bare Abram a son: and Abram called his son's name, which Hagar bare, Ishmael. ¹⁶And Abram was fourscore and six years old, when Hagar bare Ishmael to Abram.[gg]

Genesis 17 (Name Changes and Circumcision)

¹And when Abram was ninety years old and nine, the LORD appeared to Abram, and said unto him, "I am the Almighty God; walk before me, and be thou perfect. ²And I will make my covenant between me and thee, and will multiply thee exceedingly." ³And Abram fell on his face: and God talked with him, saying, ⁴"As for me, behold, my covenant is with thee, and thou shalt be a father of many nations. ⁵Neither shall thy name any more be called Abram, but thy

---

[dd] This is not as unusual or disturbing as you might think. Many families in this era and region were polygamous, and the reason for this probably had a lot to do with maximizing reproduction. One man could impregnate multiple women. The volume of children would increase his workforce and therefore his wealth.

[ee] Regardless of cultural norms, human beings can still be jealous! Furthermore, it appears that the child conceived by Hagar will still be considered Sarai's property, since Hagar is essentially a slave. Consider the complex emotions existing between the two women.

[ff] Beer-laha-iroi means "well of the Living One who sees me." (BHL)

[gg] Four score and six = 86 (FI)

name shall be Abraham; for a father of many nations have I made thee. ^{6}And I will make thee exceeding fruitful, and I will make nations of thee, and kings shall come out of thee. ^{7}And I will establish my covenant between me and thee and thy seed after thee in their generations for an everlasting covenant, to be a God unto thee, and to thy seed after thee. ^{8}And I will give unto thee, and to thy seed after thee, the land wherein thou art a stranger, all the land of Canaan, for an everlasting possession; and I will be their God."

^{9}And God said unto Abraham, "Thou shalt keep my covenant therefore, thou, and thy seed after thee in their generations. ^{10}This is my covenant, which ye shall keep, between me and you and thy seed after thee; Every man child among you shall be circumcised. ^{11}And ye shall circumcise the flesh of your foreskin; and it shall be a token of the covenant betwixt me and you. ^{12}And he that is eight days old shall be circumcised among you, every man child in your generations, he that is born in the house, or bought with money of any stranger, which is not of thy seed. ^{13}He that is born in thy house, and he that is bought with thy money, must needs be circumcised: and my covenant shall be in your flesh for an everlasting covenant. ^{14}And the uncircumcised man child whose flesh of his foreskin is not circumcised, that soul shall be cut off from his people; he hath broken my covenant."

^{15}And God said unto Abraham, "As for Sarai thy wife, thou shalt not call her name Sarai, but Sarah shall her name be. ^{16}And I will bless her, and give thee a son also of her: yea, I will bless her, and she shall be a mother of nations; kings of people shall be of her." ^{17}Then Abraham fell upon his face, and laughed, and said in his heart, "Shall a child be born unto him that is an hundred years old? and shall Sarah, that is ninety years old, bear?" ^{18}And Abraham said unto God, "O that Ishmael might live before thee!" ^{19}And God said, "Sarah thy wife shall bear thee a son indeed; and thou shalt call his name Isaac: and I will establish my covenant with him for an everlasting covenant, and with his seed after him. ^{20}And as for Ishmael, I have heard thee: Behold, I have blessed him, and will make him fruitful, and will multiply him exceedingly; twelve princes shall he beget, and I will make him a great nation. ^{21}But my covenant will I establish with Isaac, which Sarah shall bear unto thee at this set time in the next year."

^{22}And he left off talking with him, and God went up from Abraham. ^{23}And Abraham took Ishmael his son, and all that were born in his house, and all that were bought with his money, every male among the men of Abraham's house; and circumcised the flesh of their foreskin in the selfsame day, as God had said unto him. ^{24}And Abraham was ninety years old and nine, when he was circumcised in the flesh of his foreskin. ^{25}And Ishmael his son was thirteen years old, when he was circumcised in the flesh of his foreskin. ^{26}In the selfsame day was Abraham circumcised, and Ishmael his son. ^{27}And all the men of his house, born in the house, and bought with money of the stranger, were circumcised with him.

Genesis 18 (Visitations)

¹And the LORD[hh] appeared unto him in the plains of Mamre: and he sat in the tent door in the heat of the day; ²And he lift up his eyes and looked, and, lo, three men stood by him: and when he saw them, he ran to meet them from the tent door, and bowed himself toward the ground, ³And said, "My LORD,[ii] if now I have found favour in thy sight, pass not away, I pray thee, from thy servant: ⁴Let a little water, I pray you, be fetched, and wash your feet, and rest yourselves under the tree: ⁵And I will fetch a morsel of bread, and comfort ye your hearts; after that ye shall pass on: for therefore are ye come to your servant." And they said, "So do, as thou hast said." ⁶And Abraham hastened into the tent unto Sarah, and said, Make ready quickly three measures of fine meal, knead it, and make cakes upon the hearth. ⁷And Abraham ran unto the herd, and fetcht a calf tender and good, and gave it unto a young man; and he hasted to dress it. ⁸And he took butter, and milk, and the calf which he had dressed, and set it before them; and he stood by them under the tree, and they did eat. ⁹And they said unto him, "Where is Sarah thy wife?" And he said, "Behold, in the tent." ¹⁰And he said, "I will certainly return unto thee according to the time of life; and, lo, Sarah thy wife shall have a son."

And Sarah heard it in the tent door, which was behind him. ¹¹Now Abraham and Sarah were old and well stricken in age; and it ceased to be with Sarah after the manner of women. ¹²Therefore Sarah laughed within herself, saying, "After I am waxed old shall I have pleasure, my lord being old also?" ¹³And the LORD said unto Abraham," Wherefore did Sarah laugh, saying, 'Shall I of a surety bear a child, which am old?' ¹⁴Is any thing too hard for the LORD? At the time appointed I will return unto thee, according to the time of life, and Sarah shall have a son." ¹⁵Then Sarah denied, saying, "I laughed not"; for she was afraid. And he said, "Nay; but thou didst laugh."

¹⁶And the men rose up from thence, and looked toward Sodom: and Abraham went with them to bring them on the way. ¹⁷And the LORD said, "Shall I hide from Abraham that thing which I do; ¹⁸Seeing that Abraham shall surely become a great and mighty nation, and all the nations of the earth shall be blessed in him? ¹⁹For I know him, that he will command his children and his household after him, and they shall keep the way of the LORD, to do justice and judgment; that the LORD may bring upon Abraham that which he hath spoken of him." ²⁰And the LORD said, "Because the cry of Sodom and Gomorrah is great, and because their sin is very grievous; ²¹I will go down now, and see whether they have done altogether according to the cry of it, which is come unto me; and if not, I will know." ²²And the men turned their faces from thence, and went toward Sodom: but Abraham stood yet before the LORD.

²³And Abraham drew near, and said, "Wilt thou also destroy the righteous with the wicked? ²⁴Peradventure[jj] there be fifty righteous within the city: wilt thou also destroy and not spare the place for the fifty righteous that are therein? ²⁵That be far from thee to do after this manner, to slay the righteous with the wicked: and that the righteous should be as the wicked,

---

[hh] Here, "LORD" means *Yahweh*, which is the name of God (BHL)
[ii] Here, "LORD" is the word *adonai,* which could be translated as "my lords." (BHL) He is addressing the three men. Theologians generally assume these men are angels. They seem to be the same angels who later go down to the city of Sodom, in the next chapter – however, in the Sodom episode, there are only two angels.
[jj] Peradventure = What if…? (FI)

that be far from thee: Shall not the Judge of all the earth do right?" ²⁶And the LORD said, "If I find in Sodom fifty righteous within the city, then I will spare all the place for their sakes." ²⁷And Abraham answered and said, "Behold now, I have taken upon me to speak unto the LORD, which am but dust and ashes: ²⁸Peradventure there shall lack five of the fifty righteous: wilt thou destroy all the city for lack of five"? And he said, "If I find there forty and five, I will not destroy it." ²⁹And he spake unto him yet again, and said, "Peradventure there shall be forty found there." And he said, "I will not do it for forty's sake. ³⁰And he said unto him, Oh let not the LORD be angry, and I will speak: Peradventure there shall thirty be found there." And he said, "I will not do it, if I find thirty there." ³¹And he said, "Behold now, I have taken upon me to speak unto the LORD: Peradventure there shall be twenty found there." And he said, "I will not destroy it for twenty's sake." ³²And he said, "Oh let not the LORD be angry, and I will speak yet but this once: Peradventure ten shall be found there." And he said, "I will not destroy it for ten's sake." ³³And the LORD went his way, as soon as he had left communing with Abraham: and Abraham returned unto his place.

Genesis 19 (Sodom)

¹And there came two angels to Sodom at even; and Lot sat in the gate of Sodom: and Lot seeing them rose up to meet them; and he bowed himself with his face toward the ground; ²And he said, "Behold now, my lords, turn in, I pray you, into your servant's house, and tarry all night, and wash your feet, and ye shall rise up early, and go on your ways." And they said, "Nay; but we will abide in the street all night." ³And he pressed upon them greatly; and they turned in unto him, and entered into his house; and he made them a feast, and did bake unleavened bread, and they did eat. ⁴But before they lay down, the men of the city, even the men of Sodom, compassed the house round, both old and young, all the people from every quarter: ⁵And they called unto Lot, and said unto him, "Where are the men which came in to thee this night? bring them out unto us, that we may know them."[kk] ⁶And Lot went out at the door unto them, and shut the door after him, ⁷And said, "I pray you, brethren, do not so wickedly. ⁸Behold now, I have two daughters which have not known man; let me, I pray you, bring them out unto you, and do ye to them as is good in your eyes: only unto these men do nothing; for therefore came they under the shadow of my roof." ⁹And they said, "Stand back." And they said again, "This one fellow came in to sojourn, and he will needs be a judge:[ll] now will we deal worse with thee, than with them." And they pressed sore upon the man, even Lot, and came near to break the door. ¹⁰But the men[mm] put forth their hand, and pulled Lot into the house to them, and shut to the door. ¹¹And they smote the men that were at the door of the house with blindness, both small and great: so that they wearied themselves to find the door.

[kk] Know them = have sex with them. (FI) Yes. You read it right.
[ll] The "one fellow" here is Lot, who came to Sodom "to sojourn," or as a foreign traveler. The men are incensed that he, a visitor to the town, dares to play judge over them. (EP)
[mm] These men are the two angels currently inside Lot's house.

¹²And the men[nn] said unto Lot," Hast thou here any besides? son in law, and thy sons, and thy daughters, and whatsoever thou hast in the city, bring them out of this place: ¹³For we will destroy this place, because the cry of them is waxen great before the face of the LORD; and the LORD hath sent us to destroy it." ¹⁴And Lot went out, and spake unto his sons in law, which married his daughters, and said, "Up, get you out of this place; for the LORD will destroy this city." But he seemed as one that mocked unto his sons in law. ¹⁵And when the morning arose, then the angels hastened Lot, saying, "Arise, take thy wife, and thy two daughters, which are here; lest thou be consumed in the iniquity of the city." ¹⁶And while he lingered, the men laid hold upon his hand, and upon the hand of his wife, and upon the hand of his two daughters; the LORD being merciful unto him: and they brought him forth, and set him without the city. ¹⁷And it came to pass, when they had brought them forth abroad, that he said, "Escape for thy life; look not behind thee, neither stay thou in all the plain; escape to the mountain, lest thou be consumed."

¹⁸And Lot said unto them, "Oh, not so, my LORD: ¹⁹Behold now, thy servant hath found grace in thy sight, and thou hast magnified thy mercy, which thou hast shewed unto me in saving my life; and I cannot escape to the mountain, lest some evil take me, and I die: ²⁰Behold now, this city is near to flee unto,[oo] and it is a little one: Oh, let me escape thither, (is it not a little one?) and my soul shall live." ²¹And he said unto him, "See, I have accepted thee concerning this thing also, that I will not overthrow this city, for the which thou hast spoken. ²²Haste thee, escape thither; for I cannot do anything till thou be come thither." Therefore the name of the city was called Zoar. ²³The sun was risen upon the earth when Lot entered into Zoar.

²⁴Then the LORD rained upon Sodom and upon Gomorrah brimstone and fire from the LORD out of heaven; ²⁵And he overthrew those cities, and all the plain, and all the inhabitants of the cities, and that which grew upon the ground. ²⁶But his wife looked back from behind him, and she became a pillar of salt.

²⁷And Abraham gat up early in the morning to the place where he stood before the LORD: ²⁸And he looked toward Sodom and Gomorrah, and toward all the land of the plain, and beheld, and, lo, the smoke of the country went up as the smoke of a furnace. ²⁹And it came to pass, when God destroyed the cities of the plain, that God remembered Abraham, and sent Lot out of the midst of the overthrow, when he overthrew the cities in which Lot dwelt.

³⁰And Lot went up out of Zoar, and dwelt in the mountain, and his two daughters with him; for he feared to dwell in Zoar: and he dwelt in a cave, he and his two daughters. ³¹And the firstborn said unto the younger, "Our father is old, and there is not a man in the earth to come in unto us after the manner of all the earth: ³²Come, let us make our father drink wine, and we will lie with him, that we may preserve seed of our father."[pp] ³³And they made their father drink wine that night: and the firstborn went in, and lay with her father; and he perceived not when she lay down, nor when she arose. ³⁴And it came to pass on the morrow, that the firstborn said unto the

---

[nn] Again, the angels.
[oo] The city of which Lot speaks is Zoar. It will be spared for Lot's sake, while Sodom and Gomorrah will be destroyed – alas, there must not have been even 10 righteous people living there.
[pp] Preserving the male bloodline was extremely important in this culture. The only way Lot's daughters could do this was to become impregnated by their father. Remember, their husbands did not come with them out of Sodom.

younger, "Behold, I lay yesternight with my father: let us make him drink wine this night also; and go thou in, and lie with him, that we may preserve seed of our father." [35]And they made their father drink wine that night also: and the younger arose, and lay with him; and he perceived not when she lay down, nor when she arose. [36]Thus were both the daughters of Lot with child by their father. [37]And the first born bare a son, and called his name Moab: the same is the father of the Moabites unto this day. [38]And the younger, she also bare a son, and called his name Benammi: the same is the father of the children of Ammon unto this day.

Genesis 20 (Story of Abimelech, King of Gerar)

Genesis 21 (Isaac's Birth)

[1]And the LORD visited Sarah as he had said, and the LORD did unto Sarah as he had spoken. [2]For Sarah conceived, and bare Abraham a son in his old age, at the set time of which God had spoken to him. [3]And Abraham called the name of his son that was born unto him, whom Sarah bare to him, Isaac. [4]And Abraham circumcised his son Isaac being eight days old, as God had commanded him. [5]And Abraham was an hundred years old, when his son Isaac was born unto him. [6]And Sarah said, "God hath made me to laugh, so that all that hear will laugh with me." [7]And she said, "Who would have said unto Abraham, that Sarah should have given children suck? for I have born him a son in his old age." [8]And the child grew, and was weaned: and Abraham made a great feast the same day that Isaac was weaned.

[9]And Sarah saw the son of Hagar the Egyptian, which she had born unto Abraham, mocking. [10]Wherefore she said unto Abraham, "Cast out this bondwoman and her son: for the son of this bondwoman shall not be heir with my son, even with Isaac." [11]And the thing was very grievous in Abraham's sight because of his son. [12]And God said unto Abraham, "Let it not be grievous in thy sight because of the lad, and because of thy bondwoman; in all that Sarah hath said unto thee, hearken unto her voice; for in Isaac shall thy seed be called. [13]And also of the son of the bondwoman will I make a nation, because he is thy seed."

[14]And Abraham rose up early in the morning, and took bread, and a bottle of water, and gave it unto Hagar, putting it on her shoulder, and the child, and sent her away: and she departed, and wandered in the wilderness of Beersheba. [15]And the water was spent in the bottle, and she cast the child under one of the shrubs. [16]And she went, and sat her down over against him a good way off, as it were a bow shot: for she said, "Let me not see the death of the child." And she sat over against him, and lift up her voice, and wept. [17]And God heard the voice of the lad; and the angel of God called to Hagar out of heaven, and said unto her, "What aileth thee, Hagar? fear not; for God hath heard the voice of the lad where he is. [18]Arise, lift up the lad, and hold him in thine hand; for I will make him a great nation." [19]And God opened her eyes, and she saw a well of water; and she went, and filled the bottle with water, and gave the lad drink. [20]And God was with the lad; and he grew, and dwelt in the wilderness, and became an archer. [21]And he dwelt in the wilderness of Paran: and his mother took him a wife out of the land of Egypt.

Genesis 21:22-34 (Abimilech and the Well)

Genesis 22 (Isaac on the Mountain)

[1] And it came to pass after these things, that God did tempt Abraham, and said unto him, "Abraham": and he said, "Behold, here I am." [2] And he said, "Take now thy son, thine only son Isaac, whom thou lovest, and get thee into the land of Moriah; and offer him there for a burnt offering upon one of the mountains which I will tell thee of." [3] And Abraham rose up early in the morning, and saddled his ass, and took two of his young men with him, and Isaac his son, and clave the wood for the burnt offering, and rose up, and went unto the place of which God had told him.

[4] Then on the third day Abraham lifted up his eyes, and saw the place afar off. [5] And Abraham said unto his young men, "Abide ye here with the ass; and I and the lad will go yonder and worship, and come again to you." [6] And Abraham took the wood of the burnt offering, and laid it upon Isaac his son; and he took the fire in his hand, and a knife; and they went both of them together. [7] And Isaac spake unto Abraham his father, and said, "My father": and he said, "Here am I, my son." And he said," Behold the fire and the wood: but where is the lamb for a burnt offering?" [8] And Abraham said, "My son, God will provide himself a lamb for a burnt offering": so they went both of them together. [9] And they came to the place which God had told him of; and Abraham built an altar there, and laid the wood in order, and bound Isaac his son, and laid him on the altar upon the wood.

[10] And Abraham stretched forth his hand, and took the knife to slay his son. [11] And the angel of the LORD called unto him out of heaven, and said, "Abraham, Abraham": and he said, "Here am I." [12] And he said, "Lay not thine hand upon the lad, neither do thou any thing unto him: for now I know that thou fearest God, seeing thou hast not withheld thy son, thine only son from me." [13] And Abraham lifted up his eyes, and looked, and behold behind him a ram caught in a thicket by his horns: and Abraham went and took the ram, and offered him up for a burnt offering in the stead of his son. [14] And Abraham called the name of that place Jehovahjireh: as it is said to this day, "In the mount of the LORD it shall be seen."

[15] And the angel of the LORD called unto Abraham out of heaven the second time, [16] And said, "By myself have I sworn, saith the LORD, for because thou hast done this thing, and hast not withheld thy son, thine only son: [17] That in blessing I will bless thee, and in multiplying I will multiply thy seed as the stars of the heaven, and as the sand which is upon the sea shore; and thy seed shall possess the gate of his enemies; [18] And in thy seed shall all the nations of the earth be blessed; because thou hast obeyed my voice." [19] So Abraham returned unto his young men, and they rose up and went together to Beersheba; and Abraham dwelt at Beersheba.

Genesis 22: 20-24 (Genealogy)

Genesis 23-24 (Sarah Dies and Isaac Marries)

Genesis 25 (Abraham Dies)

LESSON EIGHT:
FATHER ABRAHAM AND THE COVENANT

"Father Abraham had many sons, and many sons had Father Abraham.
I am one of them, and so are you, so let's all praise the Lord…"

Thus goes the well-known children's campfire song. Indeed, this is Abraham's legacy; he is known as the great father of Israel, the patriarch of Judaism, the first person on the planet specifically called to build a formal religion around a monotheistic God. Although God has been in the picture from the very beginning of Genesis, his involvement with humanity has thus far been about teaching and enforcing moral boundaries. With Abraham, we see God reach down to one particular descendant of Noah for yet another important starting point, the beginning of a religion in which God makes grand promises and people respond through faith, obedience, and ritual. This is the beginning of the Jewish religion.

LEGENDARY HERO

Abraham's story begins in Genesis 12 at the moment of his calling, which is an archetypal element in hero stories around the world, a regular guy called away from home or out of his comfort zone by a force he cannot resist – like Luke Skywalker and Bilbo Baggins. In this case, God calls "Abram" away from his father's land and promises him a new country, not to mention sons and grandchildren to populate it. This is really huge, particularly given the setting of an ancient patriarchal culture. To leave one's father and one's land is monumental. To make things even more complicated, Abram's wife is barren, so the potential for becoming a patriarch of his own nation is slim to none. However, we know that by the end of the story, everything God promises him has come to pass. The offspring of "Father Abraham" gives root to the three most populous monotheistic religions of the world today: Judaism first, then Christianity, and finally Islam. This makes him a very unique hero of world literature.

However, there are different kinds of heroes and hero stories, and in the same way we found value in analyzing Genesis 1-11 as mythology, we should seek to identify the genre of the Abraham tale and thereby give it a context for analysis. It is not considered a myth, and for one reason in particular – the story of Abraham is more firmly grounded in historical time and place than is mythology. It does not take place at a vague "in the beginning" setting. Rather, Abraham's narrative begins with a very real city-state called Ur (10:27), overlaps with the details of an Egyptian pharaoh (Chapter 12), and relates the concretely secular details of a political battle (Chapter 14). It is clearly an attempt to tell the real life story of a man who lived his life in a real place, in the context of an identifiable historical culture, unlike the story of the Garden of Eden with its magic fruit and talking snake. By contrast, the supernatural events in Abraham's story are of a more literal nature: God speaking aloud to Abraham and sending angels against an otherwise realistic background. Abraham differs significantly from Adam as well, in that his characterization moves far beyond symbolism. We get his birth and marriage background in Chapter 11, his death and place of burial in Chapter 25, and a chronological account of the major events of his life in between. But we cannot, in a literary sense, strictly call the story a history, for it was transmitted to the writer of Genesis over many centuries of oral tradition. In fact, it shows definite signs of oral development: did you notice that Sarah sends Hagar away two times, and each time God rescues her and sends her back? Also, there are two separate episodes where Abraham pretends that his wife is his sister (the second is in chapter 20 in the story of Abimilech). It is common for orally-transmitted stories to contain repeated elements such as these. **For all these reasons, the story of Abraham is most accurately identified as a legend – more concrete and secular than a myth, less concrete and verifiable than history.**

> **NARRATIVE GENRES OF GENESIS-EXODUS**
>
> **Myth:** ancient, unverifiable, supernatural, religious, symbolic
>
> **Legend:** old, unverifiable but historically and realistically grounded, not symbolic, often showing signs of oral transmission
>
> **History:** old, verifiable, concretely detailed, attributed to a primary or secondary source

JEWISH IDENTITY

So what is the best literary angle for studying a legend? We must remember that with a legend, a presumably real person's life story was kept alive by an enduring cultural tradition for many, many years. Although it was passed along orally and could have expanded and altered over time, there was a cultural need that kept it going. In a legend, we find the hero's life story wrapped up in cultural identity. Why would the Israelite nation care for this story and nurture its survival for so long? Because the story of Abraham speaks to the self-identifying need of the Jewish people (and indeed all peoples have a need for self-identification, and so all peoples have legends). Abraham is a cultural cornerstone, like King Arthur for the English. When we study Abraham, we are learning about how the Jews view themselves as a nation and as a people of God; secondarily, we learn about the roots of Christian identity; and finally, although the Koran contains a distinctly modified version of the Abraham story, we glimpse the core of the Muslim identity as well.

The central theme of this legend must therefore shed light on the identity of the nation of Israel and the traditions of the Jewish people. Everything in the Abraham saga is centered around the theme of "covenant." Indeed, the website of the Israel Ministry of Foreign Affairs[qq] calls the Jewish people "a covenanted people," referring to God's commitment to bless Abraham's descendants in the "land of promise" as revealed to Abraham in Genesis 15: "Unto thy seed have I given this land" (18). A covenant is an agreement, a solemn promise made between two parties. God's side of the Genesis covenant is to multiply Abram's offspring into a mighty nation and give them their own special territory, and Abram's side is to be obedient and, eventually, to circumcise the men of the covenant bloodline. Both sides of this covenant continue to be fulfilled in modern times. The ceremony of religious circumcision, called a "bris," is still performed today among the Jewish people as a reflection upon their covenant identity. And in 1948 the nation of Israel was declared an independent state with territory bounded by Lebanon, Syria, Jordan, and Egypt – the same Promised Land settled by Abraham in Genesis 13. Major political conflicts over this very tract of land continue to this day.

COVENANT: THEME

This idea of a two-sided covenant between God and man doesn't exactly put God and man on the same level as equals, but it endows man with a special eye-to-eye relationship with God not common to many other religions. Zeus, for instance, would never do such a thing! One perfect example of this eye-to-eye rapport is found when Abraham debates God over the fate of Sodom. God allows Abraham to challenge him, and in fact makes concessions along the way. When Abram gets impatient and impregnates Hagar, God doesn't get angry; rather, he extends a

---

[qq] "About the Jewish Religion." *Israel Ministry of Foreign Affairs.* State of Israel, 2013. Web. March 2014.
   <www.mfa.gov.il/aboutisrael/spotlight/pages/about%20the%20jewish%20religion.aspx>

measure of blessing to Hagar's child, too. In the entire Old Testament, we see that God is always "top dog" in his dealing with humanity, but humanity – particularly Israel – enjoys a special status of dignity and blessing, which comes with special responsibilities.

Each time God establishes a covenant with the Jews, the covenant is enacted with a sacred ceremony and accompanied by a physical token of remembrance. The first time we observed such an event was with Noah – following his altar of thanksgiving after the flood, God promised that he would never again destroy human life. His token was a rainbow, and Noah's side of the covenant was to replenish the earth. The covenant with Abram picks up where Noah's covenant left off. Not only will God never again *destroy* mankind, but through this new covenant he will *bless* mankind (Gen. 12:2). The establishment and fulfillment of the covenant goes through several phases.

COVENANT: BLOOD

The first phase, which is something like a "proposal," takes place in chapter 12 when Abram says "yes" and follows God to Canaan. After several years go by without Sarai getting pregnant, God reiterates his promise and sets up an official covenant ceremony, which is phase two. By modern standards, this ceremony is an odd one. God has Abraham collect several animals and cut them in half (Gen. 15) and then arrange the halves so that there is a path between them. Then Abram falls asleep and has a prophetic dream; afterwards, a smoking furnace and burning lamp (presumably a representation of God's presence) move down the path between the carcasses, which completes the ceremony. A modern audience reading this passage will likely be bewildered or disgusted by this ritual, when in fact the shedding of blood was a common part of ceremonies and agreements in the ancient world, much like boys becoming "blood brothers" or a pirate contract being signed in blood. The popular Harry Potter and *Divergent* book series also contain examples of blood-based covenants, demonstrating that even modern culture recognizes blood as the Life Force and therefore symbolically potent.

The Hebrew word for covenant, *berith*, means "to cut." Similarly, the Greek phrase *horkia temnein*, meaning "to cut the oaths," was used by Homer in the *Iliad* to describe scenes where animals were sacrificed and sacred oaths were sworn.[π] These phrases call to mind the

---

[π] Karavites, Peter and Thomas E. Wren. Promise-Giving and Treaty Making: Homer and the Near East. BRILL, 1992. Google Books. Web.

seriously binding nature of a covenant. Not all covenants in the Bible involve blood, but it is a motif to be expected and should be analyzed from an ancient point of view. Christian theology will pick up this motif when, in the New Testament, it describes a "new" covenant established by Jesus at the cross. This may also help explain why Christianity relies so heavily on the blood of Christ for its message – it is the mark of a profound new agreement between God and man.

COVENANT: TOKENS & TEST

It takes more than 13 years before the covenant progresses to its next phase, and the circumstances continue to sound unusual to the modern ear. When Sarai suggests that her husband use her maidservant as a childbirth surrogate, Sarai is actually operating within an ancient legal expectation. Hammurabi's Code required that barren women provide their husbands with a fertile surrogate. After impregnating her, Abram marries Hagar (16:3). This situation seems scandalous to a modern reader, but in the ancient world, polygamy was the norm. The modern reader should also note that God has not, prior to Ishmael's birth, specified that Sarai is to be the mother of the covenant son – all Abram knows is that the son will be biological (not adoptive). Abram is not scolded or punished for his behavior with Hagar. He lives in peace until, at age 99, God changes his name to Abraham (meaning "father of many") and Sarai's name to Sarah (meaning "lady" or "princess"). He says that they will finally conceive the promised child of the covenant, who shall be named Isaac. Interestingly, the name Isaac means "laughter," for Abraham and Sarah both laugh at the news that she, who is 90 years old, will give birth to a baby. This is what we might call the third phase of the making of the covenant: name changes accompanied by the provision of a covenant token, which is circumcision. The act of cutting that takes place in circumcision, in keeping with the blood tradition already discussed, is specifically male-oriented because the Hebrew family

> **ANCIENT COVENANTS AND MODERN WEDDINGS**
>
> **The ceremony:** walking down the aisle between the two sides of the covenant
>
> **The token:** exchange of rings
>
> **The blood:** rings are a holdover from the practice of the bride and groom cutting their fingers and mingling their blood; the scar was the token
>
> **The name change:** traditionally speaking, the bride will take the groom's last name
>
> **The dinner reception:** in ancient times, sacrificed animals would be served in a feast after the ceremony

tree is patriarchal. Each time a Hebrew boy is circumcised, the very organ of reproduction is forever marked by a reminder of God's promise to multiply the Hebrew nation. Abraham, Ishmael, and all the other males of the household are circumcised, and within a year Isaac is born. The covenant is complete.

However, the story continues through a fourth phase, which we might call "The Test." This happens when Abraham is asked to sacrifice Isaac to God atop the mountain. This is something of a "catch 22" predicament. If Abraham refuses, then he breaks his promise to follow and obey; if God holds firm to his demand, then God breaks his promise to establish a blessed bloodline through Isaac. Either way, it seems, the covenant is doomed. What eventually happens, when God provides a ram to serve in Isaac's place, is the only outcome that fully satisfies both parties' obligations. Abraham has been faithful, and God has preserved Isaac. This episode provides evidence that the covenant is functional, that both God and man are fully willing to participate.

The legendary importance of the covenant cannot be exaggerated. For Jews, Christians and Muslims, the verses in Genesis that set down the terms of the covenant have global significance: "And I will make of thee a great nation, and I will bless thee, and make thy name great; and thou shalt be a blessing: And I will bless them that bless thee, and curse him that curseth thee: and in thee shall all families of the earth be blessed" (Genesis 12:2-3). This statement indicates that the nation fathered by Abraham will be a source of blessing for the entire earth, and that its enemies will be cursed. Jews, Christians and Muslims each claim this promise for themselves – an interesting fact which we will discuss further in the next lesson.

LESSON EIGHT STUDY GUIDE

Objective Information: legend, covenant, circumcision

Subjective Expression:

1) **Comparison**: Can you think of any other myths or religious legends in which a god makes a contractual agreement with a human, as opposed to just giving commands? Compare this god to Abraham's.

2) Cultural Connection: Contemporary literature and pop culture frequently allude to Lot's wife turning into salt. Furthermore, this episode is sometimes taken to be a mythical explanation for the salt deposits in Israel near the Dead Sea. Using the Internet, try to find some of these allusions and/or further information about the geological formation named after this tragic nameless woman… who might have been called Edith.

3) Opinion: Here's an interesting idea to ponder: fate versus determinism. In this story, does Abraham prosper because God makes it so, or because he is clever and persevering? This is a classic philosophical question, one addressed in many faith traditions. Even within the scope of Christianity, there are differences of opinion; for instance, Presbyterians tend to believe in a God-authored fate, called predestination. Other denominations have different perspectives. What do you think? Does Fate provide a script for your life, or do you write your own script and suffer your own consequences?

BIBLICAL LITERARY INVENTORY — NARRATIVE

Narrative: The Story of Abraham **Passage:** Genesis 12-25

I. Protagonist and Antagonist – Abraham versus the internal conflict arising from his desire for a son, alongside God's slow movement toward fulfilling his promise

II. Inciting Incident – God tells Abram to leave his home and family and start over in Canaan, accompanied by the promise that he will make of Abraham a great nation. This promise is known as the covenant.

III. Rising Action – Abraham leaves for Canaan, but has to travel onward when there is a famine. Then he returns to Canaan and, along with nephew Lot, settles into the new land. Action continues to rise as new details of the covenant come into play (circumcision and name changes) and Abraham and Sarah conspire to create an heir through the handmaiden, Hagar, who does indeed give birth to a son named Ishmael. Still, however, the covenant promise was intended for Abraham and Sarah, who as yet remain childless.

IV. Climax – The birth of Isaac: the fulfillment of the covenant promise.

V. Falling Action – God tells Abraham he must sacrifice Isaac on the mountain. Now that Abraham has what he wants, is he still wholly committed to the covenant? This is an unexpected development, further testing Abraham's faith that God will keep his covenant promise. Without Isaac, the covenant is null.

VI. Resolution – God saves Isaac with a substitutionary sacrifice. Abraham then goes on to find a suitable wife for Isaac, and he dies with the knowledge that the promised Abrahamic nation is underway.

VII. Theme – _____

_____

VIII. Symbolism – Circumcision functions as a symbol of the covenant, particularly in its patriarchal nature.

IX. Motif – There is a motif of sex and sexual reproduction throughout Abraham's saga: look for instances of polygamy, sodomy, and incest. Does God specifically condemn or punish any of these acts? Before answering, look up the following verses, which comment on the sins of Sodom: Jeremiah 23:14, Amos 4:1-11, and Ezekiel 16:49-50. _____

_____

_____

X. Character Development – Both God and Abraham are interesting and well-rounded characters in this legend. Keeping in mind the entire story of Sodom – from Abraham's argument with God to the final destruction of the city and escape of Lot – look for several character traits displayed by either God or Abraham. Remember: it is more interesting if you look for positives and negatives, or at least "expecteds" and "unexpected," in their character development.

_____

_____

_____

_____

_____

XI. Narrative Persona – The narrator in Chapter 12 and through the rest of the book of Genesis seems more interested in realistic events and concrete, chronological details than was the narrator of Genesis 1-11. Some scholars think that Genesis 1-11 came from a different original source than Genesis 12-25, where we find the Abraham story. The important thing is that our narrator, whoever he might be, is clearly concerned with faith in the Hebrew God. The storytelling style and genre might have changed, but the attitude toward God and mankind has been consistent.

XII. Irony, Contrast, Foil and/or Reversals – Compare and contrast Abraham and Lot.

_____
_____
_____

XIII. Additional Literary Devices – How is Abraham an "everyman" protagonist?

_____
_____

XIV. Historical Criticism – In the second millennium B.C.E. the Code of Hammurabi allowed a man to claim as heirs any children fathered through slave women; it also required that barren women provide their husbands with just such a surrogate. This sheds some light on the events surrounding Sarah and Hagar. Does this impact your interpretation of the sins of Abraham and Sarah? If this was a customary act and not a sexual sin, how are we to understand the root of the conflict in this part of the story?_____

_____
_____
_____

XV. Genre Awareness –

___ Mythology: Symbolically, what does the story reveal about human nature or God?

___ Legend / Epic: What themes of Judeo-Christian identity emerge?

___ History: What historical events have a practical bearing on the present and future?

___ Biography: Why is the subject of the biography worth special attention?

___ Drama: What aspects of the play a "hold a mirror up to nature"?

___ Short Story: What elements of intentional storytelling contribute to theme and unity?

___ Narrative Poetry: Why was the story told via elevated and/or figurative language?

Based on your selection, provide a response to the genre-related question provided above:

_____
_____
_____

THE MUSLIM ABRAHAM
FROM THE KORAN

[2:125] We have rendered the shrine (the Ka`aba) a focal point for the people, and a safe sanctuary. You may use Abraham's shrine as a prayer house. We commissioned Abraham and Ismail: "You shall purify My house for those who visit, those who live there, and those who bow and prostrate."

[2:126] Abraham prayed: "My Lord, make this a peaceful land, and provide its people with fruits. Provide for those who believe in GOD and the Last Day." (God) said, "I will also provide for those who disbelieve. I will let them enjoy, temporarily, then commit them to the retribution of Hell, and a miserable destiny."

[2:127] As Abraham raised the foundations of the shrine, together with Ismail (they prayed): "Our Lord, accept this from us. You are the Hearer, the Omniscient.

[2:128] "Our Lord, make us submitters to You, and from our descendants let there be a community of submitters to You. Teach us the rites of our religion, and redeem us. You are the Redeemer, Most Merciful.

[2:129] "Our Lord, and raise among them a messenger to recite to them Your revelations, teach them the scripture and wisdom, and purify them. You are the Almighty, Most Wise."

[2:130] Who would forsake the religion of Abraham, except one who fools his own soul? We have chosen him in this world, and in the Hereafter he will be with the righteous.

[2:131] When his Lord said to him, "Submit," he said, "I submit to the Lord of the universe."

QUOTABLE QUOTES

> In Arabic, the word "Islam" means *submission* or *surrender* – however, it was derived from the root word "salam." From this root word, you can also derive the words *peace* and *safety*. Many people feel that Islam implies some sort of enslavement to Allah, but others find it more helpful to define the word "Islam" as *surrender*.
>
> Rosemary Pennington
> "What is the Meaning of the Word 'Islam'?"
> *Muslim Voices.org*

[ss] The Quran: Authorized English Version. Trans. Rashad Khalifa, PhD. Masjid Tucson. Web.

LESSON NINE:
ABRAHAMIC RELIGIONS

The Koran's version of the Abraham story is different from what we find in Genesis. It includes reference to a building called the Kaaba, which is still standing today in the Muslim holy city of Mecca (pictured above). According to the Koran,[tt] the Kaaba was built by Abraham and his first son, Ishmael, the child of Hagar (the Arabic word for *Ishmael* being *Ismail*). In Muslim tradition, it is Ishmael and not Isaac who is the covenant bearer – because he was the first-born son, Muslims consider that Ishmael rightfully inherited God's covenant blessing. In the Koran excerpt you read on the previous page, you can see just how important Abraham is to the Muslim faith. Muslims, Jews and Christians would agree on the roots of the Abrahamic family tree, but they would make different claims about its two main branches. You will find on the next page a diagram accurate to the Old Testament; the left side represents the Arabic tradition, and the right side illustrates Jewish (and eventual Christian) traditions:

[tt] Also known as the Quran or Qur'an, "Koran" is a Westernized phonetic spelling.

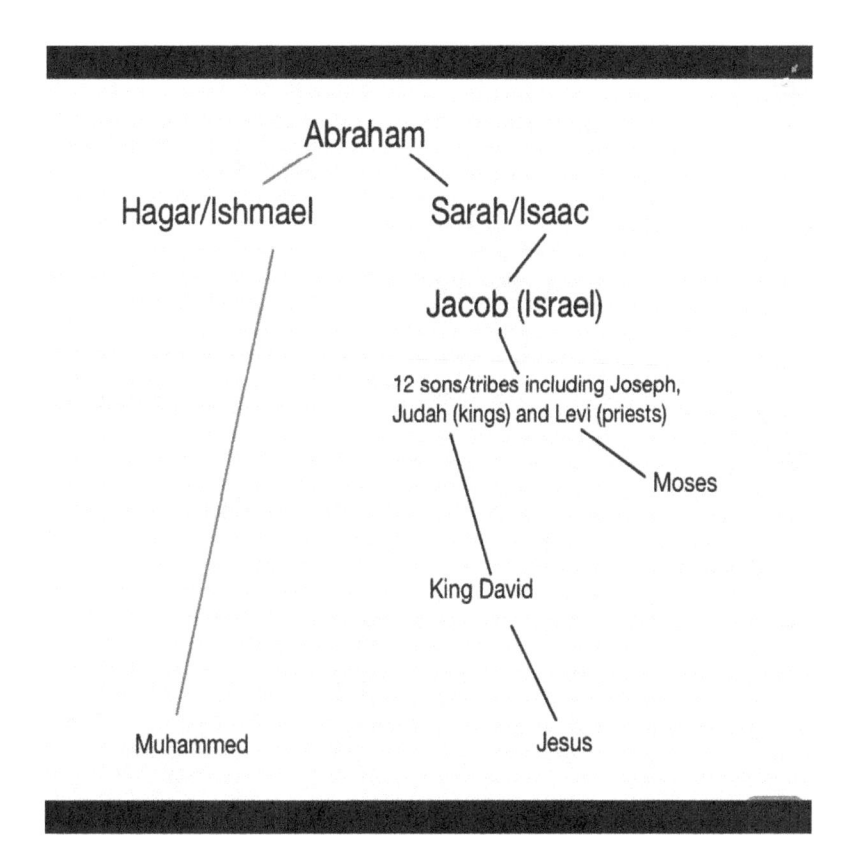

Abrahamic Family Tree Diagram:
- Abraham
  - Hagar/Ishmael → Muhammed
  - Sarah/Isaac → Jacob (Israel) → 12 sons/tribes including Joseph, Judah (kings) and Levi (priests) → Moses; King David → Jesus

The diagram is not chronologically to-scale (it does not accurately portray the length of time between generations) but it will help you visualize the blood relationships of the Abrahamic family tree according to Genesis. Isaac's son, Jacob, gets re-named "Israel" and fathers 12 sons including Joseph (who wore a famous coat of many colors) and Judah, who was the father of the kingly tribe – it is from Judah's name that we get the word *Judaism*. The royal bloodline eventually extends to King David (of the Psalms) and, according to the New Testament, to Jesus.

A Muslim point of view would focus attention on the Arabic side of the tree, whereas a Judeo-Christian point of view centers itself around the lineage of Isaac, as dictated by Genesis 17:

> And as for Ishmael, I have heard thee: Behold, I have blessed him, and will make him fruitful, and will multiply him exceedingly; twelve princes shall he beget, and I will make him a great nation. But my covenant will I establish with Isaac, which Sarah shall bear unto thee at this set time in the next year (20-21).

Muslims believe not only that Ishmael is the covenant bearer, but that it was Ishmael whom Abraham took up the mountain and nearly sacrificed. It is Ishmael who, with his father, constructs the holy Kaaba, according to the Koran. Furthermore, Muslims believe that Moses (whom we will study in the upcoming lessons) was born in the Arabic bloodline rather than the Levite tribe of the Jews. Most significantly, they believe that their chief and most holy prophet,

Muhammad, is also a descendant of Ishmael. In this fashion, Muhammad is seen as the ultimate fulfillment of the promise to Abraham, and that through Muhammad the world would be blessed:

> And I will bless them that bless thee, and curse him that curseth thee:
> and in thee shall all families of the earth be blessed. (Gen. 12:3)

Christians read the same passage and believe that Jesus fulfills this promise. Jesus, according to Christians, was born through the bloodline that started with Isaac and continued through King David, and that through Jesus the world can be saved. Jews believe that the singular fulfillment of this verse (through a Messiah) has not yet been revealed.

Before we finish up our studies of Abraham, take a look at an expanded version of our Bible Timeline, with Abraham and Muhammad added in; Abraham's dates are determined by rabbinic tradition and genealogical computations from Genesis, and Muhammad's placement is fully historical.

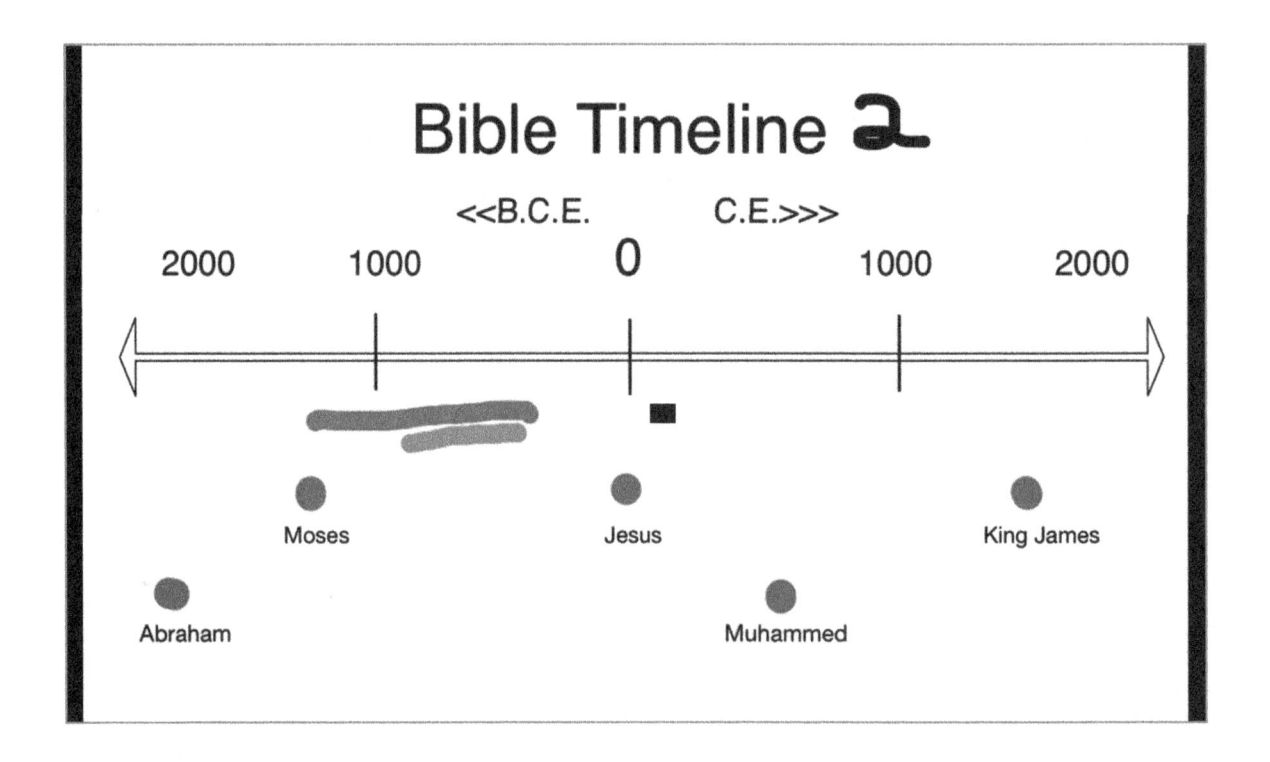

Bible Timeline 2

```
              <<B.C.E.    C.E.>>>
  2000   1000           0         1000      2000
   <|------|------------|-----------|---------|>
                 ___
                  ___
              ●           ●  ■              ●
            Moses       Jesus            King James

    ●                        ●
  Abraham                 Muhammed
```

LESSON NINE STUDY GUIDE

Objective Identification: Islam (noun), Muslim (adjective), Kaaba, Koran, Muhammad

Subjective Expression:

1) Recall: See if you can draw the Abrahamic family tree from memory. Glance back at the diagram on the previous page for a minute, and then see how accurately you can reproduce it. Keep trying until you have the basic concept committed to memory.

2) Research: See if your school library has a copy of the Koran. Flip through it to get a feel for its structure and style. You will find that, unlike the Bible, it is composed of surahs (chapters) rather than separate books. They are organized from longest to shortest, so if you'd like to read a short excerpt, you could start at the end. The surahs are not chronological.

3) Further Exploration: Abraham is an important figure throughout the rest of the Bible, including the New Testament. You may wish to explore the following mentions of Abraham:

- 2 Chronicles 1:27
- Hebrews 11:8-19
- Galatians 3:7-9
- James 2:23

Lexi

You said in the introduction that the Bible has something for everyone. I thought the art and science lessons were okay, but is there anything else of interest here for an atheist or agnostic like myself? Learning the roots of world religions isn't my number one goal for English class if you know what I mean. Thanks!

Dear Lexi,

Let's try to get an angle on the Abraham legend from a humanistic point of view – something you can do for most any Bible story if you are so inclined. As a text about human nature, the Bible scores rather well. Abraham might represent a sort of everyman prototype: the classic entrepreneur, mover-and-shaker, and leap-taker. He's also a visionary. He thinks he's heard from God, and this encounter inspires him to leave behind his entire universe and start over in a new land with no guarantees – at least no practical, physical guarantees. He is tenacious, clever, and freakishly brave. The result of his lifetime of perseverance is the birth of something huge. And although what he creates is distinctly religious (perhaps not of interest to everyone), let us not forget the humanistic value of a functioning faith community. All coherent cultures share strong beliefs in certain core principles; even secular American culture fits this pattern, with its defining faith in the principles of democracy, personal freedom, and the hope of the "American dream." The Abraham story has probably survived, in part, due to its "you can do it" philosophy, which is rather American in spirit! It's hard to find a character like this in world literature who predates Abraham.

MOSES (EXCERPTS FROM EXODUS-DEUTERONOMY)

The Book of Exodus picks up with the story of the Israelites at six generations after Abraham.[uu] They have been enslaved by an Egyptian pharaoh who fears that their growing numbers may be politically dangerous. Thus, he declares that all newborn Hebrew babies be thrown into the Nile. Moses' mother hides her son for three months in an effort to keep him alive.

Exodus 2:3-10 (Moses in the Bulrushes)

[3]And when she could not longer hide him, she took for him an ark of bulrushes,[vv] and daubed it with slime and with pitch, and put the child therein; and she laid it in the flags[ww] by the river's brink. [4]And his sister stood afar off, to wit[xx] what would be done to him.

[5]And the daughter of Pharaoh came down to wash herself at the river; and her maidens walked along by the river's side; and when she saw the ark among the flags, she sent her maid to fetch it. [6]And when she had opened it, she saw the child: and, behold, the babe wept. And she had compassion on him, and said, "This is one of the Hebrews' children." [7]Then said his sister to Pharaoh's daughter, "Shall I go and call to thee a nurse of the Hebrew women, that she may nurse the child for thee?" [8]And Pharaoh's daughter said to her, "Go." And the maid went and called the child's mother. [9]And Pharaoh's daughter said unto her, "Take this child away, and nurse it for me, and I will give thee thy wages." And the woman took the child, and nursed it. [10]And the child grew, and she brought him unto Pharaoh's daughter, and he became her son. And she called his name Moses: and she said, "Because I drew him out of the water."[yy]

After his rescue from the Nile by Pharaoh's daughter, Moses grows up in the royal family, apparently aware that he is an Israelite by birth. When he is 40 years old (Acts 7:23) he sees an Egyptian beating a Hebrew slave and in a fit of anger kills the Egyptian. In fear for his own life, Moses flees Egypt across the Sinai Peninsula (the Arabian Desert, as pictured on the map on page 14) and ends up in Midian (modern day Iran), where he starts a family and becomes a shepherd. Another 40 years go by (Acts 7:30) and God appears to Moses on Mount Horeb in the form of a burning bush. He has been chosen for a special task.

[uu] See Moses' family genealogy as reported in Exodus 6

[vv] Bulrushes = wetland grass; ark = a boat-like container, in this case woven from the bulrushes and floated upon the Nile. Many scholars believe that this story alludes to Noah's ark. In the original Hebrew, the word translated as "bulrushes" may also be defined as wicker or papyrus; the word translated as "ark" is sometimes rendered as "basket." (FI) (BHL)

[ww] Flags = reeds (FI)

[xx] To wit = to know (so that she would know) (FI)

[yy] The name *Moses* means "taken out" or "drawn forth" (FI)

Exodus 3:1-20 (The Burning Bush)

¹Now Moses kept the flock of Jethro his father in law, the priest of Midian: and he led the flock to the backside of the desert, and came to the mountain of God, even to Horeb. ²And the angel of the LORD appeared unto him in a flame of fire out of the midst of a bush: and he looked, and, behold, the bush burned with fire, and the bush was not consumed.

³And Moses said, "I will now turn aside, and see this great sight, why the bush is not burnt." ⁴And when the LORD saw that he turned aside to see, God called unto him out of the midst of the bush, and said, "Moses, Moses." And he said, "Here am I."

⁵And he said, "Draw not nigh hither: put off thy shoes from off thy feet, for the place whereon thou standest is holy ground. ⁶Moreover" he said, "I am the God of thy father, the God of Abraham, the God of Isaac, and the God of Jacob." And Moses hid his face; for he was afraid to look upon God.

⁷And the LORD said, "I have surely seen the affliction of my people which are in Egypt, and have heard their cry by reason of their taskmasters; for I know their sorrows; ⁸And I am come down to deliver them out of the hand of the Egyptians, and to bring them up out of that land unto a good land and a large, unto a land flowing with milk and honey;[zz] unto the place of the Canaanites, and the Hittites, and the Amorites, and the Perizzites, and the Hivites, and the Jebusites.[aaa] ⁹Now therefore, behold, the cry of the children of Israel is come unto me: and I have also seen the oppression wherewith the Egyptians oppress them. ¹⁰Come now therefore, and I will send thee unto Pharaoh, that thou mayest bring forth my people the children of Israel out of Egypt."

¹¹ And Moses said unto God, "Who am I, that I should go unto Pharaoh, and that I should bring forth the children of Israel out of Egypt?" ¹² And he said, "Certainly I will be with thee; and this shall be a token unto thee, that I have sent thee: When thou hast brought forth the people out of Egypt, ye shall serve God upon this mountain."[bbb]

¹³ And Moses said unto God, "Behold, when I come unto the children of Israel, and shall say unto them, 'The God of your fathers hath sent me unto you'; and they shall say to me, 'What is his name?' what shall I say unto them?" ¹⁴ And God said unto Moses, "I Am That I Am": and he said, "Thus shalt thou say unto the children of Israel, 'I Am hath sent me unto you.'"[ccc]

[zz] Frequently in the Bible, the Promised Land is referred to as "a land flowing with milk and honey." It is an image associated with agricultural abundance. (FI)

[aaa] These are all tribes that lived in the land called Canaan, which is the location of the Promised Land. (FI)

[bbb] God says that after Moses rescues his people from Egypt, he will return to Mount Horeb. (EP) Indeed he does, for this is the mountain where God will deliver the Ten Commandments. It is also called Mount Sinai. This promise functions as another covenant, with the physical token being the mountain – when Moses sees it again, it will confirm that the covenant has been fulfilled, that God has indeed used Moses to save his people.

[ccc] "I am that I am" is sometimes translated as "I will be what I will be" and is considered to be the name of the Judeo-Christian God. It is often abbreviated as "I Am" or "The Great I Am." It refers to God as a singular, independent, divine entity. This name is commonly transliterated into the Latin letters YHWH, and spelled out in English as *Yahweh*. The name *Jehovah* is another version of the same name. (FI)

When Moses goes back to Egpyt, his brother Aaron meets him in the wilderness and brings him back to the elders of their people. They must confront Pharaoh and convince him to let the Israelite people go. Because Pharaoh does not want to release his slaves, Moses performs a series of miracles and God punishes Egypt with a series of plagues that demonstrate his mighty power. The ten plagues upon Egypt are:

1. *Water of the Nile is turned to blood*
2. *Frogs infest the land*
3. *Gnats or lice infest the land*
4. *Flies infest the land*
5. *Livestock become diseased and die*
6. *Egyptians are cursed with boils*
7. *Thunder and hail*
8. *Locusts infest the land*
9. *Three days of darkness*
10. *Death of the Egyptian firstborn*

Exodus 7:6-24 (The Snake and the First Plague)

² "Thou shalt speak all that I command thee: and Aaron thy brother shall speak unto Pharaoh, that he send the children of Israel out of his land. ³ And I will harden Pharaoh's heart,[ddd] and multiply my signs and my wonders in the land of Egypt. ⁴ But Pharaoh shall not hearken unto you, that I may lay my hand upon Egypt, and bring forth mine armies, and my people the children of Israel, out of the land of Egypt by great judgments. ⁵ And the Egyptians shall know that I am the Lord, when I stretch forth mine hand upon Egypt, and bring out the children of Israel from among them."

⁶ And Moses and Aaron did as the Lord commanded them, so did they. ⁷ And Moses was fourscore years old, and Aaron fourscore and three years old, when they spake unto Pharaoh.[eee] ⁸ And the Lord spake unto Moses and unto Aaron, saying, ⁹ "When Pharaoh shall speak unto you, saying, 'Shew a miracle for you': then thou shalt say unto Aaron, 'Take thy rod, and cast it before Pharaoh, and it shall become a serpent.'"

¹⁰ And Moses and Aaron went in unto Pharaoh, and they did so as the Lord had commanded: and Aaron cast down his rod before Pharaoh, and before his servants, and it became a serpent.

¹¹ Then Pharaoh also called the wise men and the sorcerers: now the magicians of Egypt, they also did in like manner with their enchantments. ¹² For they cast down every man his rod, and

---

[ddd] God "hardens Pharaoh's heart" numerous times in this narrative. Some say this means that God causes Pharaoh to sin so that God himself may be glorified through the dramatic defeat of the pagan Egyptians. It could also be a Hebrew figure of speech or a narrative device of the storyteller, assigning responsibility for good and bad events to the sovereign control of God and thereby reflecting the storyteller's belief that God's plan – despite bad news – is not being thwarted by Pharaoh and that the promised exodus is destined to happen even if Pharaoh tries to stop it.
[eee] Moses is 80 and Aaron is 83. (FI)

they became serpents: but Aaron's rod swallowed up their rods. ¹³ And he hardened Pharaoh's heart, that he hearkened not unto them; as the Lord had said.

¹⁴ And the Lord said unto Moses, "Pharaoh's heart is hardened, he refuseth to let the people go. ¹⁵ Get thee unto Pharaoh in the morning; lo, he goeth out unto the water; and thou shalt stand by the river's brink against he come; and the rod which was turned to a serpent shalt thou take in thine hand. ¹⁶ And thou shalt say unto him,

> The Lord God of the Hebrews hath sent me unto thee, saying, "Let my people go, that they may serve me in the wilderness: and, behold, hitherto thou wouldest not hear." ¹⁷ Thus saith the Lord, "In this thou shalt know that I am the Lord": behold, I will smite with the rod that is in mine hand upon the waters which are in the river, and they shall be turned to blood. ¹⁸ And the fish that is in the river shall die, and the river shall stink; and the Egyptians shall lothe to drink of the water of the river.

¹⁹ And the Lord spake unto Moses, "Say unto Aaron,

> Take thy rod, and stretch out thine hand upon the waters of Egypt, upon their streams, upon their rivers, and upon their ponds, and upon all their pools of water, that they may become blood; and that there may be blood throughout all the land of Egypt, both in vessels of wood, and in vessels of stone."

²⁰ And Moses and Aaron did so, as the Lord commanded; and he lifted up the rod, and smote the waters that were in the river, in the sight of Pharaoh, and in the sight of his servants; and all the waters that were in the river were turned to blood. ²¹ And the fish that was in the river died; and the river stank, and the Egyptians could not drink of the water of the river; and there was blood throughout all the land of Egypt. ²² And the magicians of Egypt did so with their enchantments: and Pharaoh's heart was hardened, neither did he hearken unto them; as the Lord had said. ²³ And Pharaoh turned and went into his house, neither did he set his heart to this also. ²⁴ And all the Egyptians digged round about the river for water to drink; for they could not drink of the water of the river.

Exodus 11 (The Tenth Plague)

¹And the LORD said unto Moses, "Yet will I bring one plague more upon Pharaoh, and upon Egypt; afterwards he will let you go hence: when he shall let you go, he shall surely thrust you out hence altogether. ²Speak now in the ears of the people, and let every man borrow of his neighbour, and every woman of her neighbour, jewels of silver and jewels of gold." ³And the LORD gave the people favour in the sight of the Egyptians. Moreover the man Moses was very great in the land of Egypt, in the sight of Pharaoh's servants, and in the sight of the people.[fff]

[fff] Apparently, Moses was very popular among Pharaoh's servants, perhaps because he was by this time a legend in his own time, a Hebrew slave raised to royal status and now fighting for the rights of the slaves. The Egyptians, too, are favorably impressed with Moses and his people, enough that they are willing to donate silver and gold to the cause. Most translations besides the KJV say that the Israelites "asked for" rather than "borrowed" the valuables.

⁴And Moses said, [to Pharaoh]

> Thus saith the LORD, "About midnight will I go out into the midst of Egypt: ⁵And all the firstborn in the land of Egypt shall die, from the first born of Pharaoh that sitteth upon his throne, even unto the firstborn of the maidservant that is behind the mill; and all the firstborn of beasts. ⁶And there shall be a great cry throughout all the land of Egypt, such as there was none like it, nor shall be like it any more. ⁷But against any of the children of Israel shall not a dog move his tongue, against man or beast": that ye may know how that the LORD doth put a difference between the Egyptians and Israel. ⁸And all these thy servants shall come down unto me, and bow down themselves unto me, saying, "Get thee out, and all the people that follow thee": and after that I will go out.

And he went out from Pharaoh in a great anger. ⁹And the LORD said unto Moses, "Pharaoh shall not hearken unto you; that my wonders may be multiplied in the land of Egypt." ¹⁰And Moses and Aaron did all these wonders before Pharaoh: and the LORD hardened Pharaoh's heart, so that he would not let the children of Israel go out of his land.

Exodus 12:1-17 (The Passover)

¹And the LORD spake unto Moses and Aaron in the land of Egypt saying, ² "This month shall be unto you the beginning of months: it shall be the first month of the year to you.[ggg] ³Speak ye unto all the congregation of Israel, saying, In the tenth day of this month they shall take to them every man a lamb, according to the house of their fathers, a lamb for an house: ⁴And if the household be too little for the lamb, let him and his neighbour next unto his house take it according to the number of the souls; every man according to his eating shall make your count for the lamb.[hhh]

⁵Your lamb shall be without blemish, a male of the first year: ye shall take it out from the sheep, or from the goats: ⁶And ye shall keep it up until the fourteenth day of the same month: and the whole assembly of the congregation of Israel shall kill it in the evening. ⁷And they shall take of the blood, and strike it on the two side posts and on the upper door post of the houses, wherein they shall eat it.[iii]

[ggg] The first month on the Jewish calendar is Nissan, and it corresponds to March or April on the Gregorian/Christian calendar. Passover is always associated with the month of Nissan. For an excellent overview of the Jewish calendar, check out the "Jewish Calendar" page on the Judaism 101 website (unaffiliated with Bible 101).

[hhh] The number of the souls = the number of people in the families (EP)

[iii] This ritual describes the sacrifice of a perfect lamb, whose blood will be smeared to the left and right and above each family's front door. This blood will serve as a sign that the families have completed the sacrifice and followed all of God's instructions. (EP)

⁸ "And they shall eat the flesh in that night, roast with fire, and unleavened bread; and with bitter herbs they shall eat it.[jjj] ⁹Eat not of it raw, nor sodden at all with water, but roast with fire; his head with his legs, and with the purtenance thereof.[kkk] ¹⁰And ye shall let nothing of it remain until the morning; and that which remaineth of it until the morning ye shall burn with fire. ¹¹And thus shall ye eat it; with your loins girded, your shoes on your feet, and your staff in your hand; and ye shall eat it in haste: it is the LORD's passover.[lll]

¹² "For I will pass through the land of Egypt this night, and will smite all the firstborn in the land of Egypt, both man and beast; and against all the gods of Egypt I will execute judgment: I am the LORD. ¹³And the blood shall be to you for a token upon the houses where ye are: and when I see the blood, I will pass over you, and the plague shall not be upon you to destroy you, when I smite the land of Egypt. ¹⁴And this day shall be unto you for a memorial; and ye shall keep it a feast to the LORD throughout your generations; ye shall keep it a feast by an ordinance for ever.

¹⁵"Seven days shall ye eat unleavened bread; even the first day ye shall put away leaven[mmm] out of your houses: for whosoever eateth leavened bread from the first day until the seventh day, that soul shall be cut off from Israel. ¹⁶And in the first day there shall be an holy convocation, and in the seventh day there shall be an holy convocation to you; no manner of work shall be done in them, save that which every man must eat, that only may be done of you. ¹⁷And ye shall observe the feast of unleavened bread; for in this selfsame day have I brought your armies out of the land of Egypt: therefore shall ye observe this day in your generations by an ordinance for ever."[nnn]

Exodus 12:29-42 (The Exodus)

²⁹ And it came to pass, that at midnight the Lord smote all the firstborn in the land of Egypt, from the firstborn of Pharaoh that sat on his throne unto the firstborn of the captive that was in the dungeon; and all the firstborn of cattle. ³⁰ And Pharaoh rose up in the night, he, and all his servants, and all the Egyptians; and there was a great cry in Egypt; for there was not a house where there was not one dead.

³¹ And he called for Moses and Aaron by night, and said, "Rise up, and get you forth from among my people, both ye and the children of Israel; and go, serve the Lord, as ye have said. ³² Also

---

[jjj] The meat was to be roasted over fire and the bread unleavened (baked without first rising it with yeast) for the sake of speed. The food preparation had to be quick, so that the Israelites would be prepared to depart Egypt first thing in the morning. The bitter herbs are said to be symbolic: a reminder of the afflictions of their enslavement. (FI)

[kkk] The prohibitions in this verse may suggest the singularly distinctive qualities of the Passover lamb, not just in comparison to pagan practices but also compared to other Hebrew sacrificial meals. Pagan sacrifices sometimes involved the eating of raw or bloody meat (as in the worship of Dionysus among the Greeks), the dismemberment of a live sacrifice (also associated with Dionysus) as well as divination performed with the intestines of the sacrificed animal (as practiced by the Babylonians). (FI)

[lll] Loins girded = essentially, dressed and with one's pants on. The Israelites were to eat this meal standing, dressed, and ready to exit Egypt. (EP)

[mmm] Leaven = yeast (FI)

[nnn] To this day, many Jews celebrate Passover with a seven day observance that begins and ends with prayer services and requires that all leavened bread products be removed from the house or at least not consumed during the holiday. (FI)

take your flocks and your herds, as ye have said, and be gone; and bless me also." ³³ And the Egyptians were urgent upon the people, that they might send them out of the land in haste; for they said, "We be all dead men."

³⁴ And the people took their dough before it was leavened, their kneading troughs being bound up in their clothes upon their shoulders. ³⁵ And the children of Israel did according to the word of Moses; and they borrowed of the Egyptians jewels of silver, and jewels of gold, and raiment: ³⁶ And the Lord gave the people favour in the sight of the Egyptians, so that they lent unto them such things as they required. And they spoiled the Egyptians.

³⁷ And the children of Israel journeyed from Rameses to Succoth,[ooo] about six hundred thousand on foot that were men, beside children. ³⁸ And a mixed multitude went up also with them; and flocks, and herds, even very much cattle. ³⁹ And they baked unleavened cakes of the dough which they brought forth out of Egypt, for it was not leavened; because they were thrust out of Egypt, and could not tarry, neither had they prepared for themselves any victual.[ppp]

⁴⁰ Now the sojourning of the children of Israel, who dwelt in Egypt, was four hundred and thirty years.[qqq] ⁴¹ And it came to pass at the end of the four hundred and thirty years, even the selfsame day it came to pass, that all the hosts of the Lord went out from the land of Egypt. ⁴² It is a night to be much observed unto the Lord for bringing them out from the land of Egypt: this is that night of the Lord to be observed of all the children of Israel in their generations

Moses leads his people out of Egypt, following behind a divine pillar of clouds by day and a pillar of fire by night. In this way, God leads them to travel an unexpected route. Rather than a straight line north to the Promised Land, which would take them through enemy territory and risk war and discouragement, God sends them east through the desert toward the Red Sea, which they will now have to cross. Meanwhile, Pharaoh is having second thoughts about having released them.

Exodus 14:5-31 (Crossing the Red Sea)

⁵And it was told the king of Egypt that the people fled: and the heart of Pharaoh and of his servants was turned against the people, and they said, "Why have we done this, that we have let Israel go from serving us?" ⁶And he made ready his chariot, and took his people with him: ⁷And he took six hundred chosen chariots, and all the chariots of Egypt, and captains over every one of them. ⁸And the LORD hardened the heart of Pharaoh king of Egypt, and he pursued after the children of Israel: and the children of Israel went out with an high hand. ⁹But the Egyptians pursued after them, all the horses and chariots of Pharaoh, and his horsemen, and his army, and overtook them encamping by the sea, beside Pihahiroth, before Baalzephon.[rrr] ¹⁰And when

---

[ooo] Rameses and Succoth = these appear to be towns in the eastern delta of the Nile (FI)
[ppp] Victual = food (FI)
[qqq] Sojouorning = living away from home, in Egypt. 430 years = the length of their time in Egypt. (FI)
[rrr] Seaside location assumed to be near the Gulf of Suez (FI)

Pharaoh drew nigh, the children of Israel lifted up their eyes, and, behold, the Egyptians marched after them; and they were sore afraid: and the children of Israel cried out unto the LORD.

[11]And they said unto Moses, "Because there were no graves in Egypt, hast thou taken us away to die in the wilderness? wherefore hast thou dealt thus with us, to carry us forth out of Egypt? [12]Is not this the word that we did tell thee in Egypt, saying, 'Let us alone, that we may serve the Egyptians?' For it had been better for us to serve the Egyptians, than that we should die in the wilderness." [13]And Moses said unto the people, "Fear ye not, stand still, and see the salvation of the LORD, which he will shew to you to day: for the Egyptians whom ye have seen to day, ye shall see them again no more for ever. [14]The LORD shall fight for you, and ye shall hold your peace."

[15]And the LORD said unto Moses, "Wherefore criest thou unto me? speak unto the children of Israel, that they go forward: [16]But lift thou up thy rod, and stretch out thine hand over the sea, and divide it: and the children of Israel shall go on dry ground through the midst of the sea. [17]And I, behold, I will harden the hearts of the Egyptians, and they shall follow them: and I will get me honour upon Pharaoh, and upon all his host, upon his chariots, and upon his horsemen. [18]And the Egyptians shall know that I am the LORD, when I have gotten me honour upon Pharaoh, upon his chariots, and upon his horsemen."

[19]And the angel of God, which went before the camp of Israel, removed and went behind them; and the pillar of the cloud went from before their face, and stood behind them: [20]And it came between the camp of the Egyptians and the camp of Israel; and it was a cloud and darkness to them, but it gave light by night to these: so that the one came not near the other all the night.

[21]And Moses stretched out his hand over the sea; and the LORD caused the sea to go back by a strong east wind all that night, and made the sea dry land, and the waters were divided.[sss] [22]And the children of Israel went into the midst of the sea upon the dry ground: and the waters were a wall unto them on their right hand, and on their left. [23]And the Egyptians pursued, and went in after them to the midst of the sea, even all Pharaoh's horses, his chariots, and his horsemen.

[24]And it came to pass, that in the morning watch the LORD looked unto the host of the Egyptians through the pillar of fire and of the cloud, and troubled the host of the Egyptians, [25]And took off their chariot wheels, that they drave them heavily: so that the Egyptians said, "Let us flee from the face of Israel; for the LORD fighteth for them against the Egyptians." [26]And the LORD said unto Moses, "Stretch out thine hand over the sea, that the waters may come again upon the Egyptians, upon their chariots, and upon their horsemen. [27]And Moses stretched forth his hand over the sea, and the sea returned to his strength when the morning appeared; and the Egyptians fled against it; and the LORD overthrew the Egyptians in the midst of the sea. [28]And the waters returned, and covered the chariots, and the horsemen, and all the host of Pharaoh that came into the sea after them; there remained not so much as one of them.

[sss] An east wind blows upon the north-to-south stretch of the Red Sea (possibly the Gulf of Suez or the Gulf of Aqaba), causing the waters to separate like two walls on either side of a wide path, thereby allowing the Israelites to cross the sea on dry ground. Modern scholars believe that a better translation of "Red Sea" (*Yam Suph*, from Exodus 13:18) could be the "sea of reeds," which would put this iconic crossing near the tip of the Gulf of Aqaba or perhaps at a now-dry lake in eastern Egypt. (FI) (ASB)

[29]But the children of Israel walked upon dry land in the midst of the sea; and the waters were a wall unto them on their right hand, and on their left. [30]Thus the LORD saved Israel that day out of the hand of the Egyptians; and Israel saw the Egyptians dead upon the sea shore. [31]And Israel saw that great work which the LORD did upon the Egyptians: and the people feared the LORD, and believed the LORD, and his servant Moses.

After their escape from the Egyptians, the Israelites travel on to Mount Sinai (also known as Mount Horeb) where God will provide the Ten Commandments as well as an extensive set of laws for daily life and religious ritual. (The Book of Leviticus, which comes right after Exodus, contains most of these religious laws.) On the way to Sinai, the people get hungry and again begin to fear for their lives.

Exodus 16 (Quail and Manna)

[1]And they took their journey from Elim, and all the congregation of the children of Israel came unto the wilderness of Sin, which is between Elim and Sinai, on the fifteenth day of the second month after their departing out of the land of Egypt.

[2] And the whole congregation of the children of Israel murmured against Moses and Aaron in the wilderness: [3] And the children of Israel said unto them, "Would to God we had died by the hand of the Lord in the land of Egypt, when we sat by the flesh pots, and when we did eat bread to the full; for ye have brought us forth into this wilderness, to kill this whole assembly with hunger."

[4] Then said the Lord unto Moses, "Behold, I will rain bread from heaven for you; and the people shall go out and gather a certain rate every day, that I may prove them, whether they will walk in my law, or no.[ttt] [5] And it shall come to pass, that on the sixth day they shall prepare that which they bring in; and it shall be twice as much as they gather daily."

[6] And Moses and Aaron said unto all the children of Israel, "At even,[uuu] then ye shall know that the Lord hath brought you out from the land of Egypt: [7] And in the morning, then ye shall see the glory of the Lord; for that he heareth your murmurings against the Lord: and what are we, that ye murmur against us?"

[8] And Moses said, "This shall be, when the Lord shall give you in the evening flesh to eat, and in the morning bread to the full; for that the Lord heareth your murmurings which ye murmur against him: and what are we? your murmurings are not against us, but against the Lord."

[9-12 the people are reminded of God's glory]

[13] And it came to pass, that at even the quails came up, and covered the camp: and in the morning the dew lay round about the host. [14] And when the dew that lay was gone up, behold, upon the

---

[ttt] "that I may prove them" – the people's obedience to God's specific instructions about food will prove whether or not they are committed to following Him
[uuu] Even = evening

face of the wilderness there lay a small round thing, as small as the hoar[vvv] frost on the ground. ¹⁵ And when the children of Israel saw it, they said one to another, "It is manna": for they wist not what it was.[www] And Moses said unto them, "This is the bread which the Lord hath given you to eat. ¹⁶ This is the thing which the Lord hath commanded, Gather of it every man according to his eating, an omer for every man, according to the number of your persons; take ye every man for them which are in his tents."[xxx]

¹⁷ And the children of Israel did so, and gathered, some more, some less. ¹⁸ And when they did mete it with an omer, he that gathered much had nothing over, and he that gathered little had no lack; they gathered every man according to his eating. ¹⁹ And Moses said, "Let no man leave of it till the morning." ²⁰ Notwithstanding they hearkened not unto Moses; but some of them left of it until the morning, and it bred worms, and stank: and Moses was wroth with them. ²¹ And they gathered it every morning, every man according to his eating: and when the sun waxed hot, it melted.

²² And it came to pass, that on the sixth day they gathered twice as much bread, two omers for one man: and all the rulers of the congregation came and told Moses. ²³ And he said unto them, "This is that which the Lord hath said, 'To morrow is the rest of the holy sabbath unto the Lord: bake that which ye will bake to day, and seethe that ye will seethe; and that which remaineth over lay up for you to be kept until the morning.'"

²⁴ And they laid it up till the morning, as Moses bade: and it did not stink, neither was there any worm therein. ²⁵ And Moses said, "Eat that to day; for to day is a sabbath unto the Lord: to day ye shall not find it in the field. ²⁶ Six days ye shall gather it; but on the seventh day, which is the sabbath, in it there shall be none."

²⁷ And it came to pass, that there went out some of the people on the seventh day for to gather, and they found none. ²⁸ And the Lord said unto Moses, "How long refuse ye to keep my commandments and my laws? ²⁹ See, for that the Lord hath given you the sabbath, therefore he giveth you on the sixth day the bread of two days; abide ye every man in his place, let no man go out of his place on the seventh day." ³⁰ So the people rested on the seventh day.

³¹ And the house of Israel called the name thereof Manna: and it was like coriander seed, white; and the taste of it was like wafers made with honey. ³² And Moses said, "This is the thing which the Lord commandeth, Fill an omer of it to be kept for your generations; that they may see the bread wherewith I have fed you in the wilderness, when I brought you forth from the land of Egypt." ³³ And Moses said unto Aaron, "Take a pot, and put an omer full of manna therein, and lay it up before the Lord, to be kept for your generations." ³⁴ As the Lord commanded Moses, so Aaron laid it up before the Testimony, to be kept. ³⁵ And the children of Israel did eat manna forty years, until they came to a land inhabited; they did eat manna, until they came unto the borders of the land of Canaan. ³⁶ Now an omer is the tenth part of an ephah.

[vvv] Hoar = gray
[www] Other versions of the Bible do not translate this as a statement but as a question: "When the Israelites saw it, they said to each other, 'What is it?' For they did not know what it was" (NIV).
[xxx] Omer = a unit of measurement probably equal to 3.64 litres, which is just a little less than a U.S. gallon (FI)

Exodus 20:1-17 (The Ten Commandments)

¹And God spake all these words, saying, ² "I am the LORD thy God, which have brought thee out of the land of Egypt, out of the house of bondage.

³Thou shalt have no other gods before me.

⁴Thou shalt not make unto thee any graven image,[yyy] or any likeness of any thing that is in heaven above, or that is in the earth beneath, or that is in the water under the earth. ⁵Thou shalt not bow down thyself to them, nor serve them: for I the LORD thy God am a jealous God, visiting the iniquity[zzz] of the fathers upon the children unto the third and fourth generation of them that hate me; ⁶And shewing mercy unto thousands of them that love me, and keep my commandments.

⁷Thou shalt not take the name of the LORD thy God in vain;[aaaa] for the LORD will not hold him guiltless that taketh his name in vain. ⁸Remember the sabbath day, to keep it holy.[bbbb] ⁹Six days shalt thou labour, and do all thy work: ¹⁰But the seventh day is the sabbath of the LORD thy God: in it thou shalt not do any work, thou, nor thy son, nor thy daughter, thy manservant, nor thy maidservant, nor thy cattle, nor thy stranger that is within thy gates: ¹¹For in six days the LORD made heaven and earth, the sea, and all that in them is, and rested the seventh day: wherefore the LORD blessed the sabbath day, and hallowed it.

¹²Honour thy father and thy mother: that thy days may be long upon the land which the LORD thy God giveth thee.

¹³Thou shalt not kill.

¹⁴Thou shalt not commit adultery.[cccc]

¹⁵Thou shalt not steal.

¹⁶Thou shalt not bear false witness against thy neighbour.[dddd]

¹⁷Thou shalt not covet[eeee] thy neighbour's house, thou shalt not covet thy neighbour's wife, nor his manservant, nor his maidservant, nor his ox, nor his ass, nor any thing that is thy neighbour's."

[yyy] Graven image = an idol representing God (FI)
[zzz] Iniquity = sins (FI)
[aaaa] In vain = for no purpose. In other words, it is a sin to speak God's name as a swear-word or an exclamation. His name should only be invoked when he is being seriously and respectfully addressed. (EP)
[bbbb] Sabbath = seventh (FI)
[cccc] The crime of adultery is not simply premarital sex. It specifically relates to the act of a man having sex with another man's wife. Premarital or extramarital sex is called *fornication* and is not addressed in the Ten Commandments. (BHC – Clarke's Commentary)
[dddd] Do not lie about your neighbor in a court of law. This commandment should be read also as an "exhortation to honest speech." (WBD)
[eeee] Covet = to desire for yourself (FI)

God also gives Moses instructions for building a tabernacle, a portable structure that will serve as their temple, and a holy "ark" within which the commandments are to be stored and carried. This container is known as the Ark of the Covenant, and we learn in the Book of Numbers (after Leviticus) that only priests will be allowed to touch these sacred objects.

Exodus 25:10-16   (Instructions for the Ark of the Covenant)

[10] "And they shall make an ark of shittim wood:[ffff] two cubits and a half shall be the length thereof, and a cubit and a half the breadth thereof, and a cubit and a half the height thereof.[gggg] [11] And thou shalt overlay it with pure gold, within and without shalt thou overlay it, and shalt make upon it a crown of gold round about. [12] And thou shalt cast four rings of gold for it, and put them in the four corners thereof; and two rings shall be in the one side of it, and two rings in the other side of it. [13] And thou shalt make staves of shittim wood, and overlay them with gold.[hhhh] [14] And thou shalt put the staves into the rings by the sides of the ark, that the ark may be borne with them. [15] The staves shall be in the rings of the ark: they shall not be taken from it. [16] And thou shalt put into the ark the testimony which I shall give thee."

While Moses is on the mountain receiving these commandments and instructions from God, Aaron and the Israelite people become impatient, committing one of the Old Testament's greatest sins against God: the building and worshiping of a pagan idol.

Exodus 32 (The Golden Calf)

[1] And when the people saw that Moses delayed to come down out of the mount, the people gathered themselves together unto Aaron, and said unto him, "Up, make us gods, which shall go before us; for as for this Moses, the man that brought us up out of the land of Egypt, we wot not[iiii] what is become of him."

[2] And Aaron said unto them, "Break off the golden earrings, which are in the ears of your wives, of your sons, and of your daughters, and bring them unto me." [3] And all the people brake off the golden earrings which were in their ears, and brought them unto Aaron. [4] And he received them at their hand, and fashioned it with a graving tool, after he had made it a molten calf: and they said, "These be thy gods, O Israel, which brought thee up out of the land of Egypt." [5] And when Aaron saw it, he built an altar before it; and Aaron made proclamation, and said, "To morrow is a feast to the Lord." [6] And they rose up early on the morrow, and offered burnt offerings, and brought peace offerings; and the people sat down to eat and to drink, and rose up to play.

[ffff] Shittim wood = acacia wood, which is fragrant, produces a medicinal gum, and is hard and dense and thereby resistant to decay (FI)
[gggg] Cubit = about 18 inches. The ark would have been 45 x 27 x 27 inches. (FI)
[hhhh] Staves = poles. Two golden poles, one running down each side and affixed to the ark by golden rings, would be used to carry the ark. (FI)
[iiii] Wot not = do not know

⁷ And the Lord said unto Moses, "Go, get thee down; for thy people, which thou broughtest out of the land of Egypt, have corrupted themselves: ⁸ They have turned aside quickly out of the way which I commanded them: they have made them a molten calf, and have worshipped it, and have sacrificed thereunto, and said, 'These be thy gods, O Israel, which have brought thee up out of the land of Egypt.'" ⁹ And the Lord said unto Moses, "I have seen this people, and, behold, it is a stiffnecked people: ¹⁰ Now therefore let me alone, that my wrath may wax[iiii] hot against them, and that I may consume them: and I will make of thee a great nation."

¹¹ And Moses besought the Lord his God, and said, "Lord, why doth thy wrath wax hot against thy people, which thou hast brought forth out of the land of Egypt with great power, and with a mighty hand? ¹² Wherefore should the Egyptians speak, and say, 'For mischief did he bring them out, to slay them in the mountains, and to consume them from the face of the earth?' Turn from thy fierce wrath, and repent of this evil against thy people. ¹³ Remember Abraham, Isaac, and Israel, thy servants, to whom thou swarest by thine own self, and saidst unto them, 'I will multiply your seed as the stars of heaven, and all this land that I have spoken of will I give unto your seed, and they shall inherit it for ever.'" ¹⁴ And the Lord repented of the evil which he thought to do unto his people.

¹⁵ And Moses turned, and went down from the mount, and the two tables of the testimony were in his hand: the tables were written on both their sides; on the one side and on the other were they written. ¹⁶ And the tables were the work of God, and the writing was the writing of God, graven upon the tables. ¹⁷ And when Joshua heard the noise of the people as they shouted, he said unto Moses, "There is a noise of war in the camp." ¹⁸ And he said, "It is not the voice of them that shout for mastery, neither is it the voice of them that cry for being overcome: but the noise of them that sing do I hear."

¹⁹ And it came to pass, as soon as he came nigh unto the camp, that he saw the calf, and the dancing: and Moses' anger waxed hot, and he cast the tables out of his hands, and brake them beneath the mount. ²⁰ And he took the calf which they had made, and burnt it in the fire, and ground it to powder, and strawed it upon the water, and made the children of Israel drink of it.

Moses also has 3000 Israelites slaughtered as punishment for their disloyalty to God. Appeased by these acts, God takes Moses back up the mountain and presents new tablets to him, and then the Israelites continue on toward Canaan, the Promised Land. As they draw near, scouts are sent ahead to assess the situation and bring back news regarding the Canaanites. The news is grim – the Canaanites look like giants – and the people once again falter in their faith.

[iiii] Wax = become

Numbers 14 (Forty Years of Wandering)

^{1}And all the congregation lifted up their voice, and cried; and the people wept that night. ^{2} And all the children of Israel murmured against Moses and against Aaron: and the whole congregation said unto them, "Would God that we had died in the land of Egypt! or would God we had died in this wilderness! ^{3} And wherefore hath the LORD brought us unto this land, to fall by the sword, that our wives and our children should be a prey? were it not better for us to return into Egypt?" ^{4} And they said one to another, "Let us make a captain, and let us return into Egypt."

^{5} Then Moses and Aaron fell on their faces before all the assembly of the congregation of the children of Israel. ^{6} And Joshua the son of Nun, and Caleb the son of Jephunneh, which were of them that searched the land, rent their clothes:[kkkk]

^{7} And they spake unto all the company of the children of Israel, saying, "The land, which we passed through to search it, is an exceeding good land. ^{8} If the LORD delight in us, then he will bring us into this land, and give it us; a land which floweth with milk and honey. ^{9} Only rebel not ye against the LORD, neither fear ye the people of the land; for they are bread for us: their defence is departed from them, and the LORD is with us: fear them not."

^{10} But all the congregation bade stone them with stones. And the glory of the LORD appeared in the tabernacle of the congregation before all the children of Israel. ^{11} And the LORD said unto Moses, "How long will this people provoke me? and how long will it be ere they believe me, for all the signs which I have shewed among them? ^{12} I will smite them with the pestilence,[llll] and disinherit them, and will make of thee a greater nation and mightier than they."

^{13} And Moses said unto the LORD, "Then the Egyptians shall hear it, (for thou broughtest up this people in thy might from among them;) ^{14} And they will tell it to the inhabitants of this land: for they have heard that thou LORD art among this people, that thou LORD art seen face to face, and that thy cloud standeth over them, and that thou goest before them, by day time in a pillar of a cloud, and in a pillar of fire by night. ^{15} Now if thou shalt kill all this people as one man, then the nations which have heard the fame of thee will speak, saying, ^{16}'Because the LORD was not able to bring this people into the land which he sware unto them, therefore he hath slain them in the wilderness.' ^{17} And now, I beseech thee, let the power of my lord be great, according as thou hast spoken, saying, ^{18}'The LORD is longsuffering, and of great mercy, forgiving iniquity and transgression, and by no means clearing the guilty, visiting the iniquity of the fathers upon the children unto the third and fourth generation.' ^{19} Pardon, I beseech thee, the iniquity of this people according unto the greatness of thy mercy, and as thou hast forgiven this people, from Egypt even until now."

^{20} And the LORD said, "I have pardoned according to thy word: ^{21} But as truly as I live, all the earth shall be filled with the glory of the LORD. ^{22} Because all those men which have seen my glory, and my miracles, which I did in Egypt and in the wilderness, and have tempted me now these ten times, and have not hearkened to my voice; ^{23} Surely they shall not see the land which I

[kkkk] Rent their clothes = tore their clothes, a sign of mourning or, here, severe disappointment in God's people
[llll] Pestilence = disease

sware unto their fathers, neither shall any of them that provoked me see it: [24] But my servant Caleb, because he had another spirit with him, and hath followed me fully, him will I bring into the land whereinto he went; and his seed shall possess it.

[25] (Now the Amalekites and the Canaanites dwelt in the valley.) "Tomorrow turn you, and get you into the wilderness by the way of the Red sea." [26] And the LORD spake unto Moses and unto Aaron, saying, [27] "How long shall I bear with this evil congregation, which murmur against me? I have heard the murmurings of the children of Israel, which they murmur against me. [28] Say unto them, 'As truly as I live, saith the LORD, as ye have spoken in mine ears, so will I do to you: [29] Your carcases shall fall in this wilderness; and all that were numbered of you, according to your whole number, from twenty years old and upward which have murmured against me. [30] Doubtless ye shall not come into the land, concerning which I sware to make you dwell therein, save Caleb the son of Jephunneh, and Joshua the son of Nun. [31] But your little ones, which ye said should be a prey, them will I bring in, and they shall know the land which ye have despised. [32] But as for you, your carcases, they shall fall in this wilderness.

[33] And your children shall wander in the wilderness forty years, and bear your whoredoms, until your carcases be wasted in the wilderness. [34] After the number of the days in which ye searched the land, even forty days, each day for a year, shall ye bear your iniquities, even forty years, and ye shall know my breach of promise."

The forty years draw to a close, and a new generation rises up as prophesied. A census is taken. Moses makes plans to finally invade Canaan (the Promised Land) and conquer the heathens currently inhabiting the region. Right before the conquest begins, Moses gives a series of three sermons which are recounted in the Book of Deuteronomy (the fifth and final book of the Torah). The most important passage from these sermons includes the "Shema," which is considered the central prayer in the Jewish prayer book.

Deuteronomy 6:1-8 (The Shema)

[1] "Now these are the commandments, the statutes, and the judgments, which the LORD your God commanded to teach you, that ye might do them in the land whither ye go to possess it: [2] That thou mightest fear the LORD thy God, to keep all his statutes and his commandments, which I command thee, thou, and thy son, and thy son's son, all the days of thy life; and that thy days may be prolonged.

[3] Hear therefore, O Israel, and observe to do it; that it may be well with thee, and that ye may increase mightily, as the LORD God of thy fathers hath promised thee, in the land that floweth with milk and honey.

> [4] Hear, O Israel: The LORD our God is one LORD:
> [5] And thou shalt love the LORD thy God with all thine heart,
>   and with all thy soul, and with all thy might.

⁶And these words, which I command thee this day, shall be in thine heart: ⁷And thou shalt teach them diligently unto thy children, and shalt talk of them when thou sittest in thine house, and when thou walkest by the way, and when thou liest down, and when thou risest up. ⁸And thou shalt bind them for a sign upon thine hand, and they shall be as frontlets between thine eyes.[mmmm] ⁹And thou shalt write them upon the posts of thy house, and on thy gates."

After his final sermons, Moses passes his authority onto Joshua, his most trusted soldier and one of only three people (including Moses himself and another soldier, Caleb) whom God has allowed to survive from the original generation that escaped Egypt 40 years prior. Joshua is put in charge of the conquest of Promised Land. Moses dies at the age of 120.

Deuteronomy 34 (Moses Dies)

¹And Moses went up from the plains of Moab unto the mountain of Nebo, to the top of Pisgah, that is over against Jericho. And the LORD shewed him all the land of Gilead, unto Dan, ²And all Naphtali, and the land of Ephraim, and Manasseh, and all the land of Judah, unto the utmost sea, ³And the south, and the plain of the valley of Jericho, the city of palm trees, unto Zoar. ⁴And the LORD said unto him, "This is the land which I sware unto Abraham, unto Isaac, and unto Jacob, saying, 'I will give it unto thy seed': I have caused thee to see it with thine eyes, but thou shalt not go over thither."

⁵So Moses the servant of the LORD died there in the land of Moab, according to the word of the LORD. ⁶And he buried him in a valley in the land of Moab, over against Bethpeor: but no man knoweth of his sepulchre unto this day. ⁷And Moses was an hundred and twenty years old when he died: his eye was not dim, nor his natural force abated. ⁸And the children of Israel wept for Moses in the plains of Moab thirty days: so the days of weeping and mourning for Moses were ended.

⁹And Joshua the son of Nun was full of the spirit of wisdom; for Moses had laid his hands upon him: and the children of Israel hearkened unto him, and did as the LORD commanded Moses. ¹⁰And there arose not a prophet since in Israel like unto Moses, whom the LORD knew face to face, ¹¹In all the signs and the wonders, which the LORD sent him to do in the land of Egypt to Pharaoh, and to all his servants, and to all his land, ¹²And in all that mighty hand, and in all the great terror which Moses shewed in the sight of all Israel.

[mmmm] The word translated as "sign" is *oth*, meaning a banner or a pledge. The word translated as "frontlet" is *tatapoth*, meaning a band, and which may be associated with dedication or remembrance. These commandments may be taken as figurative instructions to make a pledge and to dedicate oneself to loving God fully at all times. Some orthodox Jews interpret it literally by wearing tiny Shema scrolls in small boxes, called phylacteries, upon their foreheads and left hands. Google "phylacteries" images for a better comprehension of this practice. (BHL) (FI)

LESSON TEN: HISTORY OF A HERO

Charleton Heston as Moses in *The Ten Commandments*

A baby in the bulrushes. A burning bush. Ten plagues. Passover. The parting of the Red Sea. Ten Commandments and the Ark of the Covenant. The epic story of Moses is one of the most dramatic and renowned of all Bible tales. Its narration takes place over the course of four books, Exodus through Deuteronomy, all credited to the authorship of its protagonist. If this is true, then we can call Moses a primary source and, for the first time in our survey of the Old Testament, identify our text as a *history*.

Even if one rejects the notion of Moses' authorship, the story definitely bears the characteristics of being written down in real time with the intent of recording actual events in an objective "captain's log" style. One of the most important traits of historical literature is an abundance of concrete, specific, and secular details. In the Red Sea episode (for example) we find very specific geographical notes about passage of travel and camp sites, and we also get a detailed description of Pharaoh's troops, in number and composition. In Numbers 33 (which we didn't read in this text) there is an even more detailed list of journal-like travel records: it contains 46 verses that go back and account for every camp site pitched by the Israelites from Egypt to the Promised Land, including specific places, travel dates and durations, and even counts of palm trees and water sources. The text indicates that Moses "wrote their goings out according to their journeys by the commandment of the Lord" (33:2). Clearly, the *intent* of the narrative is historical.

Furthermore, the overall quality of the narrative resembles history more so than fiction or even memoir, due to its "come as it may" structure. Moses' life story unfolds with frequent interruptions for long lists of civil and religious laws, provided not as a separate legal document, but chronologically, as they were revealed to the Israelites. Moses is known as the great Law-Giver. Pictures of Moses holding the Ten Commandments are featured on law monuments and judicial buildings across the Western world. You may also recall that the five biblical books attributed to Moses are called the Torah, or "The Law." In his presumably autobiographical composition of Exodus through Deuteronomy, Moses goes back and forth between snippets of narrative and records of law. He does not seem to be concerned with achieving a narrative arc: there is no clear, single climax to the story, and the saga does not ever achieve a satisfactory resolution. By contrast, a fictional or orally transmitted hero story of this magnitude from the ancient world would almost certainly have taken on the archetypal hero cycle and concluded triumphantly, but this one does not. Rather, Moses dies within sight of the Promised Land, and the historical narrative of Joshua (the next book in the Old Testament) picks up right where Moses leaves off. The overall story of Moses ambles in a natural, practical, real-time style that carries all the marks of authenticity...

...Unless you simply do not believe in supernatural events like staffs turning into snakes and water turning to blood. The truth of the matter is that, even though the Moses narrative bears the textual characteristics of history, it has not been authenticated by archeology. Moses' name does not appear in any Second Millennium B.C.E. artifacts, and there is no proof that the Israelites were ever enslaved by Egypt. Alternate versions of the Moses narrative show up in Jewish, Greek and Roman literature as early as 400

ART OR HISTORY?

One feature of the Moses narrative suggests that artistic craft supercedes historical accuracy: the structure of Moses' life comes in three neat groups of 40 years. He leaves Egypt at age 40, leaves Midian at age 80, and dies at age 120. In Hebrew culture, the number 40 has symbolic significance; it is considered the number of years in a single generation or the number of years required for a man to reach full maturity. It also appears throughout the Bible as a period of temporary suffering followed by salvation or renewal (40 days of the flood and Jesus' 40 days of fasting and temptation). Of course, it is entirely possible that a real man's life fell into segments of 40 years each, but many critics find this to be an artistic feature superimposed upon the story.

B.C.E., but that is nearly 1000 years after the "real" Moses would have existed. The lack of firm evidence, along with the presence of supernatural story elements, adds up to a great deal of skepticism among historians. Few scholars consider the Moses narrative to be factual. Thus, we may still call it a work *of history* (in the sense of genre), but it would not be presented as fact in the pages of a history textbook. Alas, not all historical texts are considered trustworthy, in the same way that not all poems are considered beautiful and not all websites are considered reliable.

This lesson concludes our examination of the genres of the Old Testament narratives, including myth, legend, and history. Let's review these classifications before moving on to a closer literary examination of Moses in our next lesson.

MYTH: Ancient, orally transmitted, unverifiable, religious, supernatural, and symbolic.
Biblical example: Adam.

LEGEND: Orally transmitted, unverifiable but historically grounded, sometimes religious, sometimes supernatural, but never symbolic. Often having multiple variations of similar episodes.
Biblical example: Abraham.

HISTORY: Recorded by or traceable to a primary or secondary source, should be verifiable, never symbolic but rather concrete and detail-oriented, largely secular, and lacking a precise narrative structure or archetypal hero cycle (as one would find in fiction)
Biblical example: Moses

POSSIBLE OR IMPOSSIBLE?

Ron Wyatt was a self-proclaimed archeologist who claimed to have discovered the remains of wheels and chariots as well as human and horse bones at the bottom of the Red Sea, supposedly confirming the Exodus events as factual. His claims have been refuted and dismissed by a broad array of scientists, historians, and researchers. Wyatt also claimed to have found Noah's ark and the Tower of Babel.

Meteorologist Carl Drews, of the National Center for Atmospheric Research in Boulder, has proposed that a 63 mph wind blowing for 12 hours, called a wind set-down, could push back a wall of water and expose a land bridge for crossing. (Reported in USA Today 9/21/2010)

LESSON ELEVEN: GO DOWN, MOSES

By the time Moses leads his people out of Egypt (during the 430 years between Genesis and the Exodus) the Israelites have become "as numerous as the stars," as foretold in Abraham's covenant conversations with God. Another part of the covenant prophecy has also come to be – that the Jewish people have been enslaved in a foreign land: "And [God] said unto Abram, know of a surety that thy seed shall be a stranger in a land that is not theirs, and shall serve them; and they shall afflict them four hundred years; And also that nation, whom they shall serve, will I judge: and afterward shall they come out with great substance" (Gen. 15: 13-14). After the crossing of the Red Sea, we see that Israel has left Egypt with stockpiles of gold and silver and that the forces of Pharaoh have been judged and defeated.

Thus, the Book of Exodus seems to wrap up the theme of covenant (see Lesson Eight) and introduce a new and powerful theme of freedom. The Israelites desperately want freedom from their Egyptian oppressors, and they need a hero to make it happen. Moses is the man for the job. Moses' success in achieving national liberty for his people has been a central inspiring metaphor in United States history.

AMERICAN HISTORY

Ben Franklin's preference for the first American seal was an allegorical scene of Moses crossing the Red Sea, an image encircled by the motto "Rebellion to Tyrants is Obedience to God."[nnnn] A century later, the Exodus became an inspirational motif for the slaves, and a century after that a symbol for the continuing Civil Rights movements of the 1900's. Numerous Negro spiritual songs were inspired by the Exodus story, for instance the classic "Go Down Moses":

> When Israel was in Egypt's land:
> Let my people go,

[nnnn] Carol Meyers discusses the colonists' strong identification with the Exodus in her interview with NOVA, entitled "Moses and the Exodus" as part of NOVA's program, "The Bible's Buried Secrets," in August 2007.

Oppress'd so hard they could not stand,

Let my People go.

Go down, Moses,

way down in Egypt's land,

Tell old Pharaoh,

Let my people go.

The sentiment of freedom in this song is dressed up in religious clothes, which made it acceptable subject matter for slaves to sing openly. Many allusions to the Exodus and other Bible stories exist throughout the African American spiritual tradition.

POP CULTURE

Moses' story has had a huge impact on American pop culture as well. One of Hollywood's great epic films, <u>The Ten Commandments</u> starring Charleton Heston as Moses, is often shown on television during the week of Passover. And who hasn't heard of <u>Indiana Jones and The Raiders of the Lost Ark</u>? Understanding the origin of the ark will enhance your appreciation of the film. The ark was never to be touched by human hands, but carried on poles that ran down each side. A story elsewhere in the Bible describes a man being smitten by God for touching the ark merely to steady it at a bump in the road (II Sam. 6:1-7). The ark was said to house the very presence of God, particularly when outside the tabernacle. The Indiana Jones movie is set during the era of the Nazis, who were of course anti-Jewish, and the villains of the film are out to find and take advantage of the Jewish ark and its amazing powers. The Nazis – spoiler alert! – are not prepared for the anger of the God of the ark at the end of the film, but fortunately our hero Indiana Jones knows his Bible stories and is able to survive the revelation of its awesome power.

Additional allusions to the Moses saga appear throughout Western literature and pop culture, from Steinbeck's classic novel <u>The Grapes of Wrath</u>, where the protagonist has many Moses parallels as he saves his family from Depression era oppression, to a scene from <u>Bruce Almighty</u> when Bruce parts the seas of his tomato soup. As you continue studying Western literature, going to museums, and generally paying attention to the world around you, see how many more references to this iconic story you can spot! Here are just a few more: There are seven commandments in the novel <u>Animal Farm</u>, clearly a parallel to the Ten Commandments; there is more than one variety of plant with the common name "burning bush"; and Moses is depicted on the wall of several U.S. government buildings, including the Supreme Court great hall, because of his legacy as a lawgiver.

THE PASSOVER

The turning point of the Israelites' journey from captivity to the Promised Land, the Passover, is celebrated annually by persons of the Jewish faith. One feature of this holiday is the eating of matzah bread, which is "unleavened" (made without yeast) to commemorate the haste with which the Israelites packed and left Egypt, as there would not have been time for bread to rise for their final meal. Matzah is also considered a poor person's bread, so it helps symbolize the bondage of the Israelites before the exodus. The other central feature of modern Passover celebrations is the seder meal, which is eaten in the home by family and friends. It includes not only matzah, but also bitter herbs to signify the suffering of the Israelite slaves, and four glasses of wine to symbolize the four promises of God regarding deliverance: "I will bring you out," "I will rid you of bondage," "I will redeem you," and "I will take you unto me for a people" (Exodus 6:6-7). In this way, Passover highlights the theme of freedom from bondage found throughout Moses' story.

LESSONS TEN & ELEVEN STUDY GUIDE

Objective Identification:
Exodus, Leviticus, Numbers, Deuteronomy, bulrushes, burning bush, ten plagues, Passover, Red Sea, manna, Ten Commandments, tabernacle, Ark of the Covenant, history, Torah

Subjective Expression:
1) Comparison: Compare Moses to other national heroes, like George Washington or Napoleon. Compare Pharaoh to other national villains, like Stalin or Hitler. Do you find more similarities or differences? Are Moses and Pharaoh "classic" national heroes and villains?

2) Opinion: Many modern thinkers, including notable atheists Sigmund Freud, Richard Dawkins, and American patriot Thomas Paine, felt that Moses was a decidedly poor moral role model. You read about how he had 3000 people killed for the sin of the Golden Calf. Read Numbers 31 (and chapter 25 for some back-story) if you are interested in another very dark episode of military conquest and slaughter. What you think of Moses as a moral leader?

3) Further Reading: The saga of Moses includes several episodes that revolve around Moses' sister, Miriam, who rescued her baby brother from the Nile and delivered him to safety. After the Israelites cross the Red Sea, she is identified as a prophet: "And Miriam the prophetess, the sister of Aaron, took a timbrel in her hand; and all the women went out after her with timbrels and with dances. And Miriam answered them, 'Sing ye to the Lord, for he hath triumphed gloriously; the horse and his rider hath he thrown into the sea'" (Exodus 15:20-21). Later, in chapter 12 of Numbers, she is punished by God for speaking out against Moses; however, her other brother, Aaron, had done the same thing and is not punished. What do you think the stories of Miriam say about the role of women in ancient Hebrew culture?

3) Further Research: During the 2008 presidential campaign, Barack Obama (Democrat) and John McCain (Republican) waged a controversial battle in which Obama was compared to Moses. See if you can find any of the TV ads or articles written in response to the ads, and explain the reason for the comparison.

4) Cultural Connections: Besides the classic <u>Ten Commandments</u> and <u>Raiders of the Lost Ark</u>, good films featuring Passover depictions and themes include the animated <u>Prince of Egypt</u> (DreamWorks, 1998) and <u>The Devil's Arithmetic</u>, a made-for-TV movie starring Kirsten Dunst (1999).

QUOTABLE QUOTES

> I have wondered at times what the Ten Commandments would have looked like if Moses had run them through the US Congress.

President Ronald Reagan

LESSON TWELVE:
EPIC PROPORTIONS

Grecian urn featuring Odysseus and the Sirens, from the epic *The Odyssey*

The Moses story is huge, in scope and in impact. In fact, you could say that it is epic! We might even say that Moses is the Bible's only epic hero. Epics are long, grand adventure stories featuring a larger-than-life protagonist who represents the best qualities of his culture. True epics are novel-length poems (unlike Exodus-Deuteronomy) but the story of Moses comes pretty close to the definition in other respects. Here is a list of qualities normally associated with an epic – let's get a count of how many of these items are applicable to the Moses story:

LONG NARRATIVE POEM

Yes and no - it's long and narrative, but it's not poetic.

OPENS *IN MEDIAS RES* WITH AN INVOCATION

No – our story progresses from birth to death, chronologically, in historical fashion. It does not begin with a prayer. It is presented simply and directly, with no specialized literary packaging.

GRAND SUBJECT MATTER AND ELEVATED STYLE

Yes and no - the subject matter is about as grand and dramatic as you can get. The style, however, is not particularly elevated. As mentioned before, it has historic intent and style. It is simple and concrete, not poetic. However, it is very serious, as are epics.

IDEALISTIC NATIONAL HERO

Yes – Moses is a national hero, a savior for the Jewish people, and the deliverer of the Law. He is considered a prophet in the Jewish, Christian, and Muslim traditions. His idealistic character traits include perseverance and faith. Unlike most epic heroes, he does not possess any notable physical strength, although survival in the wilderness might constitute a certain amount of physical heartiness. However, these qualities are accompanied by doubt, temper, and, some would say, cruelty. For instance, after defeating Midian (Numbers 31) he commands the Hebrew army to kill the surviving mothers and sons and take the virgins for themselves. This doesn't seem very idealistic or good. But, again, this type of vengeance and imperfection is not uncommon among epic heroes. Odysseus, for instance, bars the doors and murders all his wife's suitors. He also conducts affairs during his twenty-year sojourn, while his wife remains faithful. There is no requirement that an epic hero be thoroughly upright, as long as he successfully demonstrates some key virtues admired by his culture of origin.

GEOGRAPHICALLY VAST SETTING

Yes – Moses' travels begin in Egypt, proceed across the Sinai Peninsula, into Arabia, and up into the "Promised Land" of modern Israel. Like Odysseus, he must wander aimlessly and backtrack frequently, and it takes a very long time to accomplish this – for Moses, more than 40 years, for Odysseus, 20. Interestingly, Moses and Odysseus travel regions that are immediately adjacent. And, while we're on the topic of similarities between Moses and Odysseus, their time setting would be very close as well, with Moses' saga taking place around 1400 BCE and the historical Trojan War occurring around 12-1300 B.C.E. They are both Bronze Age nationalistic adventures.

SUPERNATURAL FORCES

Yes – Clearly, this is a supernatural story! It contains some of the most pyrotechnical divine demonstrations in the entire Bible. It also speaks – again, like The Odyssey and Iliad – to the indisputable power of God. The hero is chosen by God, sponsored by God, and empowered by God. Moses, in particular, functions as an instrument of God, more so than many epic heroes.

MAIN CHARACTERS GIVE LONG FORMAL SPEECHES

Yes – Deuteronomy contains the three final sermons of Moses before he passes away. These are some of the most important speeches in the Bible, containing, for instance, the prayer called the Shema: "Hear, Israel, the Lord is our God, the Lord is One" (Deut. 6:4).

CATALOGUES/GENEALOGIES TO PROVIDE BROAD CONTEXT

Yes – See Numbers 16:4-16. This passage puts Moses' adventure into the historical context of the nation of Israel.

HEAVY USE OF REPETITION AND STOCK PHRASES

Yes – In Exodus 1, for example, we see a stock phrase that originated in Genesis 1: "And the children of Israel were fruitful, and increased abundantly, and multiplied" (7). The Promised Land is frequently described with the epithet "a land flowing with milk and honey." God is often identified as "the God of Abraham, the God of Isaac, the God of Jacob." And Pharaoh's heart is repeatedly "hardened."

CONCLUSION

So on a 9-item list of epic qualities, Moses' story scores a 7 (with half a point on two items and zero points on one). It is long, grand and serious, with a triumphant national hero. It is broad in scope. It is obviously supernatural. Regarding its language and conventions, it includes important speeches, genealogies, and stock phrases (epithets). What it lacks is some of the poetic qualities that a more creative writer might employ. If it was indeed Moses who recorded his own life story, he had a historical purpose in mind, and his style was largely mechanical. Homer's composition of The Odyssey and Iliad, by contrast, was a creative venture, crafted with elegant, artistic language. Moses is more of a bare-bones epic hero. And although he does not pray outright (to a muse or to God) in the opening lines of Exodus, as does Homer, Moses does pray often. This "epic" closes, rather than begins, with a prayer – Moses' final prayer before death:

> *Blessed are you, Israel!*
> *Who is like you,*
> *a people saved by the LORD?*
> *He is your shield and helper*
> *and your glorious sword.*
> *Your enemies will cower before you,*
> *and you will tread on their heights* (Deut. 33:29).

BIBLICAL LITERARY INVENTORY — NARRATIVE

Narrative: The Story of Moses (Abridged)   **Passages:** Exodus through Deuteronomy

I. Protagonist and Antagonist – Moses and the Jewish people versus Pharaoh and other obstacles that keep them from the Promised Land. (If you were to read the entire story, stretching from Exodus through Deuteronomy, you would also note a secondary antagonist: the Israelites' recurrent doubts and disobedience, which keeps them in the wilderness for 40 years.)

II. Inciting Incident – This story, as a meandering history, does not have a precise plot arc. However, the beginning of Moses' dramatic life story is his rescue from the bulrushes. You could also identify the burning bush as the moment of his archetypal "calling."

III/IV. Rising Action / Climax – Given the excerpts provided in this textbook (designed to provide a glimpse into Moses' greatest adventures) we might identify the first 80 years of his life as rising action, and the Exodus and Passover, perhaps the crossing of the Red Sea, as the climax.

V. Falling Action – The 40 years in the wilderness, including the delivery of the Ten Commandments and the rest of the Law.

VI. Resolution – Although it is not completely resolving or satisfying, Moses' death concludes his story. He is allowed to see the Promised Land from afar, but he experiences no triumphant success.

VII. Theme – _____
_____
_____

VIII. Symbolism – The fire of the burning bush could either <u>be</u> God or <u>represent</u> God; archetypally, fire suggests knowledge and power. Furthermore, some Biblical commentators think the 10 plagues each represent an attack on a different Egyptian deity, for instance the turning of the water to blood signifying the God's superiority over the god of the Nile. The plague that covered the sun may indicate the overshadowing of Ra, the Egyptian sun god and foremost among their pantheon, and the frog infestation could be interpreted as a mockery of the goddess Heket, the deity of fertility who was depicted in Egyptian hieroglyphics as a frog. Do you see any other symbolism in the Moses story? You may be interested in looking up additional symbolic interpretations of the ten plagues, which is easy to find on the Internet.
_____
_____
_____

IX. Motif – There is a motif of the number 40. Find examples (in this story and others) and interpret what the number 40 might mean:_____
_____
_____

X. Character Development – It is difficult to do a thorough character study of Moses without reading his entire story. In this text, our abridgment left out some of Moses' failures and struggles (see #2 in the previous study guide). Why do you think he has gone down in history as one of the greatest heroes of all time? _____
_____
_____
_____

XI. Narrative Persona – The speaker is third person limited, with a narrative style that is completely objective, simply relating events and quoting dialogue. The narrative persona is not poetic or interpretive; rather, the style is coldly concrete, literal, and historical.

XII. Irony, Contrast, Foil and/or Reversals – Pharaoh and Moses both have reversals of fleeing versus following and agreeing versus disagreeing. And, as mentioned earlier in this inventory, if you were to read the entire saga, you would find numerous reversals of the Israelites trusting versus doubting, praising versus complaining. What do you think is the purpose of all this vacillation throughout the story? _____

_____

_____

XIII. Additional Literary Devices – Moses has an archetypal calling, Aaron functions as an archetypal sidekick, and the crossing of the Red Sea might be seen as Moses' journey through the abyss within the archetypal hero cycle. Do you see any other archetypal elements in the story? Do you think the presence of archetype makes the story feel less historical or factual?

_____

_____

_____

XIV. Historical Criticism – Although the literary qualities of the Moses narrative are historical in nature, there are no substantiated historical records that fully support the plot details. Scholars attempting to reconcile the biblical narrative with Egyptian history disagree about which pharaoh is being described in Exodus, but it does seem clear that the story is set in the New Kingdom period (1550-1069 B.C.E.) during which time the Egyptian empire reached up through Canaan and eastward into Syria. Popular candidates for Moses' pharaoh include Rameses II, Thutmose III, or Amenhotep II. According to the *Archaeological Study Bible*, "no single theory completely harmonizes archeological evidence with biblical claims" (106). Does the lack of firm historical evidence shape your interpretation of Moses' story in any way? _____

_____

_____

XV. Genre Awareness (select one) –

___ Mythology: Symbolically, what does the story reveal about human nature or God?

___ Legend / Epic: What themes of Judeo-Christian identity emerge?

___ History: What historical events have a practical bearing on the present and future?

___ Biography: Why is the subject of the biography worth special attention?

Based on your selection, provide a response to the genre-related question provided above:

_____

_____

JONAH

¹ Now the word of the Lord came unto Jonah the son of Amittai, saying, ² "Arise, go to Nineveh, that great city, and cry against it; for their wickedness is come up before me."

³ But Jonah rose up to flee unto Tarshish from the presence of the Lord, and went down to Joppa; and he found a ship going to Tarshish: [oooo] so he paid the fare thereof, and went down into it, to go with them unto Tarshish from the presence of the Lord. ⁴ But the Lord sent out a great wind into the sea, and there was a mighty tempest in the sea, so that the ship was like to be broken.

⁵ Then the mariners were afraid, and cried every man unto his god, and cast forth the wares that were in the ship into the sea, to lighten it of them. But Jonah was gone down into the sides of the ship; and he lay, and was fast asleep. ⁶ So the shipmaster came to him, and said unto him, "What meanest thou, O sleeper? arise, call upon thy God, if so be that God will think upon us, that we perish not." ⁷ And they said every one to his fellow, "Come, and let us cast lots, that we may know for whose cause this evil is upon us." So they cast lots, and the lot fell upon Jonah.[pppp] ⁸ Then said they unto him, "Tell us, we pray thee, for whose cause this evil is upon us; What is thine occupation? and whence comest thou? what is thy country? and of what people art thou?"

⁹ And he said unto them, "I am an Hebrew; and I fear the Lord, the God of heaven, which hath made the sea and the dry land." ¹⁰ Then were the men exceedingly afraid, and said unto him. "Why hast thou done this?" For the men knew that he fled from the presence of the Lord, because he had told them. ¹¹ Then said they unto him, "What shall we do unto thee, that the sea may be calm unto us?" for the sea wrought, and was tempestuous.[qqqq] ¹² And he said unto them, "Take me up, and cast me forth into the sea; so shall the sea be calm unto you: for I know that for my sake this great tempest is upon you."

¹³ Nevertheless the men rowed hard to bring it to the land; but they could not: for the sea wrought, and was tempestuous against them. ¹⁴ Wherefore they cried unto the Lord, and said, "We beseech thee, O Lord, we beseech thee, let us not perish for this man's life, and lay not upon us innocent blood: for thou, O Lord, hast done as it pleased thee."[rrrr] ¹⁵ So they took up Jonah, and cast him forth into the sea: and the sea ceased from her raging. ¹⁶ Then the men feared the Lord exceedingly, and offered a sacrifice unto the Lord, and made vows.

[oooo] Tarshish seems to be a sea that is far away from Israel, reachable only by sea. Joppa is a Mediterranean coast port city. Ninevah would have been in the opposite direction of Tarshish. (FI)

[pppp] Casting lots was an ancient means of gambling, similar to throwing dice; here, it refers to something like drawing straws, in which case Jonah comes up with the short straw. We see from the details in this paragraph that the mariners were polytheists, and it seems that they are trying to figure out whose god is causing the storm. All signs point to Jonah and his God.

[qqqq] Wrought = moved back and forth. Tempestuous = stormy. (BHL) (FI)

[rrrr] Beseech = beg. (FI) They pray to Jonah's God that he will not punish them for throwing him overboard; they do not want to anger a foreign god by killing his servant. (EP)

¹⁷ Now the Lord had prepared a great fish to swallow up Jonah.[ssss] And Jonah was in the belly of the fish three days and three nights. **2** Then Jonah prayed unto the Lord his God out of the fish's belly, ² And said,

> "I cried by reason of mine affliction unto the Lord,
> > and he heard me;
> out of the belly of hell cried I,[tttt]
> > and thou heardest my voice.
> ³ For thou hadst cast me into the deep,
> > in the midst of the seas;
> and the floods compassed me about:
> > all thy billows and thy waves passed over me.
>
> ⁴ Then I said, I am cast out of thy sight;
> > yet I will look again toward thy holy temple.
> ⁵ The waters compassed me about,
> > even to the soul:
> the depth closed me round about,
> > the weeds were wrapped about my head.
> ⁶ I went down to the bottoms of the mountains;
> > the earth with her bars was about me for ever:
> yet hast thou brought up my life from corruption, O Lord my God.
>
> ⁷ When my soul fainted within me
> > I remembered the Lord:
> and my prayer came in unto thee,
> > into thine holy temple.
>
> ⁸ They that observe lying vanities
> > forsake their own mercy.[uuuu]
> ⁹ But I will sacrifice unto thee
> > with the voice of thanksgiving;
> I will pay that that I have vowed.
> > Salvation is of the Lord."

¹⁰ And the Lord spake unto the fish, and it vomited out Jonah upon the dry land. **3** And the word of the Lord came unto Jonah the second time, saying, ² "Arise, go unto Nineveh, that great city, and preach unto it the preaching that I bid thee."

[ssss] The original Hebrew uses the word for fish, but most people know this creature as a whale, since whales are big enough to swallow a man. (BHL)

[tttt] The word translated here as "hell" is commonly translated as "abyss" or the "realm of the dead." It is interesting to note that archetypal heroes often pass through an abyss on the way to completing their heroic calling. (BHL) (FI)

[uuuu] "They that cling to worthless idols (lying vanities) turn their backs (forsake) on God's mercy." (BHL)

³ So Jonah arose, and went unto Nineveh, according to the word of the Lord. Now Nineveh was an exceeding great city of three days' journey. ⁴ And Jonah began to enter into the city a day's journey, and he cried, and said, "Yet forty days, and Nineveh shall be overthrown."

⁵ So the people of Nineveh believed God, and proclaimed a fast, and put on sackcloth,[vvvv] from the greatest of them even to the least of them. ⁶ For word came unto the king of Nineveh, and he arose from his throne, and he laid his robe from him, and covered him with sackcloth, and sat in ashes. ⁷ And he caused it to be proclaimed and published through Nineveh by the decree of the king and his nobles, saying, "Let neither man nor beast, herd nor flock, taste any thing: let them not feed, nor drink water: ⁸ But let man and beast be covered with sackcloth, and cry mightily unto God: yea, let them turn every one from his evil way, and from the violence that is in their hands. ⁹ Who can tell if God will turn and repent, and turn away from his fierce anger, that we perish not?" ¹⁰ And God saw their works, that they turned from their evil way; and God repented of the evil, that he had said that he would do unto them; and he did it not.

4 But it displeased Jonah exceedingly, and he was very angry. ² And he prayed unto the Lord, and said, "I pray thee, O Lord, was not this my saying, when I was yet in my country? Therefore I fled before unto Tarshish: for I knew that thou art a gracious God, and merciful, slow to anger, and of great kindness, and repentest thee of the evil. ³ Therefore now, O Lord, take, I beseech thee, my life from me; for it is better for me to die than to live." ⁴ Then said the Lord, "Doest thou well to be angry?"

⁵ So Jonah went out of the city, and sat on the east side of the city, and there made him a booth,[wwww] and sat under it in the shadow, till he might see what would become of the city. ⁶ And the Lord God prepared a gourd,[xxxx] and made it to come up over Jonah, that it might be a shadow over his head, to deliver him from his grief. So Jonah was exceeding glad of the gourd. ⁷ But God prepared a worm when the morning rose the next day, and it smote the gourd that it withered.[yyyy] ⁸ And it came to pass, when the sun did arise, that God prepared a vehement east wind; and the sun beat upon the head of Jonah, that he fainted, and wished in himself to die, and said, "It is better for me to die than to live."

⁹ And God said to Jonah, "Doest thou well to be angry for the gourd?" And he said, "I do well to be angry, even unto death." ¹⁰ Then said the Lord, "Thou hast had pity on the gourd, for the which thou hast not laboured, neither madest it grow; which came up in a night, and perished in a night: ¹¹ And should not I spare Nineveh, that great city, wherein are more than sixscore[zzzz] thousand persons that cannot discern between their right hand and their left hand; and also much cattle?"

[vvvv] Fast = a period of willing abstinence from food (and sometimes drink) for the purpose of self-discipline or worship. Sackcloth = a type of course fabric customarily worn by ancient Jews during a period of penitence or mourning. Sackcloth and ashes together were worn as a sign of mourning. (FI)
[wwww] Booth = a shelter (FI)
[xxxx] Gourd = most translations say "a plant" or "a leafy plant." (BHL)
[yyyy] The worm chewed the plant so it withered.
[zzzz] Sixscore = 120 (for a total of 120,000) (FI)

LESSON THIRTEEN:
JONAH AS COMIC ANTI-HERO

"Jonah and the Whale" by Pieter Lastman

Everyone knows who Jonah is – the hero who survived three days in the belly of a whale! However, there aren't too many folks who think of Jonah as a *comic* hero. My friend's four-year-old son refused to swim in the ocean last summer while on a beach vacation because he had just heard the story of Jonah – he was afraid of being swallowed by a whale. But bear with me for just a few minutes while I make my case. Isn't it just a wee bit funny that God saves Jonah through a miracle of vomit? Just a *little* funny?

Let's go back to the beginning of the story and see what kind of message and mood the narrator might really have in mind for us. We can easily analyze the Book of Jonah as a carefully crafted short story (and some Bible scholars think it was a work of religious fiction from the ancient world). Everything about the story seems intentional, balanced, and precisely paced. Someone who knew a thing or two about good writing put it down on paper with some artistic flair. I think he had humor in mind – a few laughs to help drive home a very serious point about the nature of God. And nobody ever said God doesn't have a sense of humor.

Jonah is introduced as a prophet. But what kind of prophet is he? One that refuses to prophesy, that's what. God tells him to go to Ninevah (a prominent and wealthy ancient city) and he goes the opposite direction. He's either a really rotten guy, or he's laughable. He's the only character in the story who is supposed to know anything at all about the Real God, so he certainly understands omnipresence and omniscience, right? If so, he ignores the facts and acts like a fool. Once the storm hits, he knows God is punishing him, and so he agrees to take the heat. Here's where we realize he's not a totally bad guy, but he really should have known better all along. There is an interesting irony here as well: the heathen sailors respond more quickly and obediently to God than Prophet Jonah ever did. So they reluctantly toss him overboard, and he gets swallowed by the giant fish, the proverbial whale. It's preposterous. Like a children's tall tale. So Jonah realizes his mammoth mistake while inside the whale's mammoth gut. He prays an elegant prayer, and God decides to give him a second chance. Via vomit. The great prophet (who isn't really so great at all) gets re-inaugurated into his holy calling by being upchucked on the beach. This is a great lesson for Jonah… and a pretty funny image for readers. Consider that ancient Jewish humor was often based on exaggeration, puns, irony, and good old-fashioned funny images like this one.[aaaaa]

The second part of the story has its share of comedy as well. Jonah finally goes to Ninevah and utters what we might acknowledge as a half-hearted and half-accurate sermon: all he tells the people is that God is going to destroy the city, which isn't quite true. He doesn't deliver the warning God told him to. He delivers an inaccurate single sentence prediction. After all this business about avoiding Ninevah, almost dying in the sea, and then repenting of his error, Jonah shows up to Ninevah and preaches an eight-word sermon. Fortunately for them, the Ninevites hear and repent, hoping that God will find favor in their groveling. It's really quite a miraculously quick conversion, and so yet again we see a group of heathens who (ironically) behave more obediently than Jonah the prophet does. And then the funny part – everyone in town commences to ceremonial mourning, which consists of putting on rags and fasting – from the king right down to the cattle. Yes, the text describes cows dressed in rags, being deprived of

---

[aaaaa] Friedman, Hershey H. "Humor in the Hebrew Bible." <u>HUMOR: International Journal of Humor Research</u>. Volume 13.3. Sept. 2000. 257-285.

food and drink for God's sake. Dogs and cats in dirty clothes, everyone crying. Please tell me you find this at least somewhat humorous. It's another funny image based on exaggeration.

But the story isn't over, because Jonah has not resolved his conflict with God. He's no longer running away, but he's still rebellious in spirit. He leaves town and finds himself a comfortable place to camp, somewhere overlooking the city so he can watch the glorious spectacle of destruction that God is certainly about to deliver. Sadly for Jonah, it doesn't come. God decides to spare them. So that's good news, right? Mission accomplished? The only problem is that Jonah *really* wanted to see Ninevah get blown to bits. He's actually peeved at God for not smiting them. He wants to die he's so depressed – a bit of an exaggerated mental state, perhaps? Meanwhile, it's pretty hot outside, so God takes some pity on his servant Jonah, too, by causing a tall plant to grow beside him, providing some shade under the brutal sun. Jonah pouts for a while in relative comfort until God causes the plant to wither. And now, while Jonah stews in his anger at God for <u>sparing</u> 120 thousand people <u>from execution</u>, Jonah has the nerve to criticize God even further for <u>not sparing</u> his shoulders <u>from a sunburn</u>. And then the story ends. Maybe he didn't learn a lesson after all. So, on a scale of one to ten, how great a prophet is Jonah?

Jonah appears to fit the definition of an *antihero*. An antihero is a protagonist who embodies traits that run rather opposite to a traditional hero. An antihero is either unskilled or unintelligent, and he often has poorer-than-average morals. A good storyteller can make you root for the antihero's success even though you don't really admire him. Sometimes, an antihero is spirited or sexy, and sometimes he is simply laughable. Think Jack Sparrow or Butch Cassidy and the Sundance Kid. Jonah (clearly not spirited or sexy!) is the laughable type, a bit like Michael Scott in <u>The Office</u>. We want him to do his job well; we want him to bring salvation to the Ninevites. But we never admire him. He succeeds due to God's grace, not anything he accomplishes by heroic means.

Jonah may be seen as symbolic of the worst kind of religious zeal – something hateful and foolish rather than compassionate. Many folks consider the Book of Jonah a work of satire, targeting the religious Israelites of the day for a holier-than-thou attitude that excluded God's grace from non-Jews. The theme of the story is clear: God takes more pleasure in saving than in smiting. Jonah never quite figures this out, but a good reader does. And a little dose of comedy helps sell the message.

LESSON THIRTEEN STUDY GUIDE

Objective Identification:

comedy, antihero, satire

Subjective Expression:

1) Recall and Opinion: List three elements of the story that could be considered funny. Did you expect that any portions of the Bible would be comedic?

2) Deeper Analysis: A story's climax often functions as a sort of thematic or emotional backbone. In this story, the climax is Jonah's expulsion from the whale. Immediately prior to this moment, he prays to be rescued. The prayer appears in the form of a poem, containing all the elements of Hebrew poetry discussed in the previous lesson about Genesis 1. Take a closer look at the poem (2:1-9) and analyze its artistic elements and its theme.

3) Cultural Connections: Make a list of several other comedic antiheroes you have seen in television or film. Remember, an antihero must be the protagonist, but not a typically noble or heroic protagonist. There must be something significant in his character to dislike or despise. Still, he can't be the villain. Example: Michael Scott in <u>The Office</u>.

4) Literary Connections: Can you think of a work of comedy that actually made you do some serious thinking about an important issue? Identify the comedy and explain your reaction.

5) Comparison: Compare the three biblical heroes from this unit of study – Abraham, Moses, and Jonah – on the basis of faithfulness, strength, intellect, impact and narrative drama.

BIBLICAL LITERARY INVENTORY   NARRATIVE

Narrative – Book of Jonah

I. Protagonist and Antagonist – Jonah is clearly the protagonist, but then who or what is the antagonist? Consider internal conflict._____

II. Inciting Incident –_____

III. Rising Action – _____

IV. Climax – _____
_____

V. Falling Action – _____
_____

VI. Resolution – _____
_____

VII. Theme – _____
_____
_____

VIII. Symbolism – Because God creates the plant in order to teach Jonah a lesson, it can be considered a symbol. What does it represent? _____
_____
_____

IX. Motif – Trace a motif of comedic imagery through the story. _____
_____
_____

X. Character Development - _____
_____
_____
_____
_____

XI. Narrative Persona – If Jonah himself were the author/speaker of the story (a traditional point of view) then for some reason he chooses a third person point of view. Of what benefit it this point of view, given the negative portrayal of Jonah's behavior? _____
_____
_____

XII. Irony, Contrast, Foil and/or Reversals – What is the essential irony of the story? It involves Jonah's qualities as a prophet. _____
_____
_____

XIII. Additional Literary Devices – Consider antihero, satire, and archetype.

_____

_____

_____

XIV. Historical Criticism – There are clues in the Second Book of Kings (chapter 14) as to the historical placement of Jonah: during the reign of Jeroboam II, in the early 7th century BCE. Later in this century, Assyria began invading and conquering parts of Israel. The text of Jonah says that Ninevah (which was Assyrian) was a "great city," probably referring to size and wealth, and history tells us that they were antagonists of ancient Israel. How does this information shape your interpretation of the story? Do you think it gives the story a political angle?

_____

_____

_____

XV. Genre Awareness (select one) –

Due to its fantastical elements, many secular scholars read Jonah as a creative short story with a satirical purpose. A more traditional religious reading would classify it as history, written by the Prophet Jonah. It is found in the section of the Old Testament called the Minor Prophets. Prophets, as you will learn in the upcoming section on "Poetry and Prophecy," are designated spokesmen for God (not just fortune-tellers but authorized historians as well).

　　___ Mythology: Symbolically, what does the story reveal about human nature or God?

　　___ Legend / Epic: What themes of Judeo-Christian identity emerge?

　　___ History: What historical events have a practical bearing on the present and future?

　　___ Biography: Why is the subject of the biography worth special attention?

　　___ Drama: What aspects of the play a "hold a mirror up to nature"?

　　___ Short Story: What elements of intentional storytelling contribute to theme and unity?

　　___ Narrative Poetry: Why was the story told via elevated and/or figurative language?

Based on your selection, provide a response to the genre-related question provided above:

_____

_____

_____

POETRY & PROPHECY

To everything there is a season,
And a time to every purpose
Under the heaven

SELECTED PSALMS

Psalm 100

¹Make a joyful noise unto the LORD, all ye lands.
²Serve the LORD with gladness:
    come before his presence with singing.
³Know ye that the LORD he is God:
    it is he that hath made us, and not we ourselves;
    we are his people, and the sheep of his pasture.

⁴Enter into his gates with thanksgiving,
    and into his courts with praise:
    be thankful unto him, and bless his name.
⁵For the LORD is good; his mercy is everlasting;
    and his truth endureth to all generations.

Psalm 22

¹My God, my God, why hast thou forsaken[a] me?
    why art thou so far from helping me,
    and from the words of my roaring?
²O my God, I cry in the day time, but thou hearest not;
    and in the night season, and am not silent.

³But thou art holy,
    O thou that inhabitest the praises of Israel.[b]
⁴Our fathers trusted in thee: they trusted,
    and thou didst deliver them.
⁵They cried unto thee, and were delivered:
    they trusted in thee, and were not confounded.

⁶But I am a worm, and no man;
    a reproach of men,[c] and despised of the people.
⁷All they that see me laugh me to scorn:
    they shoot out the lip, they shake the head, saying,
⁸"He trusted on the LORD that he would deliver him:
    let him deliver him, seeing he delighted in him."

---

[a] Forsaken = abandoned (FI)
[b] Sometimes translated as "you who are enthroned on the praises of Israel" (BHL)
[c] A reproach of men = someone scorned by men (FI)

⁹But thou art he that took me out of the womb:
> thou didst make me hope
> when I was upon my mother's breasts.

¹⁰I was cast upon thee from the womb:
> thou art my God from my mother's belly.

¹¹Be not far from me;
> for trouble is near;
> for there is none to help.

¹²Many bulls have compassed me:
> strong bulls of Bashan have beset me round.[d]

¹³They gaped upon me with their mouths,
> as a ravening and a roaring lion.

¹⁴I am poured out like water,
> and all my bones are out of joint:
my heart is like wax;
> it is melted in the midst of my bowels.

¹⁵My strength is dried up like a potsherd;[e]
> and my tongue cleaveth to my jaws;
> and thou hast brought me into the dust of death.

¹⁶For dogs have compassed me:
> the assembly of the wicked have inclosed me:
> they pierced my hands and my feet.

¹⁷I may tell all my bones:
> they look and stare upon me.

¹⁸They part my garments among them,
> and cast lots upon my vesture.[f]

¹⁹But be not thou far from me, O LORD:
> O my strength, haste thee to help me.

²⁰Deliver my soul from the sword;
> my darling from the power of the dog.

²¹Save me from the lion's mouth:
> for thou hast heard me from the horns of the unicorns.[g]

²²I will declare thy name unto my brethren:
> in the midst of the congregation will I praise thee.

²³Ye that fear the LORD, praise him;
> all ye the seed of Jacob, glorify him;
> and fear him, all ye the seed of Israel.

---

[d] Bulls from the region of Bashan, an area of rich pastureland which could have produced large and fierce bulls. (BHC – Barnes' Notes)

[e] Potsherd = shard of pottery, a piece of broken-up and dry pottery

[f] Cast lots upon my vesture = gamble with my clothing as the prize (FI)

[g] The word translated in the KJV as "unicorn" is more commonly translated as "oxen." (BHL)

²⁴For he hath not despised nor abhorred
>   the affliction of the afflicted;
neither hath he hid his face from him;
>   but when he cried unto him, he heard.

²⁵My praise shall be of thee in the great congregation:
>   I will pay my vows before them that fear him.
²⁶The meek shall eat and be satisfied:
>   they shall praise the LORD that seek him:
>   your heart shall live for ever.

²⁷All the ends of the world
>   shall remember and turn unto the LORD:
and all the kindreds of the nations
>   shall worship before thee.
²⁸For the kingdom is the LORD's:
>   and he is the governor among the nations.

²⁹All they that be fat upon earth shall eat and worship:
>   all they that go down to the dust shall bow before him:
>   and none can keep alive his own soul.
³⁰A seed shall serve him;
>   it shall be accounted to the Lord for a generation.
³¹They shall come, and shall declare his righteousness
>   unto a people that shall be born,
>   that he hath done this.

Psalm 23

¹The LORD is my shepherd; I shall not want.[h]
²He maketh me to lie down in green pastures:
>   he leadeth me beside the still waters.
³He restoreth my soul:
>   he leadeth me in the paths of righteousness
>   for his name's sake.

⁴Yea, though I walk
>   through the valley of the shadow of death,
I will fear no evil:
>   for thou art with me;
thy rod and thy staff [i]
>   they comfort me.

---

[h] I shall not want = I will have no unmet needs (EP)
[i] Rod and staff = a shepherd's tools for leading sheep and protecting them from attack (FI)

⁵Thou preparest a table before me
>   in the presence of mine enemies:
thou anointest my head with oil; ʲ
>   my cup runneth over.
⁶Surely goodness and mercy shall follow me
>   all the days of my life:
and I will dwell in the house of the LORD
>   for ever.

Psalm 137

¹By the rivers of Babylon, there we sat down, yea, we wept,
>   when we remembered Zion. ᵏ
²We hanged our harps
>   upon the willows in the midst thereof.
³For there they that carried us away captive required of us a song;
>   and they that wasted us required of us mirth, saying,
>   "Sing us one of the songs of Zion."

⁴How shall we sing the LORD's song
>   in a strange land?
⁵If I forget thee, O Jerusalem,
>   let my right hand forget her cunning.
⁶If I do not remember thee,
>   let my tongue cleave to the roof of my mouth;
if I prefer not Jerusalem
>   above my chief joy.

⁷Remember, O LORD, the children of Edom ˡ
>   in the day of Jerusalem;
who said, "Rase it, rase it, ᵐ
>   even to the foundation thereof."

ʲ Anointing is a tradition of pouring oil, perfume, or spices on a person's head or body as part of a religious ritual. In the Hebrew custom, kings and priests were anointed prior to taking office. In this context, the poet suggests that God has chosen him or blessed him. In other contexts, a body might be anointed prior to burial. (FI)

ᵏ Babylon = the Babylonian Empire, which conquered and displaced the Israelites in the middle of the First Millennium B.C.E. (called the Babylonian Captivity or Babylonian Exile). The rivers of Babylon were perhaps the Tigris and Euphrates. Zion = Jerusalem. (FI)

ˡ Edom = in reference to the Edomites, who were a Semitic people said to have descended from Esau, Jacob's brother (Jacob and Esau were Abraham's grandsons, and Jacob, the younger brother, deceitfully stole his brother's birthright/inheritance). The Edomites appear frequently in the Old Testament as enemies of Israel (descended from Jacob) and therefore as a continuation of the sibling rivalry between Jacob and Esau. (FI)

ᵐ Rase = destroy, as in "erase." (FI)

⁸O daughter of Babylon, who art to be destroyed;
>happy shall he be, that rewardeth thee
>as thou hast served us.

⁹Happy shall he be, that taketh and dasheth thy little ones
>against the stones.

Psalm 139

¹O lord, thou hast searched me,
>and known me.

²Thou knowest my downsitting and mine uprising,
>thou understandest my thought afar off.

³Thou compassest my path and my lying down,
>and art acquainted with all my ways.

⁴For there is not a word in my tongue, but, lo, O LORD,
>thou knowest it altogether.

⁵Thou hast beset me behind and before, ⁿ
>and laid thine hand upon me.

⁶Such knowledge is too wonderful for me;
>it is high, I cannot attain unto it.

⁷Whither shall I go from thy spirit? ᵒ
>or whither shall I flee from thy presence?

⁸If I ascend up into heaven, thou art there:
>if I make my bed in hell, behold, thou art there.ᵖ

⁹If I take the wings of the morning,
>and dwell in the uttermost parts of the sea;

¹⁰Even there shall thy hand lead me,
>and thy right hand shall hold me.

¹¹If I say, "Surely the darkness shall cover me;"
>even the night shall be light about me.

¹²Yea, the darkness hideth not from thee;
>but the night shineth as the day:
>the darkness and the light are both alike to thee.

ⁿ You go before me as a guide, and you follow me as a protector. (EP)

ᵒ Whither = where (FI)

ᵖ The word translated as "hell" in this verse is the Hebrew sheol, which means "underworld" or "realm of death." (BHL)

¹³For thou hast possessed my reins:
>> thou hast covered me in my mother's womb. ^q
¹⁴I will praise thee; for I am fearfully and wonderfully made:
>> marvellous are thy works;
>> and that my soul knoweth right well.
¹⁵My substance was not hid from thee,
>> when I was made in secret,
>> and curiously wrought in the lowest parts of the earth.
¹⁶Thine eyes did see my substance, yet being unperfect;
>> and in thy book all my members were written,
>> which in continuance were fashioned, when as yet there was none of them.

¹⁷How precious also are thy thoughts unto me, O God!
>> how great is the sum of them!
¹⁸If I should count them,
>> they are more in number than the sand:
when I awake,
>> I am still with thee.

¹⁹Surely thou wilt slay the wicked, O God:
>> depart from me therefore, ye bloody men.
²⁰For they speak against thee wickedly,
>> and thine enemies take thy name in vain.
²¹Do not I hate them, O LORD, that hate thee?
>> and am not I grieved with those that rise up against thee?
²²I hate them with perfect hatred:
>> I count them mine enemies.

²³Search me, O God, and know my heart: try me, and know my thoughts:
>> ²⁴And see if there be any wicked way in me, and lead me in the way everlasting.

---

[q] The NIV says "For you have created my inmost being" for the first line of verse 13. The word rendered as "reins" in the KJV is the Hebrew word *kilyah*, which means "kidneys." The NIV renders the second line of the verse as "you knit me together in my mother's womb." (BHL)

LESSON FOURTEEN:
SONGS OF LAMENT AND PRAISE

The Book of Psalms is a collection of Hebrew poems that were composed as song lyrics for the lyre or harp. The word *psalm* comes from the Hebrew *zmr*, which means "to pluck," referring to a stringed instrument. Most of these poems are attributed to the authorship of King David, who lived nearly 1000 years before Jesus. The Bible features David as one of the most important kings of Israel, his life story narrated in the books of Samuel, I Kings, and I Chronicles in the Old Testament. This is the same character who, as a boy, kills the giant Goliath with a slingshot (I Samuel 17). He is also the king who falls in love with the beautiful Bathsheba and orders her husband sent to the front lines of war so that he will be killed (II Samuel 11). David subsequently marries Bathsheba, and they give birth to Solomon – traditionally recognized as the author of Proverbs, Song of Solomon, and Ecclesiastes (which we will study in the next lesson). David is best known as a king, warrior, poet, and musician.

Many psalms were written about the topic of singing, as illustrated in Psalm 100. Other psalms mention dancing and musical instruments. The Psalms, whether sung or recited, remain an important part of modern day worship for both Jews and Christians. They often appear in Jewish liturgy, particularly as part of the morning service, or *Shacharit*. Psalms 113-118 are called *Hallel* (Hebrew for "praise") and recited in their entirety on holidays. In Christian churches, Psalm 22 is often read during Lent, and many psalms have inspired traditional hymns as well as contemporary religious music, for instance the song "Make a Joyful Noise," based on Psalm 100. The first book ever printed in North America was called <u>The Bay Psalm Book</u>, which contained metrical translations of psalms into English, for the purpose of congregational singing.

We begin our literary analysis with Psalm 22, largely because it is the most frequently quoted psalm in the New Testament (and we will refer back to it in a later lesson). It is also an interesting combination of two of the most common themes in the entire Psalms collection: *lament* and *praise*. The Psalms are intensely emotional, and Psalm 22 begins with the poet in an extreme state of grief, so much so that he feels God has "forsaken" him, left him behind to be devoured by his enemies. You will find that this and most other psalms express their emotional intent through common, earthy, physical imagery: worms, a mother's breast, bulls, roaring lions, bones, dried and broken pottery, dust, wild dogs, and wounded flesh appear in Psalm 22. This poetry is not delicate or bashful; it is poetry for the common people. If you can't find a psalm to match your mood, you're not looking hard enough. The Book of Psalms as a whole grapples with life's deepest despair and its most resounding joy, using earthy imagery and poetic repetition to help a singing congregation express honest feelings. There is a wonderful assumption here that God doesn't mind an honest complaint or two. The poets in this book do not shy away from horror, grief, hatred, or anger – even anger directed at God. By the end of Psalm 22, however, the grieving poet does in fact acknowledge a profound hope in God with sweeping descriptions of a future day of redemption. All these emotions, positive and negative, find a home in the Psalms, side by side in the context of faith.

Psalm 23 is probably the most famous of all the psalms. The imagery grounds the entire sentiment in places and objects that would have been very familiar to the original audience: a shepherd's staff, pastures, rivers, valleys, shadows, a wine glass at a banquet table. Psalm 23 is also rich in pattern and sound, which no doubt contributes to its popularity. The opening line has four strong beats, and the next two lines are pleasingly structured with simple repetition: he maketh, he leadeth, he restoreth. The next verse is heavily rhythmic, followed by another repetitive set: thou preparest, thou anointest. The last verse is conclusive, finishing with another strong four-beat phrase: "I will <u>dwell</u> in the <u>house</u> of the <u>Lord</u> for<u>ev</u>er." It is easy to chant, easy to sing, easy to imagine, easy to remember. This is the power of a psalm.

Psalm 137 is a historically important poem. It was written during the time of Babylonian captivity, an era when the Jewish people were conquered, transported away from the Promised Land, and forced to live under the harsh hand of the Babylonians. This era of biblical history, called the Exile, occurs right around the halfway point of the first millennium B.C. This poem, therefore, is not attributed to King David, who ruled over Jerusalem during an earlier period of political success (followed by his son, King Solomon, who is known for his excessive wealth). On the next page, you will find another update of our timeline, to help you put David, Solomon, and the Exile into a historical perspective.

The period of the Babylonian Exile is an important setting and topic throughout the Old Testament, and because of its prominent position in the Bible, it appears frequently in Western literature. Often, an allusion to Babylon will serve as a metaphor for captivity and oppression. Because Babylon also appears in the Book of Revelation, where it is depicted as the embodiment

Bible Timeline 3

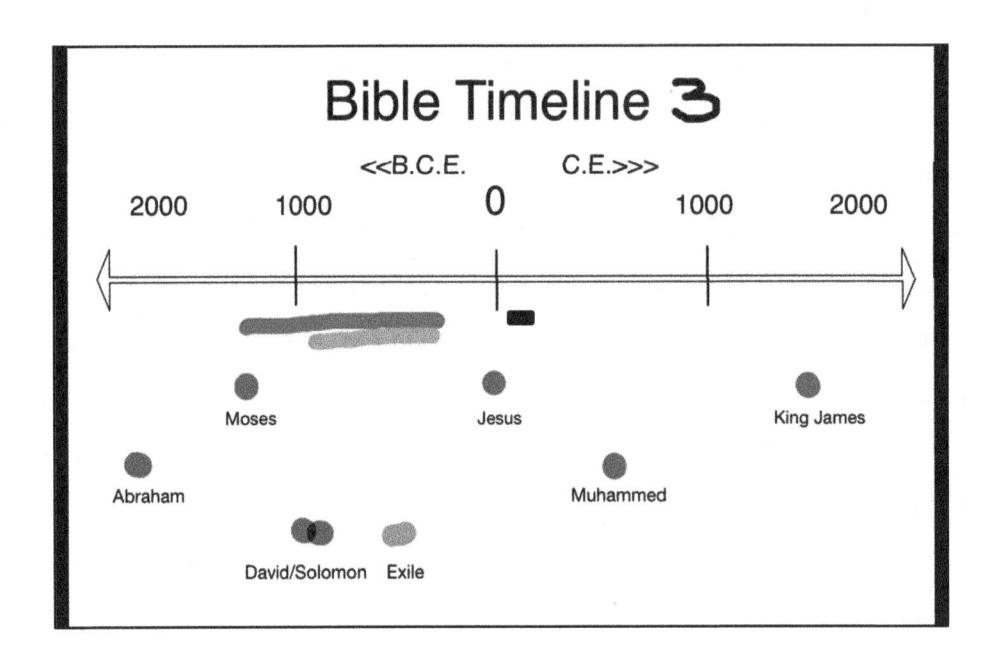

<<B.C.E.   C.E.>>>

2000   1000   0   1000   2000

- Moses
- Jesus
- King James
- Abraham
- Muhammed
- David/Solomon
- Exile

of godlessness, an allusion to Babylon may suggest either a bustling urban setting or an evil empire. Let us not forget also that the Babel of Genesis 12, site of the infamous tower, is thought to be synonymous with Babylon. The speaker of Psalm 137 is begrudgingly trapped in this undesirable place, where he cries out to God in his yearning for "Zion," which is a synonym for Jerusalem. Zion, like Babylon, has broad cultural implications, and it is often used in Christian contexts as a metaphor for heaven; elsewhere it may simply suggest a lost homeland or utopia. In the African American spiritual tradition, as well as in Rastafarian reggae, both Babylon and Zion appear frequently in these symbolic capacities. In the movie <u>The Matrix</u>, Zion is the name of the last city on Earth, and the final hope for humanity.

Let's explore some additional literary qualities of this poem using an analysis inventory – not the narrative version used thus far in our text, but one revised to suit the analysis of biblical poetry: our **Inventory for Poetry.**

BIBLICAL LITERARY INVENTORY — POETRY

Poem: Psalm 137

I. Imagery and Mood – Weeping by a river, a harp hanging in a tree, happy songs, a tongue stuck to the roof of its dry mouth, and babies being dashed to death upon rocks. Aside from the happy songs, each of these images is negative, ranging from sad to horrific. A closer reading of the "happy songs" image reveals that they are being sung under duress, which is not happy at all – it is mockery. The final image is particularly violent and heart-wrenching. The mood is dark and mournful.

II. Persona and Tone – The speaker is in captivity in Babylon and yearning for home in Zion. The tone is in keeping with the mood – mournful, yearning, heartbroken, vengeful, and yet hopeful. He confidently believes there will come a day when Zion will be restored.

III. Interpretation of Figurative Language and Analysis of Diction – The idea of a harp hanging in a tree is notable, for psalms are songs typically written with harp accompaniment; the harp image is certainly referring to the speaker's reluctance to sing psalms, but it is a temporary situation. If all hope were lost, the harp would have been cast to the ground. The hanging harp represents hope that sometime in the future, there will be occasion to pick up the harp and sing again. Later in the poem, the speaker promises never to forget his homeland, and if he does, his mouth will dry up, unable to sing – this, he implies, will never happen. Likewise, he says his right hand would forget "her cunning," which could refer losing the ability to play the harp or, perhaps, to write poetry.

IV. Structure and Movement – The poem begins at the scene of the speaker's contemplation and moves first to a memory of being captured, and then to the imagination of an undesirable future (if he were to forget Jerusalem) and finally to a desirable future (the punishment of Babylon). It begins with weeping and ends with happiness – albeit a cruel, vengeful happiness.

V. Theme – The poem comments on ideas of home, oppression, hope, and vengeance. It suggests that there is nothing so sad as losing loved ones and leaving one's home behind. It also expresses a profound hope in God, even in the worst of circumstances.

VI. Additional Literary Devices – The "right hand" in verse 5 is symbolic. When the right hand "loses its cunning" it essentially loses its skill. The right hand is associated with strength, skill, and authority in the Jewish tradition (see "right hand" in Wycliffe Bible Dictionary). It is often associated with God himself. To forget the cunning of the right hand would be to forget not only God, but the strength and honor invested in Jerusalem by God. Furthermore, in the context of this poem, a hand that has lost its skill could no longer play the harp or write poetry.

VII. Historical Criticism – This psalm is one of few with a concrete, un-debated historical placement: during the Babylonian Captivity of the 6th Century B.C. The Edomites, mentioned in verse 7, were also enemies of Israel (they were the descendants of Jacob's brother Esau, not the favored bloodline of Israel). It is rather easy to understand the extreme pain and anger experienced by the poet as he and his family are torn away from their homeland and forced to serve their enemies. This poem speaks to the emotional state of its original audience.

VIII. Genre Awareness (select one) –

    _____ **Lyric Poetry** (expressing personal emotions of the speaker): Can you relate to the emotions of the speaker? How do the speaker's emotions interact with his faith?

    _____ **Prophetic Poetry** (spoken on behalf of God as a call to faith and/or action; frequently cryptic): What warning, promise, or prediction is being proclaimed to whom?

    _____ **Narrative Poetry** (a story set down in poetic lines rather than prose): Why do you think the storyteller chose elevated, poetic language for the telling of this particular story?

    _____ **Proverbs** (short, wise, folk sayings heavy in figurative language, imagery and/or parallelism): How does this reflect universal truth and/or faith-based common sense?

Based on your selection, provide a response to the genre-related question provided above:

_____

_____

_____

Finally, let's take a closer look at Psalm 139, another well-known passage attributed to David. For the purpose of this lesson, it shall serve as a review of various qualities of the Psalms previously discussed. It is a praise poem, specifically regarding the omnipresence of God. It is patterned and rhythmic: "<u>Thou knowest</u> my downsitting and mine uprising, <u>thou understandest</u> my thought afar off. <u>Thou compasseth</u> my path and my lying down" (139:2-3). Familiar images ground the poem in everyday experience: walking on a path, the darkness of night and brightness of morning, and a pregnant mother. Some of the language is figurative, for instance the "wings of morning" (139:9) and the metaphorical "hand" of God (139:10). The emotional range goes from thankfulness and amazement to hatred. Indeed, the language of the Psalms provides a platform for examining the many emotional realities of human life, some of them intensely dark and some beautifully bright. Their musicality calls people together to express these emotions communally, under the watchful eye of God.

LESSON FOURTEEN STUDY GUIDE

Objective Identification:

David, liturgy, Babylon, exile, Zion, imagery, mood, persona, tone, figurative language, diction

Subjective Expression:

1) Deeper Analysis: Using a blank poetic inventory from the appendices, go back and analyze Psalm 22 and/or 23 more closely.

2) Cultural Connections: Where have you encountered words or images from Psalm 23 before, for instance "walking through the valley of the shadow of death"? How about the word *Zion*? Did any of these poems seem familiar to you, even if you've never studied the Bible before?

3) Research: Psalm 22:21 contains the surprising image of a unicorn, which is not only a mythical beast but a *European* mythical beast, not part of ancient Jewish folklore at all. Using the Internet, look up some alternative translations of this verse – what words have other translators used in place of *unicorn*? You may also wish to make use of an Internet lexicon, which will show you the original Hebrew word, which in this case is *raam*. Simply search "lexicon" and "Psalm 22:21." Which word seems to be the most literal translation of *raam*? Why do you think the King James writers chose *unicorn*?

4) Cultural Connections: Is there any aspect of your life that is enhanced by poetry? Certainly you can come up with one example outside of school in which poetry figures into your life!

5) Creative Response: Do an artistic rendering inspired by one of the poems in this section. Try to do more than just depict literal imagery – see if you can use visual rhythm to echo the literary rhythm of the poem itself. Try to make color choices that capture the poem's tone and mood.

6) Opinion: If the poet of Psalm 137 is divinely inspired, do you think God is therefore condoning the killing of babies in the last verse? Or does God merely allow the human poet to freely take his emotions in whatever direction he wishes? Many readers find the image incongruent with holiness. What do you make of this detail?

7) Further Exploration: Read some additional psalms, perhaps in a different translation, like <u>The Message</u>. Find one that you particularly like and share it with the class. If it is particularly meaningful to you, memorization and recitation might enhance your connection to the poem.

PROVERBS   SELECTED CHAPTERS

Proverbs 1

¹The proverbs of Solomon the son of David, king of Israel;

²To know wisdom and instruction;
    to perceive the words of understanding;
³To receive the instruction of wisdom,
    justice, and judgment, and equity;
⁴To give subtilty to the simple,[r]
    to the young man knowledge and discretion.
⁵A wise man will hear, and will increase learning;
    and a man of understanding shall attain unto wise counsels:
⁶To understand a proverb, and the interpretation;
    the words of the wise, and their dark sayings.
⁷The fear of the LORD is the beginning of knowledge:
    but fools despise wisdom and instruction.

⁸My son, hear the instruction of thy father,
    and forsake not the law of thy mother:
⁹For they shall be an ornament of grace unto thy head,
    and chains about thy neck.

¹⁰My son, if sinners entice thee,
    consent thou not.
¹¹If they say, Come with us, let us lay wait for blood,
    let us lurk privily[s] for the innocent without cause:
¹²Let us swallow them up alive as the grave;
    and whole, as those that go down into the pit:
¹³We shall find all precious substance,
    we shall fill our houses with spoil:
¹⁴Cast in thy lot among us;
    let us all have one purse:
¹⁵My son, walk not thou in the way with them;
    refrain thy foot from their path:
¹⁶For their feet run to evil,
    and make haste to shed blood.
¹⁷Surely in vain the net is spread
    in the sight of any bird.
¹⁸And they lay wait for their own blood;
    they lurk privily for their own lives.

---
[r] Subtilty = craftiness, prudence (BHL)
[s] Lurk privily = secretly lie in wait, like a sniper (EP)

¹⁹So are the ways of every one that is greedy of gain;
>   which taketh away the life of the owners thereof.

²⁰Wisdom crieth without; [t]
>   she uttereth her voice in the streets:
²¹She crieth in the chief place of concourse,
>   in the openings of the gates: in the city she uttereth her words, saying,

²² "How long, ye simple ones, will ye love simplicity?
>   and the scorners delight in their scorning,
>   and fools hate knowledge?
²³Turn you at my reproof: behold,
>   I will pour out my spirit unto you,
>   I will make known my words unto you.
²⁴Because I have called, and ye refused;
>   I have stretched out my hand, and no man regarded;
²⁵But ye have set at nought all my counsel,
>   and would none of my reproof: [u]
²⁶I also will laugh at your calamity;
>   I will mock when your fear cometh;
²⁷When your fear cometh as desolation,
>   and your destruction cometh as a whirlwind;
>   when distress and anguish cometh upon you.

²⁸Then shall they call upon me, but I will not answer;
>   they shall seek me early, but they shall not find me:
²⁹For that they hated knowledge,
>   and did not choose the fear of the LORD:
³⁰They would none of my counsel:
>   they despised all my reproof.
³¹Therefore shall they eat of the fruit of their own way,
>   and be filled with their own devices.
³²For the turning away of the simple shall slay them,
>   and the prosperity of fools shall destroy them.
³³But whoso hearkeneth unto me shall dwell safely, [v]
>   and shall be quiet from fear of evil."

---

[t] Wisdom here is being personified. The person of Wisdom (a woman, as you will see in upcoming verses) "crieth without" which means to shout (cry) outside (without). (FI)

[u] You have set a value of naught (nothing) upon my words, and you would not accept my correction. (EP)

[v] Hearkeneth = listen (FI)

Proverbs 10:1-12

The proverbs of Solomon.

A wise son maketh a glad father:
>but a foolish son is the heaviness of his mother.

² Treasures of wickedness profit nothing:
>but righteousness delivereth from death.

³ The Lord will not suffer the soul of the righteous to famish:
>but he casteth away the substance of the wicked.

⁴ He becometh poor that dealeth with a slack hand:
>but the hand of the diligent maketh rich.

⁵ He that gathereth in summer is a wise son:
>but he that sleepeth in harvest is a son that causeth shame.

⁶ Blessings are upon the head of the just:
>but violence covereth the mouth of the wicked.

⁷ The memory of the just is blessed:
>but the name of the wicked shall rot.

⁸ The wise in heart will receive commandments:
>but a prating fool shall fall.[w]

⁹ He that walketh uprightly walketh surely:
>but he that perverteth his ways shall be known.

¹⁰ He that winketh with the eye causeth sorrow:
>but a prating fool shall fall.

¹¹ The mouth of a righteous man is a well of life:
>but violence covereth the mouth of the wicked.

¹² Hatred stirreth up strifes:
>but love covereth all sins.

Proverbs 31: 10-31 (Epilogue)

¹⁰ Who can find a virtuous woman?
>for her price is far above rubies.

¹¹ The heart of her husband doth safely trust in her,
>so that he shall have no need of spoil.[x]

---

[w] Prating = chattering, babbling (BHL)
[x] So that he will have no lack of gain, no fear of coming to ruin (BHL)

¹² She will do him good and not evil
    all the days of her life.
¹³ She seeketh wool, and flax,
    and worketh willingly with her hands.
¹⁴ She is like the merchants' ships;
    she bringeth her food from afar.
¹⁵ She riseth also while it is yet night,
    and giveth meat to her household,
    and a portion to her maidens.
¹⁶ She considereth a field, and buyeth it:
    with the fruit of her hands she planteth a vineyard.
¹⁷ She girdeth her loins with strength,[y]
    and strengtheneth her arms.
¹⁸ She perceiveth that her merchandise is good:
    her candle goeth not out by night.
¹⁹ She layeth her hands to the spindle,
    and her hands hold the distaff.[z]
²⁰ She stretcheth out her hand to the poor;
    yea, she reacheth forth her hands to the needy.
²¹ She is not afraid of the snow for her household:
    for all her household are clothed with scarlet.
²² She maketh herself coverings of tapestry;
    her clothing is silk and purple.
²³ Her husband is known in the gates,
    when he sitteth among the elders of the land.
²⁴ She maketh fine linen, and selleth it;
    and delivereth girdles unto the merchant.
²⁵ Strength and honour are her clothing;
    and she shall rejoice in time to come.
²⁶ She openeth her mouth with wisdom;
    and in her tongue is the law of kindness.
²⁷ She looketh well to the ways of her household,
    and eateth not the bread of idleness.
²⁸ Her children arise up, and call her blessed;
    her husband also, and he praiseth her.
²⁹ Many daughters have done virtuously,
    but thou excellest them all.
³⁰ Favour is deceitful, and beauty is vain:
    but a woman that feareth the Lord, she shall be praised.
³¹ Give her of the fruit of her hands;
    and let her own works praise her in the gates.

---

[y] She dresses herself with strength (EP)
[z] The distaff and the spindle are tools used in spinning thread. (FI)

ECCLESIASTES 1 & 3

Ecclesiastes 1 – King James Version

[1] The words of the Preacher, the son of David, king in Jerusalem.
[2] "Vanity of vanities,"
    saith the Preacher,
"vanity of vanities; all is vanity."

[3] What profit hath a man of all his labour
    which he taketh under the sun?
[4] One generation passeth away, and another generation cometh:
    but the earth abideth for ever.
[5] The sun also ariseth, and the sun goeth down,
    and hasteth to his place where he arose.
[6] The wind goeth toward the south, and turneth about unto the north;
    it whirleth about continually, and the wind returneth again according to his circuits.
[7] All the rivers run into the sea;
    yet the sea is not full;
unto the place from whence the rivers come,
    thither they return again.
[8] All things are full of labour;
    man cannot utter it:
the eye is not satisfied with seeing,
    nor the ear filled with hearing.
[9] The thing that hath been, it is that which shall be;
    and that which is done is that which shall be done:
    and there is no new thing under the sun.
[10] Is there any thing whereof it may be said,
    "See, this is new"?
It hath been already of old time,
    which was before us.
[11] There is no remembrance of former things;
    neither shall there be any remembrance
of things that are to come
    with those that shall come after.

[12] I the Preacher was king over Israel in Jerusalem. [13] And I gave my heart to seek and search out by wisdom concerning all things that are done under heaven: this sore travail hath God given to the sons of man to be exercised therewith. [14] I have seen all the works that are done under the sun; and, behold, all is vanity and vexation of spirit.

    [15] That which is crooked cannot be made straight:
        and that which is wanting cannot be numbered.

¹⁶I communed with mine own heart, saying, Lo, I am come to great estate, and have gotten more wisdom than all they that have been before me in Jerusalem: yea, my heart had great experience of wisdom and knowledge. ¹⁷And I gave my heart to know wisdom, and to know madness and folly: I perceived that this also is vexation of spirit. ¹⁸For in much wisdom is much grief: and he that increaseth knowledge increaseth sorrow.

Ecclesiastes 3 – King James Version

¹To every thing there is a season,
    and a time to every purpose under the heaven:
²A time to be born, and a time to die;
a time to plant, and a time to pluck up that which is planted;
³A time to kill, and a time to heal;
a time to break down, and a time to build up;
⁴A time to weep, and a time to laugh;
a time to mourn, and a time to dance;
⁵A time to cast away stones, and a time to gather stones together;
a time to embrace, and a time to refrain from embracing;
⁶A time to get, and a time to lose;
a time to keep, and a time to cast away;
⁷A time to rend, and a time to sew;
a time to keep silence, and a time to speak;
⁸A time to love, and a time to hate;
a time of war, and a time of peace.

⁹What profit hath he that worketh in that wherein he laboureth? ¹⁰I have seen the travail, which God hath given to the sons of men to be exercised in it. ¹¹He hath made every thing beautiful in his time: also he hath set the world in their heart, so that no man can find out the work that God maketh from the beginning to the end. ¹²I know that there is no good in them, but for a man to rejoice, and to do good in his life. ¹³And also that every man should eat and drink, and enjoy the good of all his labour, it is the gift of God. ¹⁴I know that, whatsoever God doeth, it shall be for ever: nothing can be put to it, nor any thing taken from it: and God doeth it, that men should fear before him.

    ¹⁵That which hath been is now;
        and that which is to be hath already been;
        and God requireth that which is past.

¹⁶And moreover I saw under the sun
    the place of judgment, that wickedness was there;
    and the place of righteousness, that iniquity was there.

¹⁷I said in mine heart,
    God shall judge
        the righteous and the wicked:

for there is a time there for every purpose
    and for every work.

[18] I said in mine heart concerning the estate of the sons of men, that God might manifest them,[aa] and that they might see that they themselves are beasts. [19] For that which befalleth the sons of men befalleth beasts; even one thing befalleth them: as the one dieth, so dieth the other; yea, they have all one breath; so that a man hath no preeminence above a beast: for all is vanity. [20] All go unto one place; all are of the dust, and all turn to dust again. [21] Who knoweth the spirit of man that goeth upward, and the spirit of the beast that goeth downward to the earth?

[22] Wherefore I perceive that there is nothing better, than that a man should rejoice in his own works; for that is his portion:[bb] for who shall bring him to see what shall be after him?

Ecclesiastes 3:1-15 – *The Message*

[1] There's an opportune time to do things, a right time for everything on the earth:
[2-8] A right time for birth and another for death,
A right time to plant and another to reap,
A right time to kill and another to heal,
A right time to destroy and another to construct,
A right time to cry and another to laugh,
A right time to lament and another to cheer,
A right time to make love and another to abstain,
A right time to embrace and another to part,
A right time to search and another to count your losses,
A right time to hold on and another to let go,
A right time to rip out and another to mend,
A right time to shut up and another to speak up,
A right time to love and another to hate,
A right time to wage war and another to make peace.

[9-13] But in the end, does it really make a difference what anyone does? I've had a good look at what God has given us to do—busywork, mostly. True, God made everything beautiful in itself and in its time—but he's left us in the dark, so we can never know what God is up to, whether he's coming or going. I've decided that there's nothing better to do than go ahead and have a good time and get the most we can out of life. That's it—eat, drink, and make the most of your job. It's God's gift. [14] I've also concluded that whatever God does, that's the way it's going to be, always. No addition, no subtraction. God's done it and that's it. That's so we'll quit asking questions and simply worship in holy fear.

[15] Whatever was, is.
    Whatever will be, is.
    That's how it always is with God.

[aa] God might manifest them = God will test them and show them, or God may prove to them that… (BHL)
[bb] His portion = his lot in life, his inheritance (FI)

LESSON FIFTEEN:
WISDOM LITERATURE

"The Judgment of Solomon" by Raphael

Psalms, Proverbs, Ecclesiastes, the Song of Solomon, and the Book of Job are collectively known by Bible scholars as the "wisdom books." Three of the five – Proverbs, Ecclesiastes, and of course Song of Solomon – are traditionally attributed to the authorship of Solomon. King Solomon of Israel, whose stories are recounted in some of the Old Testament's historical books, has become a Western icon of wisdom. One of the most enduring stories concerning Solomon's problem-solving skills comes from the Book of Kings and is known as "The Judgment of Solomon." As the tale goes, two women come to King Solomon with a baby, each woman claiming to be the child's mother. Solomon orders that a sword be brought and that the baby be cut in half. One woman agrees to the solution and one woman is so horrified that she offers to give up the child if only his life will be spared. Solomon deduces that the woman willing to save the child yet part with him must therefore be his real mother, and she is granted custody. Thus, Solomon passes into legend as the wise king of Israel.

Solomon's wisdom writings contain poetry that expresses everyday advice and contemplates topics ranging from work, to love, to knowledge itself. Passages from these two wisdom books have been selected for this textbook because of their cultural impact; even if you've never read the Bible before, you have very likely heard allusions to Proverbs and Ecclesiastes. From Proverbs, you may have heard that "pride goes before a fall" (16:18) and that "iron sharpens iron" (27:17). Ecclesiastes chapter one inspired the saying "there is nothing new under the sun" (look up Shakepeare's Sonnet 59 for an example), and the chapter three poem about time is widely quoted in literature and popular music – you may recognize this line from a popular Sixties folk ballad: "To everything, turn, turn, turn / There is a season, turn, turn, turn / And a time for every purpose under heaven." Indeed, Solomon's ideas endure throughout Western art and literature.

PROVERBS

The Book of Proverbs is a collection of sayings presented within the framework of a father teaching his son how to live a productive and respectable lifestyle. A *proverb* by definition is a type of "quotable quote," a saying passed down by word of mouth from generation to generation. Proverbs get passed down in the first place because they are smart and practical, like when Grandma says, "An apple a day keeps the doctor away!" Proverbs are often memorable because of their clever figurative language, familiar imagery, or rhythmic parallelism. Consider the first verse in chapter 10, for instance: "A wise son maketh a glad father: but a foolish son is the heaviness of his mother." This statement features classic Hebrew parallelism, with the second half of the proverb saying basically the same thing as the first, but from the opposite side of the coin. Verse 5, in additional to parallelism, uses imagery familiar to the common Israelite: "He that gathereth in summer is a wise son: but he that sleepeth in harvest is a son that causeth shame." Verse 12 is a good example of both parallelism and clever figurative language: "Hatred stirreth up strifes: but love covereth all sins."

Regarding the genre of Proverbs, the *NIV Archaeology Study Bible* says that "the pat statements so plentiful in Proverbs are not promises from God but general principles – similar to the reference to long life as the result of honoring one's parents found in the Ten Commandments" (958). For example, when Solomon says "train up a child in the way he should go: and when he is old, he will not depart from it" (22:6) he is probably offering parental advice more so than a guarantee for the future. When chapter one closes with the pronouncement that wise living will ensure insure safety from harm, this is true in a general sense but it is probably not to be read as a divine promise of good fortune. Such is the nature of a *proverb*.

After setting the scene of a father speaking to his son at the beginning of the book, Solomon goes on to personify wisdom as a woman shouting in the streets. She is being ignored by the "simple" people who refuse to gather knowledge. This character is commonly referred to as Lady Wisdom. Proverbs builds a strong theme with numerous passages about Lady Wisdom. Chapter after chapter expounds upon the fruits of wise living, the joy of studying – specifically the study of scripture – and the supreme importance of knowledge. One of the most well-known principles from Proverbs 1 is that "the fear of the Lord is the beginning of knowledge" (1:7). Indeed, all of Solomon's wisdom writing maintains that God is the cornerstone of all knowledge and wisdom. Even when Solomon goes to his darkest place, revealed in Ecclesiastes 3, he ties his hopeless feelings straight to the reality of God. It is an interesting paradox that begins with faith, proceeds through utter emptiness, and ends with faith – not the kind of faith that sings cheerful praise choruses by a campfire, but the kind of faith that stands soberly firm, with eyes wide open, and refuses to budge. The theme of Proverbs is that faith in a benevolent God is the starting point for understanding the world, and therefore is the cornerstone of wisdom. The personified figure of Lady Wisdom helps bring these ideas to life.

Proverbs ends with a passage often called the "Epilogue: The Wife of Noble Character" (as labeled in the NIV). This fits nicely within the father-to-son framing device. Frequently throughout the book, the speaker mentions his son's mother, and he finishes with a poem praising his wife's central place of value in the home. This is particularly interesting given the patriarchal nature of ancient Jewish culture. The "wife of noble character" is not only a hard worker, but an entrepreneur, a humanitarian, a stylish dresser, and a wise teacher. This image paired with the personified Lady Wisdom lends an interesting counterbalance to Genesis 2-3, where Eve is characterized as secondary to Adam. It lets us know that Jewish wisdom and instruction are not solely the domain of men.

ECCLESIASTES

Only part of Ecclesiastes is poetic, and the excerpt you read exemplifies this; notice the combination of poetic lines and prose paragraphs. As a whole, we might call the genre of Ecclesiastes an internal monologue, which by nature can be meandering and loosely structured. Compared to the Book of Proverbs, it is an advanced work of literature – not folksy at all – and designed for a serious student of religion and philosophy. The speaker is, presumably, Solomon himself, and the word *ecclesiastes* literally means "the preacher" or "the teacher."

Ecclesiastes begins with a premise that a casual Bible reader might not be expecting: that life is "vanity." Other translations use the words "emptiness" or "nonsense." The original Hebrew words (*havel* and *havalim*) mean "breath" or "vapor." Certainly a devout Jewish writer would not express such a thought! How can someone find life meaningless and yet believe in God at the same time? Indeed, religious scholars have argued about this book for centuries. Some consider it to be the antithesis of the New Testament message of "good news."[cc] Some consider Solomon's argument loose and illogical. Indeed, it is difficult to trace a clear pattern of logic through its pages. However, the central themes are consistent: the seasons of life go from one extreme to another, and nothing at either end is new or surprising. There are no satisfying answers to life's biggest questions. No matter how hard we work or how wise we are, everyone dies. In the meantime, Solomon says we should "eat and drink, and enjoy the good of all [our] labour" – or, as we see in chapter eight and have certainly heard countless times in songs and movies, we should "eat, drink and be merry!" All these ideas flow in and out of and around each other through the 12 chapters of Ecclesiastes, in one giant circular discussion that stops where it started: "Then shall the dust return to the earth as it was: and the spirit shall return unto God who gave it. Vanity of vanities, saith the preacher; all is vanity" (12:7-8). And just like the Psalms and Proverbs, all these thoughts and emotions find their habitat under the umbrella of faith. This is indeed a strange kind of wisdom, one that labors for 12 chapters to find an Answer to life's biggest Question, and all the speaker manages to grasp is the simple Existence of God.

In Proverbs and Ecclesiastes, Solomon is showing us two different sides of faithful living. The books have similar topics, but if they were songs, one would be written in a major key and one in a minor: Proverbs is pithy, confident, concrete, and fairly easy to read (a major

---

[cc] The first four books of the New Testament are called the Gospels; "gospel" literally means "good news" and is associated with the message of Jesus.

key) while Ecclesiastes is meandering, complex, abstract, and ambiguous (a minor key). The two books' conclusions about wisdom are also different: Proverbs, that wisdom brings enlightenment to life, and Ecclesiastes, that with or without wisdom, we all must make our way through the dark. And yet the two books are grounded in the same worldview, that God is at the center of the wisdom we do possess, and that he also encompasses the dark and empty spaces where we see no wisdom at all.

BIBLICAL LITERARY INVENTORY — POETRY

Poem: Proverbs 1

I. Imagery and Mood – Father and mother teaching, garland around the head, chain adorning the neck, sinners looking to attack someone, a pit, plundered houses, bloodshed, a net spread out in front of birds (bird hunting). Continue your list with verse 20: _____
_____
_____

II. Persona and Tone – Note that the speaking persona shifts at verse 22. Describe the shift in tones from strophe to strophe throughout the chapter: _____
_____

III. Interpretation of Figurative Language and Analysis of Diction – Select two figures of speech and two interesting words worthy of your interpretive attention: _____
_____
_____
_____

IV. Structure and Movement – The poem begins with an abstract introduction to the topic of wisdom, prudence, and learning. Verse 9 gets more personal, with the speaker directly addressing his son and giving him heartfelt advice for wise, successful living. Next, wisdom gets personified as a woman – and she takes over the speaking role for the rest of the chapter (and, in fact, for eight more chapters).

V. Theme – _____
_____

VI. Additional Literary Devices – The primary poetic device of Solomon's proverbs is parallelism. Look back at the passage and see how the parallel structure creates rhythm, and how each strophe is held together by internal parallelism and a unified topic.

VII. Historical Criticism – Most Near East religions surrounding ancient Israel depicted their male deities as having a female counterpart, and some scholars see a monotheistic version of this in Proverbs' Lady Wisdom (in particular, see Proverbs 8:22-30, where Lady Wisdom describes her origins). The trend of female wisdom deities existed throughout the ancient world, for instance, the Greek goddess Athena. However, it should also be noted that the Hebrew word for wisdom, *Chokmah*, is a female noun – another fact that could account for the female personification. What do you imagine to be the reason for the female Wisdom character in Proverbs? Consider this historical information as well as the father and mother motif found throughout the book. _____

_____

_____

_____

VIII. Genre Awareness (select one) –

_____ **Lyric Poetry** (expressing personal emotions of the speaker): Can you relate to the emotions of the speaker? How do the speaker's emotions interact with his faith?

_____ **Prophetic Poetry** (spoken on behalf of God as a call to faith and/or action; frequently cryptic): What warning, promise, or prediction is being proclaimed to whom?

_____ **Narrative Poetry** (a story set down in poetic lines rather than prose): Why do you think the storyteller chose elevated, poetic language for the telling of this particular story?

_____ **Proverbs** (short, wise, folk sayings heavy in figurative language, imagery and/or parallelism): How does this reflect universal truth and/or faith-based common sense?

Based on your selection, provide a response to the genre-related question provided above:

_____

_____

_____

BIBLICAL LITERARY INVENTORY — POETRY

Poem: Ecclesiastes 3

I. Imagery and Mood – _____
_____

II. Persona and Tone – The speaker is said to be Solomon, "the preacher." He is questioning life and coming up rather empty. Still, he seems convinced about certain truths and the reality of God. Provide two interesting adjectives to describe the tone he takes toward life and God:
_____

III. Interpretation of Figurative Language and Analysis of Diction – This passage is not very figurative; rather, it is direct and literal. See if you can find one figurative thought and two interesting word choices to interpret: _____
_____
_____

IV. Structure and Movement – Chapter three was probably not intended to be studied as a separate entity; however, the internal structure of the "song" part of the passage is quite simple, built on rhythmic repetition. The entire monologue is punctuated with passages of poetry. What do you think the poetry adds to the style or character of the discourse? Why did he bother with the occasional bursts of poetry? _____
_____
_____

V. Theme – _____
_____

VI. Additional Literary Devices – Rhetorical questions are an important feature of this passage. Find two of these and explain what you think they add to the flavor of the passage:
_____
_____

VII. Historical Criticism – Scholars hotly debate the authorship of Ecclesiastes. Two details in favor of Solomon include the identifying information in 1:1 as well as the details that describe riches, leisure, and money throughout the book – Solomon would have been king at the height of Israel's wealth and power. Other scholars date Ecclesiastes as post-Exilic (hundreds of years after Solomon, after the Jews return to their ravaged homeland following the Babylonian Exile). The primary reason for this position is the high number of Aramaic, Persian, and Greek words mixed in with the Hebrew. How important do you think it is to accurately identify the original author of Ecclesiastes? _____

_____

VIII. Genre Awareness (select one) –

_____ **Lyric Poetry** (expressing personal emotions of the speaker): Can you relate to the emotions of the speaker? How do the speaker's emotions interact with his faith?

_____ **Prophetic Poetry** (spoken on behalf of God as a call to faith and/or action; frequently cryptic): What warning, promise, or prediction is being proclaimed to whom?

_____ **Narrative Poetry** (a story set down in poetic lines rather than prose): Why do you think the storyteller chose elevated, poetic language for the telling of this particular story?

_____ **Proverbs** (short, wise, folk sayings heavy in figurative language, imagery and/or parallelism): How does this reflect universal truth and/or faith-based common sense?

Based on your selection, provide a response to the genre-related question provided above:

_____

_____

_____

QUOTABLE QUOTES

> By three methods we may learn wisdom: First, by reflection, which is noblest; second, by imitation, which is easiest; and third by experience, which is the bitterest.

Confucius

LESSON FIFTEEN STUDY GUIDE

Objective Identification:

Solomon, liturgy, wisdom literature, proverb, parallelism, internal monologue, imagery, mood, tone, figurative language, diction, strophe

Subjective Expression:

1) Cultural Connections: What sources would you go to when trying to find wisdom? Where do you think your parents and/or teachers get their definitions of wisdom? Where do you think Americans generally go when in search of wisdom? Is American wisdom different than wisdom from other parts of the world?

2) Deeper Analysis: Proverbs asserts that "the fear of God is the beginning of wisdom." Why *fear*? Some people think it ridiculous that an almighty God would require people to fear him. What are the connotations of *fear* in this context? Is this fear similar to the way one might fear an angry Aphrodite or Zeus, or the type of fear a child experiences when a respected teacher catches him cheating? What other thoughts do you have regarding the "fear of God?"

3) Opinion: Do you think the speaker in Ecclesiastes 3 comes to a reasonable, satisfying conclusion? If you disagree, explain why.

4) Opinion: *The Message* is a Bible *paraphrase*, not a translation, written by Eugene Peterson. The reasoning behinds its composition is that the original Bible texts were written in the local vernacular, and were therefore much more easily accessible to the original readers, and that today's modern reader deserves access to the Bible in a modern vernacular and idiom. Do you like what Peterson did with his *Message* paraphrase? Why or why not? Look up additional passages in *The Message* if you wish.

PROPHECIES OF ISAIAH

Isaiah 9:1-7 (A Messiah is Prophesied)

¹Nevertheless the dimness shall not be such as was in her vexation, when at the first he lightly afflicted the land of Zebulun and the land of Naphtali, and afterward did more grievously afflict her by the way of the sea, beyond Jordan, in Galilee of the nations. [dd]

² The people that walked in darkness
    have seen a great light:
they that dwell in the land of the shadow of death,
    upon them hath the light shined.
³ Thou hast multiplied the nation,
    and not increased the joy:
they joy before thee according to the joy in harvest,
    and as men rejoice when they divide the spoil.
⁴ For thou hast broken the yoke of his burden,
    and the staff of his shoulder,
    the rod of his oppressor, as in the day of Midian.[ee]
⁵ For every battle of the warrior is with confused noise,
    and garments rolled in blood;
but this shall be with burning
    and fuel of fire.[ff]

⁶ For unto us a child is born,
    unto us a son is given:
    and the government shall be upon his shoulder:
and his name shall be called
    Wonderful, Counsellor, The mighty God,
    The everlasting Father, The Prince of Peace.
⁷ Of the increase of his government and peace
    there shall be no end,
upon the throne of David,
    and upon his kingdom,

[dd] Paraphrase: "The dimness which Israel experienced during her time of vexation, or extreme trouble, will go away. During this time of vexation, God treated the land of Abraham's descendants with troubles. At a later time, God changed the picture." The Hebrew word translated here as "grievously afflict," *kabad*, can be defined either as "burdensome, weighty" or as "honored, glorified." Talk about opposite meanings! Many Bible translators think the verse means that God will eventually glorify Israel through the region of Galilee. This translation supports a Christian interpretation of the verse, since Jesus will eventually live in Galilee. (BHL) (FI)

[ee] The NIV translation reads: "For as in the day of Midian's defeat, you have shattered the yoke that burdens them, the bar across their shoulders, the rod of their oppressor." This alludes to a story in the Book of Judges, when the Midianites were treating Israel with cruelty. It does not reference the massacre from Numbers. (FI)

[ffff] The image of burning may be associated with the utter destruction of the enemy or with the final achievement of peace, given that the burning of a vanquished enemy's armor was customary in the ancient world. (BHC – Barnes' Notes and Clarke's Commentary). It might also be noted that fire is sometimes used as a symbol of cleansing.

to order it, and to establish it
> with judgment and with justice
>> from henceforth even for ever.
The zeal of the Lord of hosts
> will perform this.

Isaiah 40:1-11, 25-31 (Words of Comfort)

"Comfort ye, comfort ye my people,"
> saith your God.
² "Speak ye comfortably to Jerusalem,
> and cry unto her,
that her warfare is accomplished,
> that her iniquity is pardoned:
for she hath received of the Lord's hand
> double for all her sins."

³ The voice of him that crieth
> in the wilderness,
"Prepare ye
> the way of the Lord,
make straight in the desert
> a highway for our God.
⁴ Every valley shall be exalted,
> and every mountain and hill shall be made low:
and the crooked shall be made straight,
> and the rough places plain:
⁵ And the glory of the Lord shall be revealed,
> and all flesh shall see it together:
>> for the mouth of the Lord hath spoken it."

⁶ The voice said, "Cry."
> And he said, "What shall I cry?" [gg]

"All flesh is grass,
> and all the goodliness thereof is as the flower of the field:
⁷ The grass withereth, the flower fadeth:
> because the spirit of the Lord bloweth upon it:
> surely the people is grass.
⁸ The grass withereth, the flower fadeth:
> but the word of our God shall stand for ever."

[gg] Note that there are two "quoted" speakers at the beginning this chapter: God himself, and someone who is crying from the wilderness. Isaiah reports that God is telling the wilderness speaker what to say to Israel. In verse 9, when the quotation marks end, the speaking voice reverts to Isaiah himself. Isaiah's words do not appear in quotation marks. Note also that the original Hebrew does not use quotation marks, and the King James Version does not use them either. They are a modern convention. The quotation marks appearing here are identical to those used in the New International Version.

⁹ O Zion, that bringest good tidings,
> get thee up into the high mountain;
O Jerusalem, that bringest good tidings,
> lift up thy voice with strength;
lift it up, be not afraid;
> say unto the cities of Judah,
> "Behold your God!"[hh]
¹⁰ Behold, the Lord God will come with strong hand,
> and his arm shall rule for him:
behold, his reward is with him,
> and his work before him.
¹¹ He shall feed his flock like a shepherd:
> he shall gather the lambs with his arm,
and carry them in his bosom,
> and shall gently lead those that are with young.

²⁵ "To whom then will ye liken me,
> or shall I be equal?" saith the Holy One.
²⁶ Lift up your eyes on high,
> and behold who hath created these things,
that bringeth out their host by number:
> he calleth them all by names by the greatness of his might,
for that he is strong in power;
> not one faileth.

²⁷ Why sayest thou, O Jacob,
> and speakest, O Israel,
"My way is hid from the Lord,
> and my judgment is passed over from my God?"
²⁸ Hast thou not known?
> hast thou not heard,
that the everlasting God, the Lord,
> the Creator of the ends of the earth,
fainteth not, neither is weary?
> there is no searching of his understanding.
²⁹ He giveth power to the faint;
> and to them that have no might he increaseth strength.
³⁰ Even the youths shall faint and be weary,
> and the young men shall utterly fall:
³¹ But they that wait upon the Lord
> shall renew their strength;
they shall mount up with wings as eagles;
> they shall run, and not be weary;
> and they shall walk, and not faint.

[hh] The quoted speaker in this verse is a personified Jerusalem (the Israelites). For the remainder of the chapter, pay close attention to speaker identification. Where there are no quotation marks, the speaker is Isaiah.

Isaiah 53:1-10 (More Messianic Prophecy)

¹Who hath believed our report?
     and to whom is the arm of the LORD revealed?
²For he shall grow up before him as a tender plant,
     and as a root out of a dry ground:
he hath no form nor comeliness; and when we shall see him,
     there is no beauty that we should desire him.
³He is despised and rejected of men;
     a man of sorrows, and acquainted with grief:
and we hid as it were our faces from him;
     he was despised, and we esteemed him not.

⁴Surely he hath borne our griefs,
     and carried our sorrows:
yet we did esteem him stricken,
     smitten of God, and afflicted.
⁵But he was wounded for our transgressions,
     he was bruised for our iniquities:
the chastisement of our peace was upon him;
     and with his stripes we are healed.
⁶All we like sheep have gone astray;
     we have turned every one to his own way;
and the LORD hath laid on him the iniquity of us all.

⁷He was oppressed, and he was afflicted,
     yet he opened not his mouth:
he is brought as a lamb to the slaughter,
     and as a sheep before her shearers is dumb,
     so he openeth not his mouth.
⁸He was taken from prison and from judgment:
     and who shall declare his generation?
for he was cut off out of the land of the living:
     for the transgression of my people was he stricken.
⁹And he made his grave with the wicked,
     and with the rich in his death;
because he had done no violence,
     neither was any deceit in his mouth.

¹⁰Yet it pleased the LORD to bruise him; he hath put him to grief:
     when thou shalt make his soul an offering for sin,
he shall see his seed, he shall prolong his days,
     and the pleasure of the LORD shall prosper in his hand.

Isaiah 65:17-25 (New Heaven and Earth)

[17] "For, behold, I create
>new heavens and a new earth:
and the former shall not be remembered,
>nor come into mind.
[18] But be ye glad and rejoice for ever
>in that which I create:
for, behold, I create Jerusalem a rejoicing,
>and her people a joy.
[19] And I will rejoice in Jerusalem,
>and joy in my people:
and the voice of weeping shall be no more heard in her,
>nor the voice of crying.

[20] There shall be no more thence an infant of days,
>nor an old man that hath not filled his days:
for the child shall die an hundred years old;
>but the sinner being an hundred years old shall be accursed. [ii]
[21] And they shall build houses,
>and inhabit them;
and they shall plant vineyards,
>and eat the fruit of them.
[22] They shall not build, and another inhabit;
>they shall not plant, and another eat:
for as the days of a tree are the days of my people,
>and mine elect shall long enjoy the work of their hands.
[23] They shall not labour in vain,
>nor bring forth for trouble; [jj]
for they are the seed of the blessed of the Lord,
>and their offspring with them.
[24] And it shall come to pass, that before they call, I will answer;
>and while they are yet speaking, I will hear.
[25] The wolf and the lamb shall feed together,
>and the lion shall eat straw like the bullock:
>and dust shall be the serpent's meat.
They shall not hurt nor destroy
>in all my holy mountain,"
>saith the Lord.

[ii] There will be no more infants dying days after their birth (no more infant mortality); rather, everyone will live past 100 years; it will seem like a curse to die before 100 years of age. (EP)

[jj] God's people will not work hard with no results (they will prosper), and they will not give birth to children who lead troubled lives. (EP)

LESSON SIXTEEN:
POET, PROPHET, PROGNOSTICATOR

"Tiresias Appears to Ulysses" by Henry Fuseli (1780-1785)

Prophets have existed in many different cultures and eras, not just in "Bible times." Sometimes they have been called *seers*, *oracles*, *soothsayers* or *shamans*. Some famous prophets, like the Greek Tiresias, have been depicted as blind, with spiritual sight substituted for physical vision. Indeed, a prophet is gifted in seeing divine messages where average mortals cannot, and he is charged with proclaiming these messages from the spiritual realm to mankind. An Old Testament prophet was something like a televangelist, politician, poet, priest, and crystal ball reader combined. They were bold. They laid down the law, predicted the future, experienced divine visions and described them with intense poetic language. They spoke with the authority of God, and if their predictions proved false, they were to be stoned to death. The most important prophet from the Old Testament, besides Moses, is probably Isaiah.

Prophecy as a genre of literature is mystical and usually poetic in nature. In all cultures that have prophets, the ability to prophesy is considered a special gift; it is therefore a special type of literature, one that can be difficult to figure out. Prophets sometimes hear their messages straight from God (like Moses) or an angel (like Muhammad) and sometimes they are given visions (like Isaiah). Sometimes they have to interpret physical signs, like numbers on dice (casting lots) or stars or dreams (like Joseph, Abraham's great-grandson). The cryptic and spiritual nature of prophecy is well suited for the elegant and figurative nature of poetry.

> **PROPHETIC CHARACTERS IN LITERATURE WITH IMPAIRED VISION**
>
> Tiresias in Greek myth including The Odyssey and Oedipus Rex
>
> Sybil Trelawney in Harry Potter
>
> "Blind Seer" in O Brother, Where Art Thou
>
> "Seer" or "Little Girl" in Once Upon a Time
>
> Neo in The Matrix Revolutions
>
> G'Kar in Babylon 5
>
> Toph in Avatar: The Last Airbender

Another important aspect of understanding prophecy is identifying its historical context and its intended audience. Prophets tend to deliver messages directly to specific people; therefore, their messages can be misinterpreted as the result of an inaccurate understanding of setting and audience. In the Book of Isaiah, this important information comes in the first chapter, first verse: "The vision of Isaiah the son of Amoz, which he saw concerning Judah and Jerusalem in the days of Uzziah, Jotham, Ahaz, and Hezekiah, kings of Judah." Thus, we know that Isaiah's message was intended for the people of Jerusalem, the capital city of Judah – and it is helpful to know that at this time in history, the descendants of Abraham had split into two countries, Israel (to the north) and Judah (to the south). The nation of Judah included the people of the bloodline of King David.

The nature of Isaiah's prophecy is both political and spiritual. Some of it concerns military events that happened during and after Isaiah's lifetime, and some of it concerns a more distant future, what he calls the "end of days." Early in the book, he predicts how the Assyrians will conquer the northern kingdom of Israel but how the southern kingdom of Judah will be miraculously spared. He also predicts the Babylonian Exile and its conclusion due to a Persian victory over Babylon. All of these prophecies do in fact come true… but from a scholar's perspective, we have no proof that the prophecies *were written down before* the actual events came to pass, rather than *written down afterwards*, so it is impossible to historically confirm that the actual Prophet Isaiah had accurate foresight. In fact, many historians speculate that parts of the Book of Isaiah were composed by other writers, long after the lifetime of Isaiah himself. One hypothetical writer (called Deutero-Isaiah) is believed to have written during the Babylonian Exile, and one (called Trito-Isaiah) is believed to have written after the Jews returned home from the Exile. Your interpretation of the text will depend on whether or not you trust modern secular historians, and whether or not you believe in supernatural prophecy. In the updated Bible Timeline below, you can see the historical placement of the "original" Isaiah, and you can imagine the placement of the additional hypothetical contributors in relation to the Exile.

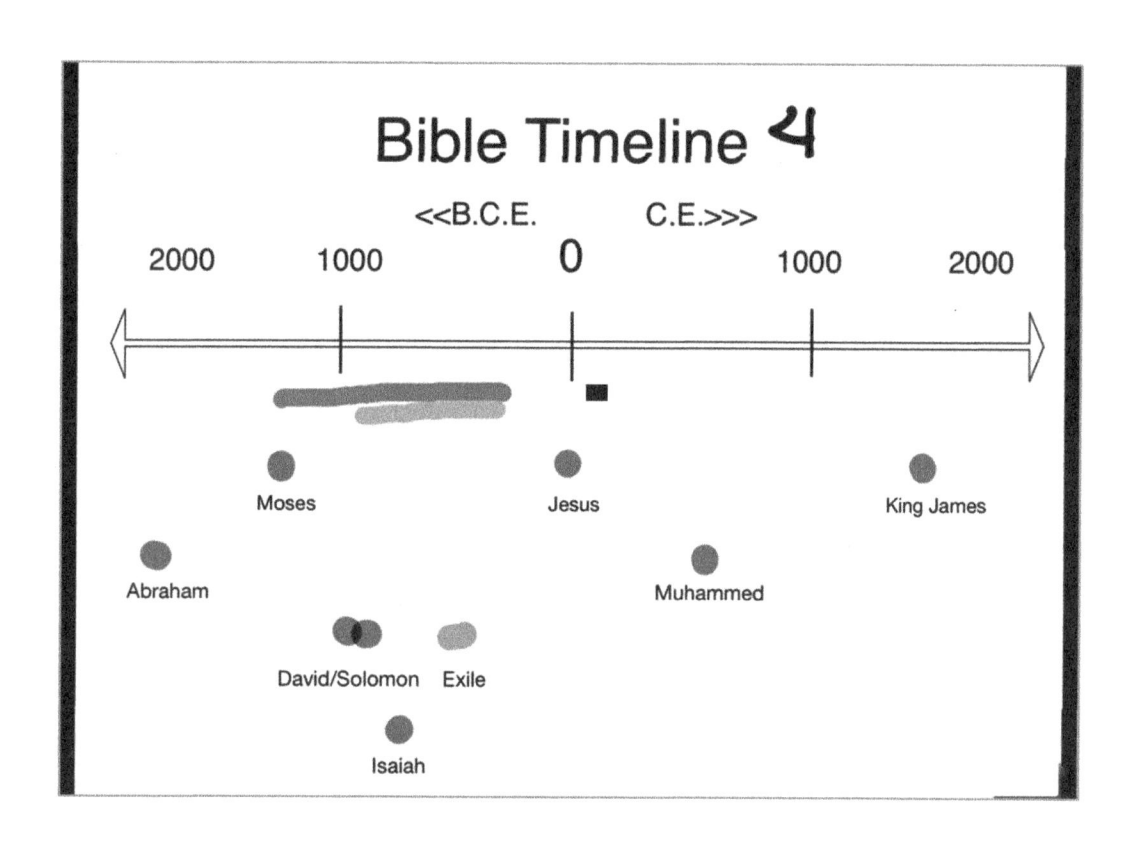

Bible Timeline

<<B.C.E.   C.E.>>>

2000   1000   0   1000   2000

- Moses
- Jesus
- King James
- Abraham
- Muhammed
- David/Solomon   Exile
- Isaiah

The format of the Book of Isaiah is a collection of prophetic poems, separated by occasional paragraphs that tell Isaiah's story as he interacts with kings and priests. The structure, in general, is (1) description of a sinful Israel and Judah, (2) prophecies of Assyria, (3) prophecies of Babylon and other ancient states, (4) description of the dark times God's people will endure, and (5) description of restoration and the glory of God in the "end of days." Frequently, Isaiah will pause in his political prophecies and woeful descriptions to remind his people that, in the midst of their suffering, God has plans to bring about a happy ending. The three passages you read from Isaiah in this textbook are pulled from these moments of hope and encouragement.

Chapter Nine may have sounded familiar to you, particularly if you have attended a Christmas performance of Handel's famous choral work called The Messiah, which contains the popular Hallelujah Chorus. You may recognize verse six: "For unto us a child is born, unto us a son is given: and the government shall be upon his shoulder: and his name shall be called Wonderful, Counsellor, The mighty God, The everlasting Father, The Prince of Peace." The child described here is a character known as the "Messiah."

Messiah prophecies are an important part of both the Jewish and Christian understandings of Isaiah, and this topic will figure into our interpretation of the entire New Testament of the Bible later in this textbook. This Messiah character seems to be a man who will bring a final resolution to the suffering of God's people, moving the world toward that big happy ending Isaiah describes at the end of his book. Note that the description of the Messiah in Isaiah 9 features very earthy, political details: "Of the increase of his government and peace there shall be no end, upon the throne of David, and upon his kingdom, to order it, and to establish it with judgment and with justice from henceforth even for ever" (9:7). Also, note that the Messiah is supposed to be born in the family line of King David, a member of the tribe of Judah (the royal tribe, as Judah was the firstborn son), to whom this prophecy is directed. But who exactly is this Messiah? There is more than one answer to that question.

The Hebrew word for Messiah is *mashiach*, which means "anointed one." In our lesson on Psalm 23, we learned that *anointing* is a Jewish tradition signifying the divine appointment of a king. The word does not mean "savior," as many Christians assume (see the website Judaism 101 for an excellent explanation of this misunderstanding). The Hebrew concept of Messiah is understood not as an incarnation of God but a God-appointed human leader of royal Davidic lineage who will set things right, once and for all, among God's people at some point in the future. Isaiah does not use the word "Messiah" in his writings, but he repeatedly refers to a man on whom the Spirit of God will rest, someone who will be a servant of the Lord, someone who will be a key to the happy ending of Isaiah 66. This person can be identified as the Messiah.

Christians believe that Jesus (born about 700 years after Isaiah) fulfilled the Messiah prophecies. Jews do not. One reason for this is that Jesus never had the "government…upon his shoulder" and that he did not bring peace for Israel. Jews believe that the Messiah has not yet appeared, for they expect him to be a successful military leader as well as a religious leader. Conversely, the Christian perspective is that Jesus established a *spiritual* kingdom and that he rescued the entire human race from *spiritual* bondage. That, in a nutshell, is the primary difference in opinion between the Christian and Jewish religions.

Chapter 40 offers comfort to the Jews, acknowledging that "hard service" is in their future and that people will die "like grass," but that the promises of God will endure and that his glory will be revealed. Until that time, God's people are encouraged to take heart and be patient: "But they that wait upon the Lord shall renew their strength; they shall mount up with wings as eagles; they shall run, and not be weary; and they shall walk, and not faint" (40:31). This is an often-quoted verse and an example of Isaiah's powerful poetry. We have already learned that ancient Hebrew poetry was not only rhythmic and parallel, but chock full of earthy images like highways in the desert, shepherds in the field, and eagles in the sky. Like all good poetry, the imagery in the Book of Isaiah evokes strong emotions, both hellish and heavenly. Isaiah insists that both suffering and salvation are part of the big picture.

It is impossible to identify a time frame for the prophecies at the end of the book. As you read in the Chapter 65 excerpt, Isaiah tells Judah that God will create "a new heavens and a new earth" (17). The poetry is powerful and, perhaps, figurative. Will *only* Jerusalem receive these heavenly blessings, as suggested in 65:18-19? Will actual lions lay down with actual lambs, or is this a metaphor? Perhaps more so than any other genre of biblical writing, prophecy is difficult to interpret, and disagreements abound. What do you think? Select your favorite of the three excerpts presented here (9, 40, or 65) and perform your own analysis in the following **Inventory**.

BIBLICAL LITERARY INVENTORY — POETRY

Poem: Isaiah's Prophecy   **Chapter/Verses:** _____

I. Imagery and Mood – _____

_____

_____

II. Persona and Tone – _____

_____

III. Interpretation of Figurative Language and/or Analysis of Diction –

_____
_____
_____

IV. Structure and Movement – All three excerpts presented here are primarily concerned with good news for the Jews, which is only part of the overall message of the book. Chapter 9 is an early "bright spot" found in the darker first half. Chapter 40 appears at the turning point in the book, when Isaiah begins focusing on comfort and redemption. Chapter 65, near the end, concerns the end times of the earth.

V. Theme – _____
_____
_____

VI. Additional Literary Devices – Consider characterization of the Messiah, of God, or of God's people. _____
_____
_____
_____

VII. Historical Criticism – One reason that many scholars date parts of Isaiah to after the Babylonian Exile is that the text specifically mentions Cyrus, the historical figure responsible for conquering Babylon and allowing the Jews to return to their homeland (see Isaiah 45). Scholars who do not believe in supernatural prophecy assume this to be evidence that portions of Isaiah must have been written after the victory of Cyrus. There are additional arguments for the multiple-author theory as well: Isaiah's name is not used in the text past Chapter 39 and literary scholars believe that the theme, style, and vocabulary of the book change at Chapter 40. Try an Internet search of "Cyrus" and "Isaiah" if you are interested in researching this controversy. As you can see, sometimes historical context has an important bearing upon faith and interpretation. What do you think: one author or multiple authors?_____
_____
_____
_____

VIII. Genre Awareness (select one) –

_____ **Lyric Poetry** (expressing personal emotions of the speaker): Can you relate to the emotions of the speaker? How do the speaker's emotions interact with his faith?

_____ **Prophetic Poetry** (spoken on behalf of God as a call to faith and/or action; frequently cryptic): What warning, promise, or prediction is being proclaimed to whom?

_____ **Narrative Poetry** (a story set down in poetic lines rather than prose): Why do you think the storyteller chose elevated, poetic language for the telling of this particular story?

_____ **Proverbs** (short, wise, folk sayings heavy in figurative language, imagery and/or parallelism): How does this reflect universal truth and/or faith-based common sense?

Based on your selection, provide a response to the genre-related question provided above:

_____

_____

_____

LESSON SIXTEEN STUDY GUIDE

Objective Identification:

prophet, Judah, Messiah

Subjective Expression:

1) Cultural Connections: Where else in the world do you see prophets or prophecy – anyone claiming to have foreknowledge of the future, or specialized spiritual insights? Come up with several examples, at least one of them ancient and one of them modern. Do you believe in any of them? Why or why not?

2) Recall: Explain the concept of Messiah and the difference between the Jewish expectation and the Christian interpretation.

3) Cultural Connections: Listen to a recording of Handel's <u>Messiah</u>. Do you hear quotations from the Book of Isaiah?

4) Cultural Connections: Check out one of the books, movies, or TV shows listed on page 171 as having an example of the sight-impaired seer.

THE BIOGRAPHY OF JESUS

This is my blood of the new testament, which is shed for many.

THE NATIVITY OF JESUS CHRIST

Matthew 1

¹ The book of the generation of Jesus Christ, the son of David, the son of Abraham.
² Abraham begat Isaac; and Isaac begat Jacob; and Jacob begat Judas and his brethren;
³ And Judas begat Phares and Zara of Thamar; and Phares begat Esrom; and Esrom begat Aram;
⁴ And Aram begat Aminadab; and Aminadab begat Naasson; and Naasson begat Salmon;
⁵ And Salmon begat Booz of Rachab; and Booz begat Obed of Ruth; and Obed begat Jesse;
⁶ And Jesse begat David the king; and David the king begat Solomon of her that had been the wife of Urias;
⁷ And Solomon begat Roboam; and Roboam begat Abia; and Abia begat Asa;
⁸ And Asa begat Josaphat; and Josaphat begat Joram; and Joram begat Ozias;
⁹ And Ozias begat Joatham; and Joatham begat Achaz; and Achaz begat Ezekias;
10 And Ezekias begat Manasses; and Manasses begat Amon; and Amon begat Josias;
¹¹ And Josias begat Jechonias and his brethren, about the time they were carried away to Babylon:
¹² And after they were brought to Babylon, Jechonias begat Salathiel; and Salathiel begat Zorobabel;
¹³ And Zorobabel begat Abiud; and Abiud begat Eliakim; and Eliakim begat Azor;
¹⁴ And Azor begat Sadoc; and Sadoc begat Achim; and Achim begat Eliud;
¹⁵ And Eliud begat Eleazar; and Eleazar begat Matthan; and Matthan begat Jacob;
¹⁶ And Jacob begat Joseph the husband of Mary, of whom was born Jesus, who is called Christ.
¹⁷ So all the generations from Abraham to David are fourteen generations; and from David until the carrying away into Babylon are fourteen generations; and from the carrying away into Babylon unto Christ are fourteen generations.

¹⁸ Now the birth of Jesus Christ was on this wise:[kk] When as his mother Mary was espoused to Joseph, before they came together, she was found with child of the Holy Ghost. ¹⁹ Then Joseph her husband, being a just man, and not willing to make her a public example, was minded to put her away privily.

²⁰ But while he thought on these things, behold, the angel of the Lord appeared unto him in a dream, saying, "Joseph, thou son of David, fear not to take unto thee Mary thy wife: for that which is conceived in her is of the Holy Ghost. ²¹ And she shall bring forth a son, and thou shalt call his name Jesus: for he shall save his people from their sins."[ll]

²² Now all this was done, that it might be fulfilled which was spoken of the Lord by the prophet, saying, ²³ "Behold, a virgin shall be with child, and shall bring forth a son, and they shall call his name Emmanuel, which being interpreted is, God with us."[mm] ²⁴ Then Joseph being raised from

---

[kk] On this wise = happened in this fashion (FI)
[ll] The angel assures Joseph, Mary's fiancé, that her unborn child is not the result of sexual sin with another man, but that the Holy Spirit placed the baby in her womb. The angel tells him to name the baby Jesus – in Hebrew, the name is *Yeshua*, which means "to deliver" or "to rescue." (FI)
[mm] The angel quotes from Isaiah 7:14, one of the Messiah prophecies.

sleep did as the angel of the Lord had bidden him, and took unto him his wife: ^{25} and knew her not[nn] till she had brought forth her firstborn son: and he called his name Jesus.

Luke 2

^{1}And it came to pass in those days, that there went out a decree from Caesar Augustus that all the world should be taxed. ^{2}(And this taxing was first made when Cyrenius was governor of Syria.) ^{3}And all went to be taxed, every one into his own city. ^{4}And Joseph also went up from Galilee, out of the city of Nazareth, into Judaea, unto the city of David, which is called Bethlehem; (because he was of the house and lineage of David:) ^{5}To be taxed with Mary his espoused wife, being great with child.

^{6}And so it was, that, while they were there, the days were accomplished that she should be delivered. ^{7}And she brought forth her firstborn son, and wrapped him in swaddling clothes, and laid him in a manger; because there was no room for them in the inn.

^{8}And there were in the same country shepherds abiding in the field, keeping watch over their flock by night. ^{9}And, lo, the angel of the Lord came upon them, and the glory of the Lord shone round about them: and they were sore afraid. ^{10}And the angel said unto them,

> "Fear not: for, behold, I bring you good tidings of great joy, which shall be to all people.
> ^{11} For unto you is born this day in the city of David a Saviour, which is Christ the Lord.
> ^{12} And this shall be a sign unto you; Ye shall find the babe wrapped in swaddling
>   clothes, lying in a manger."

^{13} And suddenly there was with the angel a multitude of the heavenly host praising God, and saying,

> ^{14}"Glory to God in the highest,
>   and on earth peace, good will toward men."

^{15} And it came to pass, as the angels were gone away from them into heaven, the shepherds said one to another, "Let us now go even unto Bethlehem, and see this thing which is come to pass, which the Lord hath made known unto us." ^{16} And they came with haste, and found Mary, and Joseph, and the babe lying in a manger. ^{17} And when they had seen it, they made known abroad the saying which was told them concerning this child. ^{18} And all they that heard it wondered at those things which were told them by the shepherds. ^{19} But Mary kept all these things, and pondered them in her heart. ^{20} And the shepherds returned, glorifying and praising God for all the things that they had heard and seen, as it was told unto them. ^{21} And when eight days were accomplished for the circumcising of the child, his name was called Jesus, which was so named of the angel before he was conceived in the womb.

[nn] Joseph did not have sex with Mary until after Jesus was born. In this way, he confirmed that this was a virgin birth. (EP)

LESSON SEVENTEEN:
JESUS - FACT OR FICTION?

"The Adoration of the Kings" by Jan Mabuse (painted 1500-1515)

The story of Jesus' birth, celebrated around the world at Christmas, is the stuff of legend, history, song, and sermon. You have just read a small part of this story, excerpted from two different Bible books. It is clearly a tale of supernatural wonder. It is also a tale set in real time with real geography and verifiably real people, for instance Caesar Augustus (Luke 2:1). Historians willingly acknowledge that there was indeed a man known as Jesus who lived in the Jewish region of the Roman Empire during the early First Century C.E. For two thousand years, the life of this man has touched nearly every aspect of Western culture, not the least of which is the calendar system itself. What I just referred to as "C.E." (the "Common Era" or the "Christian Era") is often called "A.D," meaning Anno Domino or "in the year of our Lord" in reference to Jesus. This calendar, known as the Gregorian or Christian calendar, is the most widely used calendar in the world. It is only one example of the global impact made by Jesus and his followers. But how did modern readers come into possession of the details of Jesus' birth, his life, his death, or even his legacy?

> **DID SAINT MATTHEW THE APOSTLE WRITE THE GOSPEL OF MATTHEW?**
>
> **YES:**
> Papias (c.70-155) was one of the earliest church spokesmen, and he served as Bishop of Hierapolis. He is quoted in the Ecclesiastical History, written by Bishop Eusebius of Caesarea (c. 260-c.340), as saying, **"So then Matthew wrote the oracles in the Hebrew language…"** (3.39.14-15). Papias was a second generation Christian and was considered by Second Century church fathers to be a reliable witness to original apostolic traditions; they also believed Papias to have personally known several of the disciples.
>
> **NO:**
> Upon closer examination of Papias' statement, critics note that "the Hebrew language" refers to Aramaic. However, the Gospel writer's Greek does not have the marks of translated material, and critics therefore doubt that it was originally penned in Aramaic. Furthermore, the Gospel narrative is not an "oracle," a collection of sayings. Critics have concluded that Papias was not describing the Gospel of Matthew.
>
> **NOTE:** There are additional document-based arguments both for and against the authorship of Saint Matthew the Apostle.

PRIMARY & SECONDARY SOURCES?

The "official" biography of Jesus comes to us through four separate books found at the beginning of the New Testament: The Gospel of Matthew, The Gospel of Mark, The Gospel of Luke, and The Gospel of John. The Greek word *gospel* means "good news," and these books were named as such because their writers believed that the story of Jesus contained very good news for all of humanity. It has long been presumed that these writers – Matthew, Mark, Luke, and John – were primary or secondary sources to the life and times of Jesus. Matthew and John have been identified as Jesus' disciples, and Mark and Luke as companions of the disciples Peter and Paul (respectively).[oo] It should be noted, however, that none of the gospel books include direct author identification within their text. Nevertheless, from the Second Century or earlier, these four books were

---

[oo] A disciple is a student and follower of a teacher or philosopher. Jesus' disciples traveled with him, lodged with him, ate with him, and studied under him. His disciples would have considered Jesus their rabbi.

grouped together and titled as "The Gospel of Matthew" or "The Gospel according to Matthew," and so on.[pp] These traditional assumptions of authorship went relatively unquestioned until the 1700's, when rationalist scholars began asking questions about biblical origins. Today, there are theories involving alternative and additional authors (see the sidebars on this page and the previous page for examples).

OTHER GOSPELS

It should also be noted that there were other ancient gospels besides those of Matthew, Mark, Luke, and John. The other gospels have either been lost, rejected due to questionable authorship, or discounted as "gnostic" and therefore heretical.[qq] Today, many scholars and spiritual seekers have revived an interest in these non-canonical gospels, particularly the gnostic texts (for instance the Gospel of Thomas of The DaVinci Code fame). The established Church, however, has not changed its stance on the four canonical gospels in 1900 years, and thus all New Testaments begin with the Gospels of Matthew, Mark, Luke, and John.

DID SAINT MARK WRITE THE GOSPEL OF MARK?

YES:
Clement (c.150-c.215) was the Bishop of Alexandria, Egypt, and is cited in Eusebius' Ecclesiastical History: **"Peter's hearers…were not content with the unwritten teaching of the divine Gospel…they besought Mark, a follower of Peter, and the one whose Gospel is extant, that he would leave them a written monument…"** (2.15.1-2). It should be noted that there are additional scholarly arguments for the authorship of Mark, based on the book's linguistic qualities, as well as documented attestations in addition to that of Clement.

NOT ENTIRELY:
Because Mark's narrative is thematically focused on Jesus' miracles and death – evidently a work of carefully structured, didactic narrative rather than an objective work of journalism – some critics conclude that the writer pieced together stories and sayings of Jesus that had been part of an oral tradition for an entire generation.[rr] Critics conclude that Mark (who may or may not be the same Mark that followed Peter) did not simply write down Peter's eyewitness accounts verbatim, and therefore cannot be called a secondary historical source.

[pp] Gigot, Francis. "Gospel and Gospels." The Catholic Encyclopedia. Vol. 6. New York: Robert Appleton Company, 1909. 25 Mar. 2014 <http://www.newadvent.org/cathen/06655b.htm>.

[qq] "Gnostic" means "knowledge" or "enlightenment." Gnosticism is a strain of thought found in several ancient religions. For a more complete discussion of Gnosticism and the gnostic gospels, turn to the end of this lesson and read our response to Fatima's letter.

[rr] White, L. Michael. "The Gospel of Mark: A story of secrecy and misunderstanding." From Jesus to Christ: The First Christians. Frontline. WGBH educational foundation, April 1998. 27 Mar. 2014.
<www.pbs.org/wgbh/pages/frontline/shows/religion/story/mark.html>

HISTORICITY

Of course, we have no concrete proof that these writers told the whole truth and nothing but the truth! That's a separate issue, largely concerned with your personal faith perspective. We do know that several secular historians mentioned Jesus (or someone who appears to be Jesus) in their documents and letters,[ss] and we know that copies of the gospels quickly passed into widespread use throughout the Roman empire and were considered holy scripture for the new religion of Christianity. However, because there are so few overlaps between documented secular history and the details and events described in the gospels, many scholars today are uncomfortable labeling the gospels as true biographies. They could not be reliable biography, of course, if the supernatural events they describe were fictionalized by religious zealots – again, because belief in the supernatural is more an issue of faith than of scholarship. For the purposes of our studies, we will acknowledge that the gospels are at least a *unique type* of biography, narrating the life of a man whose singular message changed the face of Western culture. The word *gospel* is very specific to Christianity; it refers *only* to a biography of Jesus Christ, and it may or may not bear important similarities with other ancient biographies (see sidebar). The gospels may be considered the most broadly influential biographical literature in the Western world.

> **BIOGRAPY IN THE ANCIENT WORLD**
>
> Ancient writers produced different genres and styles of texts than we do today, in the same way that your grandparents watched different kinds of TV shows than you do. For instance, you may have never seen a "variety" show like the Dean Martin Comedy Hour (1965-74), and your grandparents may have never watched any "reality" TV like Jersey Shore.
>
> Likewise, biographies were quite different in the Roman world than they are today. They tended to focus on a few select anecdotes and speeches (rather than presenting all the major biographical events of the subject's life) for the didactic purpose of painting a moral picture of the subject. Many ancient biographies included mythical birth stories, miracles, and omens, and they were considered a separate genre from histories.
>
> Scholars continue to debate the similarities and differences between the gospels and various examples of ancient biography.

[ss] Such documentation includes that of Tacitus (c.56-c.117), a Roman senator who wrote about Nero's infamous fire, Pliny the Younger (61-c.112)), a Roman provincial governor, and Josephus (37-c.100), a Jewish historian.

GETTING STARTED WITH MARK

Before reading our first excerpt from the Gospel of Mark, make sure you recall the meaning of the word "Messiah" (see Lessons 1 and 16) and that "Christ" is the Greek word for Messiah. We learned in our study of Isaiah that the Messiah would be born in the bloodline of the great King David (author of the Psalms), and this expectation is repeated in the opening chapters of Matthew and Luke. The Gospel of Mark begins with a direct quote from chapter 40 of Isaiah. Following this lesson, we will study the Gospel of Mark from start to finish (minus a few chapters for the sake of brevity).

Why Mark? For starters, the Gospel of Mark is the shortest of the four gospels. Most contemporary scholars also believe that Mark's gospel was the first, and so he essentially wrote the "prototype." Both Matthew and Luke copy many passages from Mark's original, adding in their own additional knowledge and themes, to produce much longer books. Matthew and Luke are the only Bible writers who tell us about Jesus' birth in Bethlehem, a tale known as the "nativity." All four gospels relate the story of Jesus' death.

Mark's gospel seems to be written for a Roman audience that needed to hear a powerful, motivational story to keep them encouraged during times of intense religious persecution. Mark tells us a tale with an adventurous edge. His rendition is fast-paced with very little detail and few sermons. If you have a picture of Jesus in your head that is mild and pale and sweet, then you might be surprised by the characterizing details you find in the first few chapters of Mark. Jesus does a lot of really good, really generous things, but he's fierce. Some of the other gospel writers include scenes of Jesus with children, images of singing angels and praying women, but not Mark. Aside from some minor plot inconsistencies,[tt] the four gospels tell the same overall story but with different styles and purposes to shape them. Think of it this way: if multiple authors were writing the story of your life, one of them your grandmother and one of them your best pal from your middle school days, wouldn't the stories be somewhat different? Even if they were completely harmonious in factual detail, the image of you painted by Grandma might be different from the image painted by your childhood best friend. Mark's image of Jesus is young, sassy, bold, and mysterious.

[tt] One example: Mark says there is one angel (described as a young man in white) at Jesus' tomb on Easter morning, whereas John says there are two (clearly identified as angels). Theologians argue that there is an important difference between a narrative variation such as this and an actual *contradiction*: it would have been *contradictory* had Mark said there was one angel in the empty tomb and John that there was one angel standing beside Jesus' corpse. Many theologians argue that no true contradictions occur among the gospels or anywhere else in the Bible.

Fatima

I've read The DaVinci Code, and I just don't see how the church could be so narrow-minded about the gnostic gospels. Why exactly did they get rejected, and why aren't they in this textbook?

Dear Fatima,

There are at least 50 gnostic gospels in existence, and most were probably written sometime during the second, third, and fourth centuries. As we have discussed earlier, one of the central principles among the church leaders who selected and approved Bible texts was that they be written by primary or secondary sources – in other words, by people who knew Jesus or knew his friends and family. The Gospel of Thomas (the one featured in The DaVinci Code) is one of the earliest of the gnostic gospels, and it was probably written in the mid-100's, a full century after Jesus' lifetime. Most religious scholars believe that Christian Gnosticism is something that grew *out of* Christianity, rather than something *inspired directly by* Jesus during the First Century. As always, positions on scriptural authorship and dating are controversial, and scholarship favoring an earlier date for the Gospel of Thomas is trendy. That fact notwithstanding, one reason for the initial exclusion of the gnostic gospels from the biblical canon was clearly the issue of dating and primary/secondary source proximity. Church leaders in the Second Century thought that Matthew, Mark, Luke, and John passed these tests and that the other gospels did not.

The other criterion was that the message of the New Testament collection be consistent within itself. The canonical gospels include reports of Jesus' words and actions that are theologically consistent with each other. As you will read in the Gospel of Mark, Jesus is described as the Son of God, the Jewish Messiah. The message in the gnostic gospels is a bit different, and, in fact, the very style of the gnostic gospels is also different from the gospel accounts you find in the Bible. Gnosticism as a philosophy is more mystical than is traditional

Christianity, and the gnostic "god concept" is more similar to pantheism or cosmic humanism than the Christian deity. In fact, there are gnostic texts in other religious traditions as well. Gnostic theology is not consistent with mainstream Christian theology, and most readers find that the gnostic gospels are incongruent with the canonical gospels. That being said, you should be your own judge of gnostic texts, copies of which are very easy to find. Many readers are drawn to them for the very reason that church authorities rejected them: because they teach an alternate theology, one of finding spiritual truths within oneself rather than through the church. The Gospel of Thomas can be accessed online with just a few clicks.

Scott

It seems like the writers of this textbook have thrown a lot of questionable opinions into this lesson and are trying to prove that the Bible isn't reliable. My pastor, who used to be an atheist, says he did all sorts of historical research and came to the conclusion that the Bible is God's Word, and it is perfect. I don't understand why you are being so pushy about non-Christian perspectives on the Christian holy book.

Dear Scott,

There are reputable scholars on both sides of the argument, and we think it's pretty important that you and your classmates know a little bit about this important debate. On one hand, it is true that no one can prove *who wrote* what book based on *which sources*, but on the other hand, we have excellent evidence for validating the accuracy of the *actual words they wrote*. When the same methods used to validate ancient books by Homer, Caesar, and Thucydides are applied to the ancient New Testament manuscripts, the New Testament texts "pass the test" with high marks. <u>The Archaeological Study Bible</u> says, "No other ancient text is substantiated by such a wealth of ancient textual witness as is the New Testament. Roughly 5,500 manuscripts are available, variously containing anything from the entire New Testament corpus to a slight fragment of a single verse" ("The New Testament Texts," page 1859). According to the <u>Catholic Encyclopedia</u>, there are papyrus fragments from the second and third centuries and complete parchment codices from the fourth century, two examples which barely tap the top of the list. Today, thousands of ancient manuscripts can be found in museums, private collections, and the Vatican (Drum, Walter. "Manuscripts of the Bible." Vol. 9).

So, yes, we can read today's copies of the Bible knowing three things: 1) that the originals were almost certainly written within 100 years of Jesus' lifetime, which is an excellent statistic, and (2) that the text we have today is probably very close to the original versions, even though the originals have been lost. Furthermore, as you saw in the sidebars on pages 181 and 182, we can acknowledge that (3) there is document-based evidence supporting primary and secondary-source authorship of the original gospels. This evidence doesn't solve all mysteries, but it is worthy of scholarly consideration.

However, there are matters that we simply can't resolve with an abundance of manuscripts. We can never be sure that the writers were telling the truth, that the document-based evidence is accurate, or that miracles are even possible. And when the manuscripts are different (as they are in the case of Mark 16:9-20, for example), we cannot be sure which manuscript is better. We also can't be sure that the church authorities made all the perfect choices when selecting some books and rejecting others from the canon. At some point, acceptance of the Bible as God's Word requires a leap of faith.

That being said, keep in mind that every single student in your class holds a few beliefs based on faith, and that's part of being human. Even scientists and atheists exercise faith. Scholarly information, whether it's "pro-Bible" or "anti-Bible," will always reach a limit. Once this limit is encountered, a brave leap of faith is required in order to move ahead. For more thoughts on this topic, check out the "Quotable Quote" from <u>Life of Pi</u> on page 214.

LESSON SEVENTEEN STUDY GUIDE

Objective Identification:

Nativity, C.E. (Current Era), A.D. (Anno Domino), Matthew, Mark, Luke, John, primary source, secondary source, gospel, gnostic/Gnosticism, messiah/Christ.

Subjective Expression:

1) Recall: Putting the accounts from Matthew and Luke together, can you summarize the nativity story? And can you name the four canonical gospels, in order?

2) Cultural Connections: What religious observances of Christmas are you familiar with? What symbols and decorations do you see during December that relate to the nativity story?

3) Opinion: Do you agree that the writers of the four gospels were primary and secondary sources to the life of Jesus, as claimed by traditional church authorities? Why or why not?

4) Further Exploration: Check out the movie or book (by Dan Brown) The DaVinci Code. The story is a gruesome murder mystery laced with history, religion, and controversy. Then read one of the many articles written by Christians in order to counter Brown's claims about Gnosticism and church history (for instance, "Breaking the DaVinci Code" by Collin Hansen at Christian History.net). Do you like the book/movie? Do you agree with the rebuttals?

THE GOSPEL OF MARK

Mark 1

Exposition: John the Baptist

[1] The beginning of the gospel of Jesus Christ, the Son of God;[a] [2] As it is written in the prophets,

> Behold, I send my messenger before thy face,
> which shall prepare thy way before thee.
> [3] The voice of one crying in the wilderness,
> Prepare ye the way of the Lord,
> make his paths straight.[b]

[4] John did baptize[c] in the wilderness, and preach the baptism of repentance for the remission of sins. [5] And there went out unto him all the land of Judaea, and they of Jerusalem, and were all baptized of him in the river of Jordan, confessing their sins.

[6] And John was clothed with camel's hair, and with a girdle of a skin about his loins[d]; and he did eat locusts and wild honey; [7] And preached, saying, There cometh one mightier than I after me, the latchet of whose shoes I am not worthy to stoop down and unloose. [8] I indeed have baptized you with water: but he shall baptize you with the Holy Ghost.

[9] And it came to pass in those days, that Jesus came from Nazareth of Galilee, and was baptized of John in Jordan. [10] And straightway coming up out of the water, he saw the heavens opened, and the Spirit[e] like a dove descending upon him: [11] And there came a voice from heaven, saying, Thou art my beloved Son, in whom I am well pleased.

[12] And immediately the spirit driveth him into the wilderness. [13] And he was there in the wilderness forty days, tempted of Satan[f]; and was with the wild beasts; and the angels ministered unto him. [14] Now after that John was put in prison, Jesus came into Galilee, preaching the gospel of the kingdom of God, [15] And saying, The time is fulfilled, and the kingdom of God is at hand: repent ye, and believe the gospel.

---

[a] Gospel = story of "good news." Christ = messiah. (FI)

[b] Mark is quoting from Isaiah 40, a passage that predicts the coming of the messiah. See Lesson 16 for further explanation.

[c] Baptism is the symbolic use of water to signify a spiritual cleansing. If done by submersion under the water (rather than by sprinkling with water atop the head as in some church traditions), baptism may also signify death and resurrection. Since our characters are in the river, we may assume that John's baptisms are submersive.

[d] John dressed in an unusual fashion for the day – a loincloth wrapped around his midsection. The clothes he wore and the food he ate suggest an uncivilized, outdoorsy, bohemian type character. This may be read as a significant connection to the Isaiah reference concerning the "wilderness."

[e] The Spirit, the Holy Spirit, and the Holy Ghost all refer to the same "person" of God in the Christian tradition. This triune concept is called the Trinity and includes Father God, the Son, and the Spirit. The Trinity is sometimes described as metaphorically similar to the nature of water – always H20 but appearing in three forms: as liquid, vapor, or ice.

[f] Forty is a number that often coincides, in the Bible, with a long period of suffering followed by salvation – Noah's flood lasted 40 days, and the Israelites wandered in the wilderness for 40 years.

Meet the Protagonist

[margin: got followers]

¹⁶ Now as he walked by the sea of Galilee, he saw Simon and Andrew his brother casting a net into the sea: for they were fishers. ¹⁷ And Jesus said unto them, Come ye after me, and I will make you to become fishers of men. ¹⁸ And straightway they forsook their nets, and followed him. ¹⁹ And when he had gone a little farther thence, he saw James the son of Zebedee, and John his brother, who also were in the ship mending their nets. ²⁰ And straightway he called them: and they left their father Zebedee in the ship with the hired servants, and went after him.

[margin: went and taught / amazed / let a sinner in]

²¹ And they went into Capernaum; and straightway on the sabbath[g] day he entered into the synagogue[h], and taught. ²² And they were astonished at his doctrine: for he taught them as one that had authority, and not as the scribes. ²³ And there was in their synagogue a man with an unclean spirit[i]; and he cried out, ²⁴ Saying, "Let us alone; what have we to do with thee, thou Jesus of Nazareth? art thou come to destroy us? I know thee who thou art, the Holy One of God."

²⁵ And Jesus rebuked him, saying, "Hold thy peace, and come out of him." ²⁶ And when the unclean spirit had torn him, and cried with a loud voice, he came out of him. ²⁷ And they were all amazed, insomuch that they questioned among themselves, saying, "What thing is this? what new doctrine is this? for with authority commandeth he even the unclean spirits, and they do obey him." ²⁸ And immediately his fame spread abroad throughout all the region round about Galilee.

[margin: miracles]

²⁹ And forthwith, when they were come out of the synagogue, they entered into the house of Simon and Andrew, with James and John. ³⁰ But Simon's wife's mother lay sick of a fever, and anon they tell him of her. ³¹ And he came and took her by the hand, and lifted her up; and immediately the fever left her, and she ministered unto them. ³² And at even, when the sun did set, they brought unto him all that were diseased, and them that were possessed with devils. ³³ And all the city was gathered together at the door. ³⁴ And he healed many that were sick of divers diseases, and cast out many devils; and suffered not the devils to speak, because they knew him.

³⁵ And in the morning, rising up a great while before day, he went out, and departed into a solitary place, and there prayed. ³⁶ And Simon and they that were with him followed after him. ³⁷ And when they had found him, they said unto him, "All men seek for thee." ³⁸ And he said unto them, "Let us go into the next towns, that I may preach there also: for therefore came I forth." ³⁹ And he preached in their synagogues throughout all Galilee, and cast out devils.

[margin: relived sins]

---

[g] Sabbath = the Jewish weekly holy day. Literally, the sabbath is the seventh day of the week: Saturday. Christians observe a "sabbath" on Sunday in honor of Jesus' resurrection, which occurred on Sunday. (FI)

[h] Synagogue = a Jewish house of worship; scribes = church officials whose job was to copy the scriptures, therefore making them experts in the details and implications of scripture and law. Their jobs in ancient times were similar to contract lawyers or royal secretaries. (FI)

[i] Unclean spirit = a demon or devil (FI)

⁴⁰ And there came a leper[j] to him, beseeching him, and kneeling down to him, and saying unto him, "If thou wilt, thou canst make me clean." ⁴¹ And Jesus, moved with compassion, put forth his hand, and touched him, and saith unto him, "I will; be thou clean." ⁴² And as soon as he had spoken, immediately the leprosy departed from him, and he was cleansed. ⁴³ And he straitly charged him, and forthwith sent him away; ⁴⁴ And saith unto him, "See thou say nothing to any man: but go thy way, shew thyself to the priest, and offer for thy cleansing those things which Moses commanded[k], for a testimony unto them." ⁴⁵ But he went out, and began to publish it much, and to blaze abroad the matter, insomuch that Jesus could no more openly enter into the city, but was without in desert places: and they came to him from every quarter.

Mark 2

Rising Action: Conflict Emerges

² And again he entered into Capernaum after some days; and it was noised that he was in the house. ² And straightway many were gathered together, insomuch that there was no room to receive them, no, not so much as about the door: and he preached the word unto them. ³ And they come unto him, bringing one sick of the palsy, which was borne of four. ⁴ And when they could not come nigh unto him for the press, they uncovered the roof[l] where he was: and when they had broken it up, they let down the bed wherein the sick of the palsy lay. ⁵ When Jesus saw their faith, he said unto the sick of the palsy, "Son, thy sins be forgiven thee."

⁶ But there was certain of the scribes sitting there, and reasoning in their hearts, ⁷ "Why doth this man thus speak blasphemies? who can forgive sins but God only?"[m] ⁸ And immediately when Jesus perceived in his spirit that they so reasoned within themselves, he said unto them, "Why reason ye these things in your hearts? ⁹ Whether is it easier to say to the sick of the palsy, 'Thy sins be forgiven thee'; or to say, 'Arise, and take up thy bed, and walk?' ¹⁰ But that ye may know that the Son of man hath power on earth to forgive sins, (he saith to the sick of the palsy,) ¹¹ I say unto thee, Arise, and take up thy bed, and go thy way into thine house." ¹² And immediately he arose, took up the bed, and went forth before them all; insomuch that they were all amazed, and glorified God, saying, "We never saw it on this fashion."

---

[j] Leper = someone suffering from leprosy, a highly contagious and fatal skin and nerve disease that may be the same as Hansen's disease in modern times. In biblical times, lepers were typically quarantined outside city limits. For Jesus to fearlessly approach and touch a leper indicates confidence and compassion. (FI)

[k] Moses received and wrote the Jewish religious law, as we studied earlier in this text. The law included rules for the healing of lepers, and Jesus is encouraging the healed man to fulfill his religious obligations with the priest. See Leviticus 14.

[l] Houses at this time often had flat roofs with stairs up the side of the house for easy access. The roof itself would have been "thatched," with branches and clay overlaying wood beams. The men in this story could have climbed the steps and then dug through the thatching to lower their friend between the roof beams. (FI)

[m] Blasphemy = any word or deed that disrespectfully violates the teachings of scripture. Here, for Jesus to forgive the man's sins is an indirect claim to be God incarnate, for only God can forgive sin. The scribes in this story do not believe that Jesus is God; therefore, they believe him to be blasphemous. (FI)

¹³ And he went forth again by the sea side; and all the multitude resorted unto him, and he taught them. ¹⁴ And as he passed by, he saw Levi the son of Alphaeus sitting at the receipt of custom[n], and said unto him, "Follow me." And he arose and followed him.

¹⁵ And it came to pass, that, as Jesus sat at meat in his house, many publicans[o] and sinners sat also together with Jesus and his disciples: for there were many, and they followed him. ¹⁶ And when the scribes and Pharisees[p] saw him eat with publicans and sinners, they said unto his disciples, "How is it that he eateth and drinketh with publicans and sinners?" ¹⁷ When Jesus heard it, he saith unto them, "They that are whole have no need of the physician, but they that are sick: I came not to call the righteous, but sinners to repentance."

¹⁸ And the disciples of John[q] and of the Pharisees used to fast: and they come and say unto him, "Why do the disciples of John and of the Pharisees fast, but thy disciples fast not?" ¹⁹ And Jesus said unto them, "Can the children of the bridechamber fast, while the bridegroom is with them?[r] as long as they have the bridegroom with them, they cannot fast. ²⁰ But the days will come, when the bridegroom shall be taken away from them, and then shall they fast in those days. ²¹ No man also seweth a piece of new cloth on an old garment: else the new piece that filled it up taketh away from the old, and the rent is made worse. ²² And no man putteth new wine into old bottles: else the new wine doth burst the bottles, and the wine is spilled, and the bottles will be marred: but new wine must be put into new bottles."

[²³⁻²⁷ Jesus allows his disciples to ignore Sabbath day rules]

Mark 3

Rising Action: Antagonists

¹ And he entered again into the synagogue; and there was a man there which had a withered hand. ² And they watched him, whether he would heal him on the sabbath day; that they might accuse him. ³ And he saith unto the man which had the withered hand, "Stand forth." ⁴ And he saith unto them, "Is it lawful to do good on the sabbath days, or to do evil? to save life, or to kill?" But they held their peace.

---

[n] Receipt of custom = a custom house, a place where taxes are collected. Levi is a tax collector. This character is known elsewhere in the Bible by the Greek name of Matthew, the same Matthew who later serves as a disciple and authors the Gospel of Matthew. (FI)

[o] Publicans = tax collectors, who were employees of Rome and therefore highly distrusted and reviled among the Jewish population. (FI)

[p] Pharisees = a group of Jewish scriptural scholars and cultural leaders. (FI)

[q] In reference to John the Baptist. Disciples are students, and in the Jewish tradition, students of scripture would attach themselves to a particular teacher, or rabbi, committing to learn that particular rabbi's philosophy of religious observance. Most rabbis taught their disciples to fast, or to go without food for a period of time in order to focus on spiritual rather than physical nourishment. Here, we see that Jesus did not require his disciples to fast. (FI)

[r] Children of the bridechamber = guests at a wedding reception; Bridegroom = the groom. (FI) This metaphor explains why Jesus does not permit his disciples to fast – because as long as he is present, the "party" is ongoing, so to speak. However, he suggests that he will indeed leave the party at some point, and when he does, then fasting will be appropriate. This foreshadows his death.

⁵ And when he had looked round about on them with anger, being grieved for the hardness of their hearts, he saith unto the man, "Stretch forth thine hand." And he stretched it out: and his hand was restored whole as the other. ⁶ And the Pharisees went forth, and straightway took counsel with the Herodians^s against him, how they might destroy him.

⁷ But Jesus withdrew himself with his disciples to the sea: and a great multitude from Galilee followed him, and from Judaea, ⁸ And from Jerusalem, and from Idumaea, and from beyond Jordan; and they about Tyre and Sidon, a great multitude, when they had heard what great things he did, came unto him. ⁹ And he spake to his disciples, that a small ship should wait on him because of the multitude, lest they should throng him. ¹⁰ For he had healed many; insomuch that they pressed upon him for to touch him, as many as had plagues. ¹¹ And unclean spirits, when they saw him, fell down before him, and cried, saying, "Thou art the Son of God."

Supporting Characters
¹² And he straitly charged them that they should not make him known. ¹³ And he goeth up into a mountain, and calleth unto him whom he would: and they came unto him. ¹⁴ And he ordained twelve^t, that they should be with him, and that he might send them forth to preach, ¹⁵ And to have power to heal sicknesses, and to cast out devils:
¹⁶ And Simon he surnamed Peter;^u
¹⁷ And James the son of Zebedee, and John the brother of James; and he surnamed them Boanerges, which is, The sons of thunder:
¹⁸ And Andrew, and Philip, and Bartholomew, and Matthew, and Thomas, and James the son of Alphaeus, and Thaddaeus, and Simon the Canaanite,
¹⁹ And Judas Iscariot, which also betrayed him: and they went into a house.

²⁰ And the multitude cometh together again, so that they could not so much as eat bread. ²¹ And when his friends heard of it, they went out to lay hold on him: for they said, "He is beside himself."

²² And the scribes which came down from Jerusalem said, "He hath Beelzebub, and by the prince of the devils casteth he out devils." ^v ²³ And he called them unto him, and said unto them in parables,^w "How can Satan cast out Satan? ²⁴ And if a kingdom be divided against itself, that kingdom cannot stand. ²⁵ And if a house be divided against itself, that house cannot stand. ²⁶ And if Satan rise up against himself, and be divided, he cannot stand, but hath an end. ²⁷ No man can enter into a strong man's house, and spoil his goods, except he will first bind the strong man; and

---
^s Herod = the king of the Jews at the time of Jesus. In the Roman Empire, local kings were permitted to reign regionally, provided taxes were paid to Rome. This Herod is probably the immediate successor to Herod the Great, who appears in the nativity stories. (FI)
^t 12 disciples were recruited by Jesus, perhaps alluding to the 12 tribes of Israel. If so, Jesus is suggesting that he is the new father of a new religion.
^u Peter = a name meaning "rock." Simon's name change to Peter is significant in the history of Christianity, symbolizing his "number one" status among the disciples – the "rock" upon which Jesus builds his church. This Peter is considered by Catholics to have been the first pope, and it is after him that St. Peter's Basilica in Vatican City is named. (FI)
^v "He hath Beelzebub" = "He (Jesus) is possessed by the demon Beelzebub." This is the only explanation the scribes can offer for Jesus' ability to do miracles. They believe his powers must come from demons, since they assume he is not God or Messiah. (FI)
^w Parable = a story used to illustrate a moral principle, often metaphorical (FI)

then he will spoil his house.^x ²⁸ Verily I say unto you, All sins shall be forgiven unto the sons of men, and blasphemies wherewith soever they shall blaspheme:^y ²⁹ But he that shall blaspheme against the Holy Ghost hath never forgiveness, but is in danger of eternal damnation."^z ³⁰ Because they said, 'He hath an unclean spirit.'"

³¹ There came then his brethren and his mother, and, standing without, sent unto him, calling him. ³² And the multitude sat about him, and they said unto him, "Behold, thy mother and thy brethren without seek for thee." ³³ And he answered them, saying, "Who is my mother, or my brethren?" ³⁴ And he looked round about on them which sat about him, and said, "Behold my mother and my brethren! ³⁵ For whosoever shall do the will of God, the same is my brother, and my sister, and mother."

Mark 4

Episodes of Teaching

And he began again to teach by the sea side: and there was gathered unto him a great multitude, so that he entered into a ship, and sat in the sea; and the whole multitude was by the sea on the land. ² And he taught them many things by parables, and said unto them in his doctrine,

³ "Hearken; Behold, there went out a sower to sow:^aa ⁴ And it came to pass, as he sowed, some fell by the way side, and the fowls of the air came and devoured it up. ⁵ And some fell on stony ground, where it had not much earth; and immediately it sprang up, because it had no depth of earth: ⁶ But when the sun was up, it was scorched; and because it had no root, it withered away. ⁷ And some fell among thorns, and the thorns grew up, and choked it, and it yielded no fruit. ⁸ And other fell on good ground, and did yield fruit that sprang up and increased; and brought forth, some thirty, and some sixty, and some an hundred." ⁹ And he said unto them, "He that hath ears to hear, let him hear."

¹⁰ And when he was alone, they that were about him with the twelve asked of him the parable. ¹¹ And he said unto them, "Unto you it is given to know the mystery of the kingdom of God: but unto them that are without, all these things are done in parables: ¹² 'That seeing they may see, and not perceive; and hearing they may hear, and not understand; lest at any time they should be converted, and their sins should be forgiven them.'"^bb

---

^x Jesus' counter argument is that demons would not sponsor the defeat of other demons. Therefore, his power must be from God. The strong man seems to be Satan, and Jesus is suggesting that he is able to bind up Satan and steal his power.

^y "Blasphemies wherewith soever they shall blaspheme" = and whatever blasphemies they utter (EP)

^z Damnation = condemnation, with a connotation of hell. Other translations say "guilty of an eternal sin." (FI)

^aa Sower = farmer; to sow = to plant seeds. (FI)

^bb Here, Jesus is quoting from Isaiah, who described a future day in which the people would "hear but not understand" God's word – that is, until the coming of the messiah (see Isaiah 6-7). Some readers think this means that Jesus used parables to disguise God's word, so that Isaiah's prophecy would be fulfilled. Some readers think Jesus is saying that the prophecy has already been fulfilled, and that parables are his way of reaching even those who had formerly "heard but not understood" God's word.

¹³ And he said unto them, "Know ye not this parable? and how then will ye know all parables?ᶜᶜ ¹⁴ The sower soweth the word. ¹⁵ And these are they by the way side, where the word is sown; but when they have heard, Satan cometh immediately, and taketh away the word that was sown in their hearts. ¹⁶ And these are they likewise which are sown on stony ground; who, when they have heard the word, immediately receive it with gladness; ¹⁷ And have no root in themselves, and so endure but for a time: afterward, when affliction or persecution ariseth for the word's sake, immediately they are offended. ¹⁸ And these are they which are sown among thorns; such as hear the word, ¹⁹ And the cares of this world, and the deceitfulness of riches, and the lusts of other things entering in, choke the word, and it becometh unfruitful. ²⁰ And these are they which are sown on good ground; such as hear the word, and receive it, and bring forth fruit, some thirtyfold, some sixty, and some an hundred."

²¹ And he said unto them, "Is a candle brought to be put under a bushel, or under a bed? and not to be set on a candlestick? ²² For there is nothing hid, which shall not be manifested; neither was any thing kept secret, but that it should come abroad. ²³ If any man have ears to hear, let him hear."ᵈᵈ

[²⁴⁻²⁹ *Jesus talks further about the Kingdom*]

³⁰ And he said, "Whereunto shall we liken the kingdom of God? or with what comparison shall we compare it? ³¹ It is like a grain of mustard seed,ᵉᵉ which, when it is sown in the earth, is less than all the seeds that be in the earth: ³² But when it is sown, it groweth up, and becometh greater than all herbs, and shooteth out great branches; so that the fowls of the air may lodge under the shadow of it." ³³ And with many such parables spake he the word unto them, as they were able to hear it. ³⁴ But without a parable spake he not unto them: and when they were alone, he expounded all things to his disciples.

Episodes of Miracles

³⁵ And the same day, when the evenᶠᶠ was come, he saith unto them, "Let us pass over unto the other side." ³⁶ And when they had sent away the multitude, they took him even as he was in the ship. And there were also with him other little ships. ³⁷ And there arose a great storm of wind, and the waves beat into the ship, so that it was now full. ³⁸ And he was in the hinder part of the ship, asleep on a pillow: and they awake him, and say unto him, "Master, carest thou not that we perish?" ³⁹ And he arose, and rebuked the wind, and said unto the sea, "Peace, be still." And the wind ceased, and there was a great calm. ⁴⁰ And he said unto them, "Why are ye so fearful? how is it that ye have no faith?" ⁴¹ And they feared exceedingly, and said one to another, "What manner of man is this, that even the wind and the sea obey him?"

ᶜᶜ Jesus is asking his disciples if they understood the previous parable of the sower. His tone has an edge to it, as if to say that if they don't understand this parable, then they won't understand any of his parables or lessons. Then Jesus breaks it down for them, just in case: the seeds are metaphors for God's word. Thus, the parable is a spiritual lesson about receiving spiritual lessons.

ᵈᵈ This line may be another allusion to Isaiah 6 – rather than people "hearing and not understanding," Jesus is inviting all people who have ears to hear God's word and fully understand it.

ᵉᵉ Mustard seeds are tiny, yet mustard plants can grow to be quite large. (FI)

ᶠᶠ Even = evening (FI)

Mark 5-7

Jesus heals a demon-possessed man, a sick woman, a dead girl, and a deaf mute. The disciples are sent out to preach village to village. John the Baptist is beheaded for having offended Herod's wife. Jesus feeds 5000 people, walks upon the water, and continues to defy and contradict the Pharisees.

Mark 8

Episodes of Miracles and Teaching

In those days the multitude being very great, and having nothing to eat, Jesus called his disciples unto him, and saith unto them, **2** "I have compassion on the multitude, because they have now been with me three days, and have nothing to eat: **3** And if I send them away fasting to their own houses, they will faint by the way: for divers[gg] of them came from far." **4** And his disciples answered him, "From whence can a man satisfy these men with bread here in the wilderness?" **5** And he asked them, "How many loaves have ye?" And they said, "Seven." **6** And he commanded the people to sit down on the ground: and he took the seven loaves, and gave thanks, and brake, and gave to his disciples to set before them; and they did set them before the people. **7** And they had a few small fishes: and he blessed, and commanded to set them also before them. **8** So they did eat, and were filled: and they took up of the broken meat that was left seven baskets. **9** And they that had eaten were about four thousand: and he sent them away.

10 And straightway he entered into a ship with his disciples, and came into the parts of Dalmanutha. **11** And the Pharisees came forth, and began to question with him, seeking of him a sign from heaven, tempting him. **12** And he sighed deeply in his spirit, and saith, "Why doth this generation seek after a sign? verily I say unto you, [hh]There shall no sign be given unto this generation."

13 And he left them, and entering into the ship again departed to the other side. **14** Now the disciples had forgotten to take bread, neither had they in the ship with them more than one loaf. **15** And he charged them, saying, "Take heed, beware of the leaven of the Pharisees, and of the leaven of Herod."[ii] **16** And they reasoned among themselves, saying, "It is because we have no bread." **17** And when Jesus knew it, he saith unto them, "Why reason ye, because ye have no bread? perceive ye not yet, neither understand? have ye your heart yet hardened? **18** Having eyes, see ye not? and having ears, hear ye not? and do ye not remember?[jj] **19** When I brake the five loaves among five thousand, how many baskets full of fragments took ye up?" They say unto

---

[gg] Divers = many (pronounced as "diverse") (FI)

[hh] Verily = truthfully (FI)

[ii] Leaven = yeast used to make bread. (FI) Jesus has just fed 4000 people with just a few loaves of bread, after which he was challenged by the Pharisees. Then, the disciples forget to bring bread aboard the boat, for dinner on the ride home. Jesus builds on a bread motif to make a point about the Pharisees to his disciples: "Be careful that you don't eat the bread of the Pharisees." He also warns them not to "eat" the bread of the followers of Herod. Herod, if you recall, is the king of the Jews.

[jj] Jesus may be alluding to Isaiah 6 again, for the disciples are "hearing without understanding." Rather than grasping Jesus' bread metaphor, they seem to think he is angry because they forgot to bring dinner on the boat! Jesus continues from this point with exasperation. How could they hear all his lessons and see all his miracles and still fail to understand his message?

him, "Twelve." ²⁰ "And when the seven among four thousand, how many baskets full of fragments took ye up?" And they said, "Seven."ᵏᵏ ²¹ And he said unto them, "How is it that ye do not understand?"

²² And he cometh to Bethsaida; and they bring a blind man unto him, and besought him to touch him. ²³ And he took the blind man by the hand, and led him out of the town; and when he had spit on his eyes, and put his hands upon him, he asked him if he saw ought.ˡˡ ²⁴ And he looked up, and said, "I see men as trees, walking." ²⁵ After that he put his hands again upon his eyes, and made him look up: and he was restored, and saw every man clearly. ²⁶ And he sent him away to his house, saying, "Neither go into the town, nor tell it to any in the town."

Foreshadowing

²⁷ And Jesus went out, and his disciples, into the towns of Caesarea Philippi: and by the way he asked his disciples, saying unto them, "Whom do men say that I am?" ²⁸ And they answered, "John the Baptist; but some say, Elias;ᵐᵐ and others, One of the prophets." ²⁹ And he saith unto them, "But whom say ye that I am?" And Peter answereth and saith unto him, "Thou art the Christ." ³⁰ And he charged them that they should tell no man of him.

³¹ And he began to teach them, that the Son of man must suffer many things, and be rejected of the elders, and of the chief priests, and scribes, and be killed, and after three days rise again. ³² And he spake that saying openly. And Peter took him, and began to rebuke him.ⁿⁿ ³³ But when he had turned about and looked on his disciples, he rebuked Peter, saying, "Get thee behind me, Satan: for thou savourest not the things that be of God, but the things that be of men."

³⁴ And when he had called the people unto him with his disciples also, he said unto them, "Whosoever will come after me, let him deny himself, and take up his cross, and follow me.ᵒᵒ ³⁵ For whosoever will save his life shall lose it; but whosoever shall lose his life for my sake and the gospel's, the same shall save it. ³⁶ For what shall it profit a man, if he shall gain the whole world, and lose his own soul? ³⁷ Or what shall a man give in exchange for his soul? ³⁸ Whosoever therefore shall be ashamed of me and of my words in this adulterous and sinful generation; of him also shall the Son of man be ashamed, when he cometh in the glory of his Father with the holy angels."

ᵏᵏ There are two episodes of Jesus feeding large crowds with just a few loaves of bread. You just read the story about 4000 people and 7 loaves. Other gospel writers report an additional episode with 5000 people and 12 loaves. (FI)

ˡˡ Ought = anything (FI)

ᵐᵐ Elias = Elijah, an Old Testament prophet. Elijah never physically died; rather, he was taken up to heaven in a chariot. (FI) The people apparently think that Jesus might be Elijah. Some people think he is the resurrected John the Baptist (who was killed by King Herod in another episode). Jesus wants to know who his disciples think he is.

ⁿⁿ Rebuke him = argue with him. (FI) Peter does not like the idea that Jesus is predicting his defeat and death, neither of which corresponds with the Jewish assumptions about the Christ (messiah).

ᵒᵒ Cross = a Roman method of execution whereby people were tortured and hung out on public display so that passers-by could see what happened to those who violated Roman law. Victims were often forced to carry their own cross to the site of execution. (FI) Jesus is using this as a metaphor, to "take up a cross" and follow him, even unto death. This can also be read as foreshadowing of Jesus' future death.

Mark 9-10

Jesus appears with Moses and Elijah in a miraculous spectacle called the Transfiguration. He heals a demon-possessed boy and a blind man, teaches, blesses children, and continues to predict his own death.

Mark 11

A New Setting: Jerusalem

And when they came nigh to Jerusalem,[pp] unto Bethphage and Bethany, at the mount of Olives, he sendeth forth two of his disciples, ² And saith unto them, "Go your way into the village over against you: and as soon as ye be entered into it, ye shall find a colt tied, whereon never man sat; loose him, and bring him. ³ And if any man say unto you, 'Why do ye this?' say ye that the Lord hath need of him; and straightway he will send him hither." ⁴ And they went their way, and found the colt tied by the door without in a place where two ways met; and they loosed him. ⁵ And certain of them that stood there said unto them, "What do ye, loosing the colt?" ⁶ And they said unto them even as Jesus had commanded: and they let them go. ⁷ And they brought the colt to Jesus, and cast their garments on him; and he sat upon him.

⁸ And many spread their garments in the way: and others cut down branches off the trees, and strawed them in the way.[qq] ⁹ And they that went before, and they that followed, cried, saying, "Hosanna; Blessed is he that cometh in the name of the Lord: ¹⁰ Blessed be the kingdom of our father David, that cometh in the name of the Lord: Hosanna in the highest."[rr]

¹¹ And Jesus entered into Jerusalem, and into the temple: and when he had looked round about upon all things, and now the eventide was come, he went out unto Bethany with the twelve. ¹² And on the morrow, when they were come from Bethany, he was hungry: ¹³ And seeing a fig tree afar off having leaves, he came, if haply[ss] he might find any thing thereon: and when he came to it, he found nothing but leaves; for the time of figs was not yet. ¹⁴ And Jesus answered and said unto it, "No man eat fruit of thee hereafter for ever."[tt] And his disciples heard it.

[pp] Jesus and his disciples have come to Jerusalem to celebrate Passover, the biggest Jewish holiday of the year. Passover refers to the events surrounding Moses' exodus from Egypt, as you learned in Lesson 11 of this text. (FI)

[qq] As Jesus arrives in Jerusalem, people greet him by laying their garments on the ground "red-carpet" style. They also lay down leaf branches in the same fashion. Tradition says that these branches were from palm trees, which are indigenous to the region. This scene inspired what Christians today call Palm Sunday, which occurs one week before Resurrection Sunday, or Easter. The week from Palm Sunday to Easter is called Holy Week in the Christian tradition. (FI)

[rr] "Our father David" = our ancestor King David. Remember that the messiah is supposed to be born in the lineage of David, and Jesus is of this lineage. (FI)

[ss] Haply = luckily, with any luck (FI)

[tt] Jesus is talking to the fig tree. He curses it so it may never bear fruit again, apparently because he is angry that it bears no figs for his breakfast.

15 And they came to Jerusalem: and Jesus went into the temple, and began to cast out them that sold and bought in the temple, and overthrew the tables of the moneychangers, and the seats of them that sold doves;[uu] 16 And would not suffer that any man should carry any vessel through the temple. 17 And he taught, saying unto them, "Is it not written, My house shall be called of all nations the house of prayer? but ye have made it a den of thieves." 18 And the scribes and chief priests heard it, and sought how they might destroy him: for they feared him, because all the people were astonished at his doctrine. 19 And when even was come, he went out of the city.

20 And in the morning, as they passed by, they saw the fig tree dried up from the roots. 21 And Peter calling to remembrance saith unto him, "Master, behold, the fig tree which thou cursedst is withered away." 22 And Jesus answering saith unto them, "Have faith in God. 23 For verily I say unto you, That whosoever shall say unto this mountain, Be thou removed, and be thou cast into the sea; and shall not doubt in his heart, but shall believe that those things which he saith shall come to pass; he shall have whatsoever he saith. 24 Therefore I say unto you, What things soever ye desire, when ye pray, believe that ye receive them, and ye shall have them. 25 And when ye stand praying, forgive, if ye have ought against any:[vv] that your Father also which is in heaven may forgive you your trespasses.[ww] 26 But if ye do not forgive, neither will your Father which is in heaven forgive your trespasses."

[*27-33 Jesus responds to another theological challenge*]

Mark 12

More Foreshadowing
And he began to speak unto them by parables.

"A certain man planted a vineyard, and set an hedge about it, and digged a place for the winefat, and built a tower, and let it out to husbandmen, and went into a far country.[xx] 2 And at the season he sent to the husbandmen a servant, that he might receive from the husbandmen of the fruit of the vineyard. 3 And they caught him, and beat him, and sent him away empty. 4 And again he sent unto them another servant; and at him they cast stones, and wounded him in the head, and sent him away shamefully handled. 5 And again he sent another; and him they killed, and many others; beating some, and killing some. 6 Having yet therefore one son, his wellbeloved, he sent him also last unto them, saying, 'They will reverence my son.' 7 But those husbandmen said among themselves, 'This is the heir; come, let us kill him, and the inheritance shall be ours.' 8 And they took him, and killed him, and cast him out of the vineyard. 9 What shall therefore the

---

[uu] Part of the celebration of Passover would have included a visit to the temple to make a sacrifice to God. (FI) According to the details in this verse, Jesus encounters merchants and bankers who have set up shop in the temple to exchange money and to sell people doves for sacrifice. The implication here – when he calls them "thieves" – is that the merchants and bankers may be cheating people. At the very least, they are attempting to profit off of the people's piety, which angers Jesus. Note that Jesus calls the temple "MY house."

[vv] "If ye have ought against any" = if you have any complaints against anyone (FI)

[ww] Trespasses = violations, sins (FI)

[xx] Vineyard = grape farm, for the purpose of making wine. Winefat = a vat for making wine. Husbandmen = tenant farmers who would live on the land and farm it in exchange for a set percentage of the crops/profits to be paid to the landowner. (FI)

lord of the vineyard do? he will come and destroy the husbandmen, and will give the vineyard unto others. **10** And have ye not read this scripture; 'The stone which the builders rejected is become the head of the corner:'[yy] **11** This was the Lord's doing, and it is marvellous in our eyes?" **12** And they sought to lay hold on him, but feared the people: for they knew that he had spoken the parable against them: and they left him, and went their way.[zz]

A Theme of Spiritual Priorities
13 And they send unto him certain of the Pharisees and of the Herodians, to catch him in his words. **14** And when they were come, they say unto him, "Master, we know that thou art true, and carest for no man: for thou regardest not the person of men, but teachest the way of God in truth: Is it lawful to give tribute to Caesar, or not? **15** Shall we give, or shall we not give?" But he, knowing their hypocrisy, said unto them, "Why tempt ye me? bring me a penny, that I may see it." **16** And they brought it. And he saith unto them, "Whose is this image and superscription?" And they said unto him, "Caesar's." **17** And Jesus answering said unto them, "Render to Caesar the things that are Caesar's, and to God the things that are God's." And they marvelled at him.

[18-27 Jesus responds to another theological challenge]

28 And one of the scribes came, and having heard them reasoning together, and perceiving that he had answered them well, asked him, "Which is the first commandment of all?" **29** And Jesus answered him, "The first of all the commandments is,

Hear, O Israel; The Lord our God is one Lord:
30 And thou shalt love the Lord thy God with all thy heart, and with all thy soul,
and with all thy mind, and with all thy strength: this is the first commandment.[aaa]

31 And the second is like, namely this, 'Thou shalt love thy neighbour as thyself.' There is none other commandment greater than these."[bbb] **32** And the scribe said unto him, "Well, Master, thou hast said the truth: for there is one God; and there is none other but he: **33** And to love him with all the heart, and with all the understanding, and with all the soul, and with all the strength, and to love his neighbour as himself, is more than all whole burnt offerings and sacrifices." **34** And when Jesus saw that he answered discreetly, he said unto him, "Thou art not far from the kingdom of God." And no man after that durst[ccc] ask him any question.

[35-40 Jesus continues to argue against the scribes]

[yy] Jesus is quoting from Psalm 118:22. This is a follow-up point to the vineyard parable.
[zz] The Pharisees are aware that, in the vineyard parable, they are portrayed as the evil husbandmen. They know the story is a threat.
[aaa] Jesus is quoting from Deuteronomy 6:4-5, which is a prayer called the "Shema" in Jewish tradition. This prayer is considered the sum of the Jewish faith. Thus, Jesus is offering a wise and informed answer to the scribe's question.
[bbb] Here, Jesus quotes from Leviticus 19:18. Thus, the complete answer to the scribe comes from quotations of Moses' Law, as given in the Old Testament and discussed in Lessons 10 and 11. Jesus cleverly aligns this commandment about neighborly love with the previously quoted commandment about love for God, which earns the approval of the scribe.
[ccc] Durst = darest, or dared to (FI)

⁴¹ And Jesus sat over against the treasury, and beheld how the people cast money into the treasury: and many that were rich cast in much. ⁴² And there came a certain poor widow, and she threw in two mites, which make a farthing.ᵈᵈᵈ ⁴³ And he called unto him his disciples, and saith unto them, "Verily I say unto you, That this poor widow hath cast more in, than all they which have cast into the treasury: ⁴⁴ For all they did cast in of their abundance; but she of her want did cast in all that she had, even all her living."

Mark 13

Jesus predicts that the temple will one day be destroyed: "Seest thou these great buildings? There shall not be left one stone upon the other, that shall not be thrown down" (13:2). Jesus also describes the future days of persecution and war, and he urges his disciples to be wary.

Mark 14

After two days was the feast of the passover, and of unleavened bread:ᵉᵉᵉ and the chief priests and the scribes sought how they might take him by craft, and put him to death. ² But they said, "Not on the feast day, lest there be an uproar of the people."

³ And being in Bethany in the house of Simon the leper, as he sat at meat, there came a woman having an alabaster box of ointment of spikenard very precious; and she brake the box, and poured it on his head.ᶠᶠᶠ ⁴ And there were some that had indignation within themselves, and said, "Why was this waste of the ointment made? ⁵ For it might have been sold for more than three hundred pence,ᵍᵍᵍ and have been given to the poor. And they murmured against her." ⁶ And Jesus said, "Let her alone; why trouble ye her? she hath wrought a good work on me. ⁷ For ye have the poor with you always, and whensoever ye will ye may do them good: but me ye have not always. ⁸ She hath done what she could: she is come aforehand to anoint my body to the burying.ʰʰʰ ⁹ Verily I say unto you, Wheresoever this gospel shall be preached throughout the whole world, this also that she hath done shall be spoken of for a memorial of her."

ᵈᵈᵈ Mites = coins of small value; even the two mites (equaling a farthing) would value one cent or less by U.S. standards. (WBD)

ᵉᵉᵉ Part of the observance of Passover involves the eating of unleavened bread, which is bread that has not been allowed to rise (leaven means yeast, and yeast causes bread to rise). Unleavened bread, often called matzah, is cracker-like. This is said to commemorate the Jews' exodus from Egypt, when they would have left in a hurry and with no time for allowing their bread dough to rise (see Exodus 12:39). Today, Jewish families still celebrate the feast of unleavened bread, also eating bitter herbs to commemorate the suffering of the Jews in Egypt and wine to celebrate their freedom following Passover. (FI)

ᶠᶠᶠ Spikenard = a flowering plant used to make a perfumed oil used by priests during church liturgy in the Old Testament. (FI) The woman in this story is pouring incense on Jesus' head, which is an act of anointing. Anointment is a religious ritual similar to crowning a king. The woman is not just giving Jesus a gift; she is making a statement about his kingship or messiah identity. It is an act of faith.

ᵍᵍᵍ Three hundred pence = the NIV says this was enough money for more than a year's wages.

ʰʰʰ Dead bodies were also anointed with oil to preserve them and prevent odor. In this way, the anointing of Jesus may be read as further foreshadowing of his death. (FI)

The Action Begins to Turn

10 And Judas Iscariot, one of the twelve, went unto the chief priests, to betray him unto them. **11** And when they heard it, they were glad, and promised to give him money. And he sought how he might conveniently betray him.

12 And the first day of unleavened bread, when they killed the passover,[iii] his disciples said unto him, "Where wilt thou that we go and prepare that thou mayest eat the passover?" **13** And he sendeth forth two of his disciples, and saith unto them, "Go ye into the city, and there shall meet you a man bearing a pitcher of water: follow him. **14** And wheresoever he shall go in, say ye to the goodman[jjj] of the house, 'The Master saith, Where is the guestchamber, where I shall eat the passover with my disciples?'[kkk] **15** And he will shew you a large upper room furnished and prepared: there make ready for us. **16** And his disciples went forth, and came into the city, and found as he had said unto them: and they made ready the passover.

17 And in the evening he cometh with the twelve. **18** And as they sat and did eat, Jesus said, "Verily I say unto you, One of you which eateth with me shall betray me." **19** And they began to be sorrowful, and to say unto him one by one, "Is it I?" and another said, "Is it I?" **20** And he answered and said unto them, "It is one of the twelve, that dippeth with me in the dish.[lll] **21** The Son of man indeed goeth,[mmm] as it is written of him: but woe to that man by whom the Son of man is betrayed! good were it for that man if he had never been born."

22 And as they did eat, Jesus took bread, and blessed, and brake it, and gave to them, and said, "Take, eat: this is my body." **23** And he took the cup, and when he had given thanks, he gave it to them: and they all drank of it. **24** And he said unto them, "This is my blood of the new testament, which is shed for many.[nnn] **25** Verily I say unto you, I will drink no more of the fruit of the vine, until that day that I drink it new in the kingdom of God."

26 And when they had sung an hymn, they went out into the mount of Olives. **27** And Jesus saith unto them, "All ye shall be offended because of me this night:[ooo] for it is written, 'I will smite[ppp] the shepherd, and the sheep shall be scattered.' **28** But after that I am risen, I will go before you

---

[iii] Killed the passover = the killing of a sacrificial lamb for the passover feast, typically done on the first day of the 8-day holiday. (FI)

[jjj] Goodman = owner. (FI)

[kkk] Guestchamber = guest room or lodging place. (BHL) The homeowner would understand that their "Master" would be their rabbi, whom they serve as disciples.

[lll] They are, perhaps, dipping bread into a shared dish of charoset, which is a fruit compote typically served with a Passover meal. To share the same dish is a sign of familial closeness. (BHC-Clarke's Commentary) (FI)

[mmm] Goeth = goes to die (FI)

[nnn] Testament = covenant. Jesus is saying that the wine should be looked upon as a representation of his blood and the symbol of a covenant. If you will recall from Lesson 8, bloodshed was a traditional part of covenant-making in the Old Testament, similar to becoming a "blood brother" or signing a contract in blood. Most Bible translations say "covenant" rather than "testament." There are no words in the original Greek that suggest the English word "new." This symbolic meal of bread and wine is called Communion or the Eucharist by Christians today and is still observed as an important ritual in the worship of Jesus. (FI)

[ooo] Be offended because of me = be ashamed of me (FI)

[ppp] Smite = strike, wound, or kill (depending on the context) (FI)

into Galilee."qqq ²⁹ But Peter said unto him, "Although all shall be offended, yet will not I." ³⁰ And Jesus saith unto him, "Verily I say unto thee, That this day, even in this night, before the cock crow twice, thou shalt deny me thrice." ³¹ But he spake the more vehemently, "If I should die with thee, I will not deny thee in any wise." Likewise also said they all.

³² And they came to a place which was named Gethsemane:rrr and he saith to his disciples, "Sit ye here, while I shall pray." ³³ And he taketh with him Peter and James and John, and began to be sore amazed, and to be very heavy; ³⁴ And saith unto them, "My soul is exceeding sorrowful unto death: tarry ye here, and watch." ³⁵ And he went forward a little, and fell on the ground, and prayed that, if it were possible, the hour might pass from him. ³⁶ And he said, "Abba, Father, all things are possible unto thee; take away this cup from me: nevertheless not what I will, but what thou wilt."

³⁷ And he cometh, and findeth them sleeping, and saith unto Peter, "Simon, sleepest thou? couldest not thou watch one hour? ³⁸ Watch ye and pray, lest ye enter into temptation. The spirit truly is ready, but the flesh is weak." ³⁹ And again he went away, and prayed, and spake the same words. ⁴⁰ And when he returned, he found them asleep again, (for their eyes were heavy,) neither wist they what to answer him. ⁴¹ And he cometh the third time, and saith unto them, "Sleep on now, and take your rest: it is enough, the hour is come; behold, the Son of man is betrayed into the hands of sinners. ⁴² Rise up, let us go; lo, he that betrayeth me is at hand."

Climax: Jesus Arrested and Tried

⁴³ And immediately, while he yet spake, cometh Judas, one of the twelve, and with him a great multitude with swords and staves, from the chief priests and the scribes and the elders. ⁴⁴ And he that betrayed him had given them a token, saying, "Whomsoever I shall kiss, that same is he; take him, and lead him away safely." ⁴⁵ And as soon as he was come, he goeth straightway to him, and saith, "Master, master"; and kissed him. ⁴⁶ And they laid their hands on him, and took him.

⁴⁷ And one of them that stood by drew a sword, and smotesss a servant of the high priest, and cut off his ear. ⁴⁸ And Jesus answered and said unto them, "Are ye come out, as against a thief, with swords and with staves to take me? ⁴⁹ I was daily with you in the temple teaching, and ye took me not: but the scriptures must be fulfilled." ⁵⁰ And they all forsookttt him, and fled.

⁵¹ And there followed him a certain young man, having a linen cloth cast about his naked body; and the young men laid hold on him: ⁵² And he left the linen cloth, and fled from them naked.

---

qqq Once again Jesus is quoting an Old Testament prophet, connecting himself with messiah prophecies. This quote from Zechariah says that when the shepherd gets wounded by God, then the sheep will run away in fear. Jesus is associating himself with the shepherd, and his disciples with the sheep. There are two implications in this metaphor: that Jesus will be killed, and that his disciples will abandon him in fear.

rrr Pronounced Geth-SEM-uh-NEE. This garden and the events that happen here are frequently mentioned in Western literature.

sss Smote = struck, wounded (past tense of smite) (FI)

ttt Forsook = forgot, abandoned (past tense of forsake) (FI)

⁵³ And they led Jesus away to the high priest: and with him were assembled all the chief priests and the elders and the scribes. ⁵⁴ And Peter followed him afar off, even into the palace of the high priest: and he sat with the servants, and warmed himself at the fire.[uuu]

⁵⁵ And the chief priests and all the council sought for witness against Jesus to put him to death; and found none. ⁵⁶ For many bare false witness against him, but their witness agreed not together.[vvv] ⁵⁷ And there arose certain,[www] and bare false witness against him, saying, ⁵⁸ "We heard him say, 'I will destroy this temple that is made with hands, and within three days I will build another made without hands.'" [xxx] ⁵⁹ But neither so did their witness agree together.

⁶⁰ And the high priest stood up in the midst, and asked Jesus, saying, "Answerest thou nothing? what is it which these witness against thee?" ⁶¹ But he held his peace, and answered nothing. Again the high priest asked him, and said unto him, "Art thou the Christ, the Son of the Blessed?" ⁶² And Jesus said, "I am: and ye shall see the Son of man sitting on the right hand of power, and coming in the clouds of heaven." ⁶³ Then the high priest rent[yyy] his clothes, and saith, "What need we any further witnesses? ⁶⁴ Ye have heard the blasphemy: what think ye?" And they all condemned him to be guilty of death. ⁶⁵ And some began to spit on him, and to cover his face, and to buffet him, and to say unto him, "Prophesy": and the servants did strike him with the palms of their hands.[zzz]

⁶⁶ And as Peter was beneath in the palace, there cometh one of the maids of the high priest: ⁶⁷ And when she saw Peter warming himself, she looked upon him, and said, "And thou also wast with Jesus of Nazareth." ⁶⁸ But he denied, saying, "I know not, neither understand I what thou sayest." And he went out into the porch; and the cock crew. ⁶⁹ And a maid saw him again, and began to say to them that stood by, "This is one of them." ⁷⁰ And he denied it again. And a little after, they that stood by said again to Peter, "Surely thou art one of them: for thou art a Galilaean, and thy speech agreeth thereto."[aaaa] ⁷¹ But he began to curse and to swear, saying, "I know not this man of whom ye speak." ⁷² And the second time the cock crew. And Peter called to mind the word that Jesus said unto him, "Before the cock crow twice, thou shalt deny me thrice." And when he thought thereon, he wept.

Mark 15

[uuu] This scene occurs outside the high priest's palace, around a fire in the courtyard, according to the Gospel of Luke
[vvv] Witness = testimony, a statement by a witness in a trial; false witness = false reports about what Jesus said or did. The fact that their witness "agreed not together" means that the testimony against him was contradictory. (FI)
[www] Some people stood up to give false testimony. (EP)
[xxx] Jesus never said that he himself would destroy the temple but that it would be "thrown down" (13:2). To say such a thing would have been a radical and violent threat.
[yyy] Rent his clothes = tore his clothes. For the Jews, this was a gesture expressing either extreme grief or indignation. (FI)
[zzz] Cover his face = to blindfold him; buffet = to beat him; strike him with the palms of their hands = to slap him. All of the actions in this verse suggest mocking. (FI)
[aaaa] They think Peter is a friend of Jesus partly due to his accent, which is clearly Galilean. Jesus is known to be from Galilee.

Falling Action: Jesus Executed

And straightway in the morning the chief priests held a consultation with the elders and scribes and the whole council, and bound Jesus, and carried him away, and delivered him to Pilate.[bbbb] [2] And Pilate asked him, "Art thou the King of the Jews?"[cccc] And he answering said unto them, "Thou sayest it." [3] And the chief priests accused him of many things: but he answered nothing. [4] And Pilate asked him again, saying, "Answerest thou nothing? behold how many things they witness against thee." [5] But Jesus yet answered nothing; so that Pilate marvelled.

[6] Now at that feast he released unto them one prisoner, whomsoever they desired.[dddd] [7] And there was one named Barabbas, which lay bound with them that had made insurrection with him, who had committed murder in the insurrection. [8] And the multitude crying aloud began to desire him to do as he had ever done unto them. [9] But Pilate answered them, saying, "Will ye that I release unto you the King of the Jews?" [10] For he knew that the chief priests had delivered him for envy. [11] But the chief priests moved the people, that he should rather release Barabbas unto them.

[12] And Pilate answered and said again unto them, "What will ye then that I shall do unto him whom ye call the King of the Jews?" [13] And they cried out again, "Crucify him." [14] Then Pilate said unto them, "Why, what evil hath he done?" And they cried out the more exceedingly, "Crucify him." [15] And so Pilate, willing to content the people, released Barabbas unto them, and delivered Jesus, when he had scourged him,[eeee] to be crucified.

[16] And the soldiers led him away into the hall, called Praetorium; and they call together the whole band. [17] And they clothed him with purple, and platted a crown of thorns,[ffff] and put it about his head, [18] And began to salute him, "Hail, King of the Jews!" [19] And they smote him on the head with a reed, and did spit upon him, and bowing their knees worshipped him. [20] And when they had mocked him, they took off the purple from him, and put his own clothes on him, and led him out to crucify him. [21] And they [did] compel one Simon a Cyrenian, who passed by, coming out of the country, the father of Alexander and Rufus, to bear his cross. [22] And they bring him unto the place Golgotha, which is, being interpreted, 'The place of a skull.'

[23] And they gave him to drink wine mingled with myrrh: but he received it not.[gggg] [24] And when they had crucified him, they parted his garments, casting lots upon them,[hhhh] what every man

---

[bbbb] Pontius Pilate was a Roman prefect, similar to a magistrate or judge. Jesus had already been convicted of blasphemy (a religious charge) in the religious court of the Jewish high priest. The priests now hand Jesus over to the local civil authority, hoping to get him executed. Pilate's job is to preserve civil order, so the priests must demonstrate that Jesus is an obstacle to civil peace. (FI)

[cccc] Apparently, the priests have told Pilate that Jesus has claimed to be the King of the Jews, which has political overtones. Of course, we as readers know that Jesus spoke of a spiritual kingdom, not a political one to rival Rome, but the priests' goal is to convince Pilate that Jesus poses a political threat.

[dddd] It appears to be customary that Pilate release one prisoner to the people as a gesture of goodwill during their annual celebration of Passover.

[eeee] Scourged = whipped (FI)

[ffff] Purple is the color of royalty; platted = braided. They are dressing him up as a king and mocking his claim to be King of Jews. (FI)

[gggg] Myrrh = a substance with medicinal qualities. (FI) This was intended as a merciful gesture, to ease Jesus' suffering.

[hhhh] Casting lots = gambling, similar to throwing dice. The soldiers gambled for Jesus' clothes. (FI)

should take. ²⁵ And it was the third hour, and they crucified him. ²⁶ And the superscription of his accusation^iiii was written over, "The King Of The Jews." ²⁷ And with him they crucify two thieves; the one on his right hand, and the other on his left. ²⁸ And the scripture was fulfilled, which saith, "And he was numbered with the transgressors."^jjjj

²⁹ And they that passed by railed on him, wagging their heads, and saying, "Ah, thou that destroyest the temple, and buildest it in three days,^kkkk ³⁰ save thyself, and come down from the cross." ³¹ Likewise also the chief priests mocking said among themselves with the scribes, "He saved others; himself he cannot save. ³² Let Christ the King of Israel descend now from the cross, that we may see and believe." And they that were crucified with him reviled him.^llll

³³ And when the sixth hour was come, there was darkness over the whole land until the ninth hour. ³⁴ And at the ninth hour Jesus cried with a loud voice, saying, "Eloi, Eloi, lama sabachthani?" which is, being interpreted, "My God, my God, why hast thou forsaken me?"^mmmm ³⁵ And some of them that stood by, when they heard it, said, "Behold, he calleth Elias."^nnnn ³⁶ And one ran and filled a spunge full of vinegar,^oooo and put it on a reed, and gave him to drink, saying, "Let alone; let us see whether Elias will come to take him down."

³⁷ And Jesus cried with a loud voice, and gave up the ghost.^pppp ³⁸ And the veil of the temple was rent in twain from the top to the bottom.^qqqq ³⁹ And when the centurion,^rrrr which stood over against him, saw that he so cried out, and gave up the ghost, he said, "Truly this man was the Son of God."

---

^iiii Superscription of his accusation = inscription of the charges against him, i.e., the reason for his execution, so that all who passed by would know his crime and the penalty for committing such a crime. (FI)

^jjjj This is another reference to an Old Testament prophet, specifically Isaiah, in reference to predictions about the messiah.

^kkkk Nowhere in the Gospel of Mark is Jesus quoted as having said this. However, the Gospel of John tells us that Jesus said, "Destroy this temple, and in three days I will raise it up" (John 2:19).

^llll Reviled him = insulted him (FI)

^mmmm Jesus is quoting the opening lines of Psalm 22. You may review this Psalm in Lesson 14 of this text.

^nnnn Elias = Elijah, an Old Testament prophet who never physically died but was taken up to heaven miraculously. Bystanders misunderstand Jesus' cry to "Eloi" (God) to be "Elias." (FI)

^oooo Most translations say "sour wine" rather than vinegar. (FI) Sour wine would have been something consumed by the poor. This could be another gesture of sympathy for Jesus' thirst, or it could be mockery, as no king would drink sour wine.

^pppp Most translations say that Jesus breathed his last breath rather than "gave up the ghost." (FI)

^qqqq In the temple, the most sacred room of all (called the "holy of holies" and into which only the high priest could go) was set apart from the rest of the temple by a blue veil, as designed by God (and dictated through Moses) in Exodus 26. At the moment of Jesus' death, the veil is "rent in twain" (torn in two) from the top to the bottom, which suggests that God himself tore it. The destruction of the veil suggests that the passageway straight into the presence of God has been opened forever, via the death of Jesus. (FI)

^rrrr Centurion = guard, soldier. (FI)

⁴⁰ There were also women looking on afar off: among whom was Mary Magdalene,^ssss and Mary the mother of James the less and of Joses, and Salome; ⁴¹ (Who also, when he was in Galilee, followed him, and ministered unto him;) and many other women which came up with him unto Jerusalem.

⁴² And now when the even was come, because it was the preparation, that is, the day before the sabbath,^tttt ⁴³ Joseph of Arimathaea, an honourable counsellor, which also waited for the kingdom of God, came, and went in boldly unto Pilate, and craved the body of Jesus. ⁴⁴ And Pilate marvelled if he were already dead: and calling unto him the centurion, he asked him whether he had been any while dead. ⁴⁵ And when he knew it of the centurion, he gave the body to Joseph. ⁴⁶ And he bought fine linen, and took him down, and wrapped him in the linen, and laid him in a sepulchre^uuuu which was hewn out of a rock, and rolled a stone unto the door of the sepulchre. ⁴⁷ And Mary Magdalene and Mary the mother of Joseph beheld where he was laid.

Mark 16

Resolution: Jesus Resurrected

And when the sabbath was past, Mary Magdalene, and Mary the mother of James, and Salome, had bought sweet spices, that they might come and anoint him.^vvvv ² And very early in the morning the first day of the week, they came unto the sepulchre at the rising of the sun. ³ And they said among themselves, "Who shall roll us away the stone from the door of the sepulchre?" ⁴ And when they looked, they saw that the stone was rolled away: for it was very great.

⁵ And entering into the sepulchre, they saw a young man sitting on the right side, clothed in a long white garment; and they were affrighted.^wwww ⁶ And he saith unto them, "Be not affrighted: Ye seek Jesus of Nazareth, which was crucified: he is risen; he is not here: behold the place where they laid him. ⁷ But go your way, tell his disciples and Peter that he goeth before you into Galilee: there shall ye see him, as he said unto you." ⁸ And they went out quickly, and fled from the sepulchre; for they trembled and were amazed: neither said they any thing to any man; for they were afraid.

---

^ssss Mary Magdalene was one of Jesus' followers; later in the chapter (9) she is identified as a woman on whom Jesus has performed an exorcism. She is the subject of many extra-biblical legends, many identifying her as an adulteress or prostitute, but the New Testament says none of this. Books such as The DaVinci Code claim that she was Jesus' wife, that they had children, and that the lineage of Jesus is alive and well in the world today. However, the Bible itself contains no indication that Jesus ever married or reproduced. (FI)
^tttt The day of preparation would have been Friday; that is, the day before Saturday (the Sabbath). On Friday, preparations would have been made so that no one would have to work on the Sabbath. (FI)
^uuuu Sepulchre = tomb. (FI)
^vvvv On Sunday (when the Sabbath was past) the same women who had seen him die went to the tomb to anoint him with spices, a standard treatment for dead bodies, similar to embalming. (FI) It is unclear why they would do such a thing after so much time had passed following death – perhaps it was an emotional or spiritual act, or perhaps they had not had time to complete the process before the Sabbath, when they were not supposed to work.
^wwww The man in white seems to be an angel. Other gospels say there was one or two angels at the scene. (FI)

Epilogue[xxxx]

⁹ Now when Jesus was risen early the first day of the week, he appeared first to Mary Magdalene, out of whom he had cast seven devils. ¹⁰ And she went and told them that had been with him, as they mourned and wept. ¹¹ And they, when they had heard that he was alive, and had been seen of her, believed not. — *didn't believe Mary*

[*Tries to prove J isn't dead*]

¹² After that he appeared in another form unto two of them, as they walked, and went into the country. ¹³ And they went and told it unto the residue:[yyyy] neither believed they them. ¹⁴ Afterward he appeared unto the eleven as they sat at meat, and upbraided them with their unbelief and hardness of heart, because they believed not them which had seen him after he was risen.

¹⁵ And he said unto them, "Go ye into all the world, and preach the gospel to every creature.[zzzz] ¹⁶ He that believeth and is baptized shall be saved; but he that believeth not shall be damned.[aaaaa] ¹⁷ And these signs shall follow them that believe; In my name shall they cast out devils; they shall speak with new tongues; ¹⁸ They shall take up serpents; and if they drink any deadly thing, it shall not hurt them; they shall lay hands on the sick, and they shall recover."

¹⁹ So then after the Lord had spoken unto them, he was received up into heaven, [*went to heaven*] and sat on the right hand of God. ²⁰ And they went forth, and preached every where, the Lord working with them, and confirming the word with signs following. Amen. — *sounds like a pastor talking*

Notes

- J has a lot of Influence, people fell on their knees for him
- Romans/scribes don't like him — J bends the rules
- Judas betrayed J for coin

[xxxx] These final 12 verses are believed to be a later addition to the text and not written by Mark himself. The NIV notation is that "the earliest manuscripts and some other ancient witnesses do not have verses 9-20."

[yyyy] Residue = the rest of the disciples, of whom there were now eleven. Other gospels account to the suicide of Judas. (FI)

[zzzz] This sentence, "Go ye into all the world and preach the gospel," is known among Christians as the Great Commission. It is Jesus' commandment that once he leaves the earth, it falls to his followers to spread the good news of his message to all people. (FI) This verse explains why Christians, perhaps more so than most religious groups, believe so heartily in telling people about their beliefs and recruiting converts. This commandment is considered by Evangelical Christians as one of the most important aspects of obeying Jesus; *evangelism* refers to the preaching of the gospel.

[aaaaa] Damned = condemned to hell (in the English tradition). However, the original Greek word translated as "damned" means something closer to "judged" or "deserving of punishment." (FI)

LESSON EIGHTEEN:
A DIFFERENT KIND OF HERO

Mark's style is fast-paced and energetic, like an adventure story or action movie... but that's sure hard to notice when you're reading the King James Version of the Bible. After all, it was translated into English some 400 years ago, and you have to stop half a dozen times per page to grab a dictionary or read footnotes. Even with Mark's frequent use of the words "straightway," "immediately" and "forthwith" (signs that he is going for a brisk narrative pace), English that was written in the days of King James and Shakespeare feels high-brow and plodding to the modern ear. But Mark certainly was not aiming for a high-brow and plodding style. Let's try to remedy that problem with a new approach: in this lesson, we will re-cast the tale as if it were an action movie. We'll leave behind all the *thee's* and *thou's* and try to uncover the vibrant heart of the story. Obviously there are no chase scenes or battles, but what we're looking for is a dramatic edge that doesn't feel as old fashioned as the King James text sounds. In your imagination, you can even dispense of the Roman-era robes and sandals.

OPENING SCENE

A sweeping desert setting with harsh winds and hot sun, a single man walking into focus. He's an oddly intense character, wild-eyed and tan and suitable for the final round of Survivor. About a hundred people follow after him while he points to the horizon and talks about Someone who is coming soon, Someone great. The people mutter amongst themselves – they and their ancestors have been waiting for centuries for this legendary hero to arrive: a rescuer greater than Moses, as they've heard in the prophecies.

This wilderness missionary, John, is standing in a narrow river dunking people under its surface and bringing them back up again as if the dirty water had the power to clean them up, to get them ready to meet their long awaited hero. Then a single figure appears on the horizon, and John goes pale as he recognizes Jesus approaching the river. The people are oblivious as Jesus makes his way through the crowd and asks to be baptized, just like them. A dove alights on his shoulder, and the voice of God booms from the heavens with a thunderclap: "This is my Son." Afterward, to the amazement of the crowd, Jesus walks back into the wilderness, over the horizon, from where he had come.

LEAD ACTOR

Let's get a closer look at the actor playing Jesus. He should be in his late 20's or early 30's, and of Middle Eastern descent – *not* Anglo-Saxon, blond, or blue-eyed. Also, Jesus would have worked as a carpenter for fifteen years at this point in his life, so our actor should be strong and fit. He should have a confident gait, an arresting voice, and a disarming smile. Remember, this was someone who over the course of three years, with no mass media support whatsoever, managed to become regionally famous and beloved by crowds of 5000.

In our next scene, Jesus is at the temple, casually discussing scripture with the scribes and scholars. A muttering, belligerent man comes into the scene, drooling and scratching himself with bloody fingernails. He shouts violently in Latin, and Jesus stops talking. Suddenly the crazed man locks eyes with Jesus. The man's eyes close and his head thrusts backward, a la The Exorcist, and he says: "I know who you are, Jesus of Nazareth! What are you here for?" Jesus simply waves his hand and replies: "Shut up and get out, all of you." The entire theatre reverberates with the man's screams, and a ghostly progression of evil spirits, looking perhaps like dementors from a Harry Potter film, stream out of his mouth. The man is left calm, gently crying on the floor of the temple, and totally healed of all his wounds. Jesus returns to his chat.

MOVIES ABOUT JESUS

Son of God (2014)
Traditional re-telling of the Jesus story with direct quotations from the gospels; edited together from a TV series.
Critics: ★ Audience: ★★★★

The Nativity Story (2006)
Traditional re-telling of the Christmas story, with authentic settings.
Critics: ★★ Audience: ★★★★

The Passion of the Christ (2004)
Graphic dramatization of the final 12 hours in the life of Jesus.
Critics: ★★ Audience: ★★★★

The Last Temptation of Christ (1988)
Controversial and creative depiction of Jesus as a man grappling with his divinity.
Critics: ★★★★ Audience: ★★★★

Godspell (1973)
Film version of Broadway musical; Jesus is depicted as a wandering minstrel in 1970's New York City.
Critics: ★★★ Audience: ★★★

The Greatest Story Ever Told (1965)
Big-budget, three-hour epic featuring an ensemble cast of 1960's movie stars.
Critics: ★★ Audience: ★★★

Ratings from Rotten Tomatoes.com

BAD GUYS AND SPECIAL EFFECTS

Meanwhile, a few gray-haired Pharisees and their henchman scribes excuse themselves from the temple and find a dark alley. *Did you see what this young upstart Jesus did? Did you hear about how he has been showing off on the Sabbath? He's not fond of rules, and he's flaunting it. Did you know that he was never even a student of the scriptures? No, I'm not kidding – he is a small town carpenter who quit his job and is now masquerading as one of us! The people don't know he's an imposter. And get this: he claims to have the authority to forgive sin. How dare he! Keep your eye on this one. He's a disrespectful little upstart, if you ask me.*

In the next scene, picture all the best special effects. Jesus is on a boat, and the winds and waves kick up. The storm starts to get out of hand, but Jesus just pushes his way through the pounding rain to the bow of the boat and screams, "Be still!" Immediately, all noise stops, and the best song from the soundtrack kicks in. We watch a montage of images while the song plays: Jesus handing out fish and bread to a mother and her hungry children; taking on demons face to face; sitting with his disciples, laughing heartily as they share a meal; warmly shaking hands with shady characters who appear to be thieves and prostitutes; and, as the song comes to a close, we see the Pharisees lurking in the background, plotting something with Judas.

VIOLENCE AND BLOOD

By now, Jesus is very popular. Wherever he goes, he draws a crowd – the ancient version of paparazzi and screaming fans. When the city of Jerusalem hears that he is coming there for Passover, everyone jams the streets trying to get a glimpse of his arrival. People start taking off their coats to throw in the dirt, letting Jesus' donkey walk over them as he passes. Jesus enters the city like a true hero, and even the chaos of the crowds is cheerful. He proceeds to the temple, and the camera zooms in on a child who is trying to buy a sacrificial dove with a single coin. The salesman says, no, the cost is five coins. The little boy walks away in tears. Next, the salesman takes five coins from an old man, puts one in the money box, and slides four of them into his pocket. Jesus grabs hold of the table and turns it upside down. "How dare you turn my father's house into a den of thieves?!" he yells at all the vendors, who start to scream and push. The people are confused and afraid, and the ones close enough to see the action stop to stare. Jesus throws, kicks, and upturns one table after another in an unexpected tirade. He climbs on top of the last table and addresses the crowd: "Just wait! One day someone is going to tear this temple down to the ground!" Then he storms down the temple steps and back into the densely packed streets. Some observers applaud, and some are afraid. His disciples follow him with worried expressions on their faces. The Pharisees look at each other and nod.

Our movie gets considerably darker from this point on. The music is dissonant and the camera work is disjointed. Jesus is in a shadowy garden late at night, and he looks scared. Judas greets him with a kiss – the soldiers' signal to grab him. They hustle him off to the palace of the high priest for a secret midnight council meeting. We hear a scribe insist that the hearing take place before sunrise so that the crowd won't intervene in the prisoner's favor. Jesus is thrust into a chair where he silently listens to a stream of seedy witnesses who offer up lies and misquotations that frame him as a dangerous heretic. The chief priest smiles with satisfaction as he orders his soldiers to tie him up and drag him to the Roman magistrate, who has the authority to pronounce a death sentence.

Think about how many great movies come to a climax during an intense courtroom scene. This story has two: the first is full of shadows and whispers, and the second is full of shouts and bloodshed. During these trials our protagonist does not look much like an action hero. Although Mark's storytelling style continues to be fast-paced and dramatic, Jesus fights no battles. He does not offer a single word in his own defense, let alone raise his voice. The fate of our hero seems to conclude with his brutal execution.

HAPPY ENDING?

Three days later, just as Jesus had predicted, several women make their way to his tomb in order to perform the ritual anointing of the corpse with oils and spices. The day prior had been the Sabbath (Saturday), and so their work had been postponed until sunrise on Sunday. This episode of the story is often depicted in churches with a golden sunrise and a glowing angel, but clues in the text suggest that our movie should create a more tense situation. The sun has just come up, so shadows are long and the silence is thick. Three women walk alone through a graveyard, and there is a very real danger of being identified as friends of the executed man, so their hope is no doubt to get in and out without being spotted. They approach the tomb – which should have been sealed tight, but which is suspiciously wide open when they arrive. Tentatively, they enter the small cavern, expecting to see a dead body, but instead they encounter a living, glowing, talking apparition who immediately tells them not to be afraid – all of which suggests that this is a moment of intense fear: these ladies certainly think that they are seeing a ghost.

In the final minutes of our movie, we see Jesus appear to several more people, not as a ghost, but somehow brighter and stronger (like Gandalf the Gray coming back as Gandalf the White). Still, the dark tone continues with weeping, disbelief, scolding, and Jesus' final words spoken of hell and serpents. Then he disappears – in this movie, I imagine it happening with a strike of lightening.

WINNING BY LOSING

Our "action movie" angle highlights something very interesting: a strong protagonist with all the typical man-versus-man and man-versus-society conflicts you might expect from a movie hero, but this hero's game plan is to *win* by *losing*. He completely gives in to his antagonists. He lets the bad guys have their way. The villains do not suffer, even at the end. Jesus carries himself with strength and dignity, and his words cut deeply but his sword does not. Many dramatic heroes of history and fiction fought their battles without violence (like Socrates, Ghandi, Jean Valjean, and Oscar Schindler) but this concept of a completely self-sacrificial lose-to-win strategy is uniquely powerful. So powerful, in fact, that gospel-based symbolism has become a major staple of Western storytelling. Examples include Gandalf, whom we've already mentioned, whose death protected the fellowship of the ring, and Superman (in Superman Returns), who sacrifices himself to save the planet, and Harry Potter, who believes that allowing Voldemort to kill him is the key to his friends' victory. This literary archetype is often called a Christ Figure.

Christ Figures are most often noble protagonists who die for the sake of someone else or for a virtuous principle, and most Christ figures, in some way, are also resurrected. Gandalf the Gray

> **ADDITIONAL CHRIST FIGURES IN BOOKS AND FILM**
>
> **Sydney Carton** in A Tale of Two Cities, by Charles Dickens
>
> **Santiago** in The Old Man and the Sea, by Ernest Hemingway
>
> **Mufasa** in The Lion King
>
> **John Connor** in The Terminator
>
> **E.T.** in E.T. the Extra Terrestrial
>
> **Optimus Prime** in Transformrers
>
> **Walt Kowalski** (Clint Eastwood) in Gran Torino
>
> **Neo** in The Matrix (particularly III)

comes back as Gandalf the White. In <u>Superman Returns</u>, Superman falls through the atmosphere in a cross-formation, and the audience is led to believe that he dies; however, he comes back at the end to bid farewell to Lois Lane. Harry Potter goes into that spooky white train station and then revives to save Hogwarts from Voldemort and the Death Eaters. Additional elements in the Potter stories add to the fullness of the Christ symbolism: his humble beginnings, fulfillment of prophecy, and his inspiring connection to an absent father.

Cultures that have been profoundly affected by the Jesus story have inevitably used Christ Figures throughout their heroic literature. Gandalf, Superman, and Harry Potter are just three of many, many examples. Some Christ figures in literature and film, like Narnia's Aslan, were designed to teach Christian principles, while others follow this Jesus-inspired lose-to-win prototype simply because it is powerful storytelling – a totally new kind of action hero.

QUOTABLE QUOTES

> This Son is a god who died in three hours, with moans, gasps and laments. What kind of a god is that? What is there to inspire in this Son?
>
> Love, said Father Martin.

Pi Patel
Protagonist in <u>Life of Pi</u>
By Yann Martel

> …Atheists are my brothers and sisters of a different faith, and every word they speak speaks of faith. Like me, they go as far as the legs of reason will carry them—and then they leap… Doubt is useful for a while. We must all pass through the garden of Gethsemane. If Christ played with doubt, so must we. If Christ spent an anguished night in prayer, if He burst out from the Cross, "My God, my God, why have you forsaken me?" then surely we are also permitted doubt. But we must move on. To choose doubt as a philosophy of life is akin to choosing immobility as a means of transportation.

Lexi

I'm not sure how I feel being labeled a "sister of a different faith." I really don't have any interest in faith or anything that can't be proven. Please remind me why this material is relevant for someone who is into science and facts, not religion or fantasy or bedtime stories.

Dear Lexi,

Thanks for hanging in there and sticking with the reading assignments. Hopefully, you will find some value in having increased your awareness of the Jesus story and Christian culture. Just to put you in good company, here is a short list of influential writers who are not Christians, but who reference the New Testament in their work – sometimes for critical purposes, and sometimes just because the biblical narrative has some poignant images that artists find useful outside of the religious sphere. At any rate, none of these writers are "preaching the gospel."

- **Ray Bradbury** (self-described "delicatessen religionist"[a]), writer of Fahrenheit 451, a sci-fi classic that includes many biblical allusions as it argues against book censorship.
- **Matt Groening** (agnostic), the man behind the TV show The Simpsons, which has frequent satirical references to numerous Bible stories.
- **Tony Kushner** (non-religious Jew), writer of Angels in America, a play that deals with the intersection of biblical faith and homosexuality.
- **Nic Pizzolato** (self-decribed as "not religious"[b]), creator/writer of the TV show True Detectives, the first season of which features a Christ figure and a variety of religious and skeptical characters.
- **John Steinbeck** (atheist[c]), great American writer of books such as The Grapes of Wrath and East of Eden, both of which contain many significant biblical allusions.

---

[a] Blake, John. "Sci-fi legend Ray Bradbury on God, 'monsters and angels.' CNN Living. 2 Aug. 2010. Web.
[b] Romano, Andrew. "'True Detectives'' Godless Universe..." The Daily Beast. 6 March 2014. Web.
[c] Gaylor, Annie Laurie. "John Steinbeck." Freedom From Religion Foundation. 26 Feb. 1980. Web.

BIBLICAL LITERARY INVENTORY — NARRATIVE

Narrative – The Gospel of Mark

I. Protagonist and Antagonist – Jesus is the protagonist, and there are multiple antagonists. Which antagonist do you think drives the action most consistently, from start to finish?
_____

II. Inciting Incident – What event do you think kicks off Jesus' campaign against his primary antagonist? _____
_____

III. Rising Action – List the major events of the rising action of the story:
_____
_____
_____

IV. Climax – The labels in this textbook identify Jesus' arrest/conviction as the climax of the story. Do you agree? What other point of action might be considered the climax? Why?
_____
_____

V. Falling Action – List the major events of the falling action of the story:
_____
_____
_____

VI. Resolution – Discovery of the resurrection.

VII. Theme – Identify a theme that is illustrated in multiple places in the story:
_____
_____
_____

VIII. Symbolism – Aside from the cross becoming the symbol of Christianity itself, the most famous symbol emerging from this story is perhaps the bread and wine of the Last Supper. Explain: _____
_____
_____

IX. Motif – One obvious motif in this story is that of miracles, particularly those of healing. Do you notice any others? _____
_____
_____
_____

X. Character Development – Look for specific character traits of Jesus that you can match to his words or actions, with chapter/verse citation. Most readers will find an abundance of "nice" traits for Jesus, but don't forget to look for something on the other side of the coin as well – he certainly is not a mild character… consider the temple and the fig tree, for starters.
_____
_____
_____
_____
_____

XI. Narrative Persona – Mark recounts the story of Jesus with a brisk pace, and a focus on miracles and action. There are few calm and peaceful scenes.

XII. Irony, Contrast, Foil and/or Reversals – There is an interesting contrast between Jesus' bold claim to be the almighty Son of God and some of his submissive actions near the end of the story. Explore this idea or another instance of irony, contrast, etc. _____
_____
_____
_____

XIII. Additional Literary Devices – The footnotes point out numerous instances of foreshadowing in the story. List several instances of foreshadowing and explain why you think they are there. _____
_____
_____
_____

XIV. Historical Criticism – Mark has been identified as John Mark, a first century missionary who traveled with Peter (1 Peter 5:13), Paul (Col. 4:10), and Barnabus (Acts 15:39). Ancient church leaders (Clement and others, as mentioned in the sidebar on page 182) attest to this theory. The composition of the book is usually dated around 70 C.E., after a failed Jewish revolt against Rome that resulted in the destruction of the temple in Jerusalem. Textual clues indicate that it was written for a non-Jewish (Gentile) audience, often assumed to be the early Roman church. It is interesting to note that in the year 64 C.E., a Great Fire tore through Rome, during the reign of Nero, and was blamed on the Christians (this according to three secondary sources, including Tacitus, a Roman senator and historian). Some scholars surmise that the Gospel of Mark was written to encourage the persecuted Christian community. If so, then the central theme of Mark's Gospel is bravery and perseverance. Do you see ample evidence of this theme in the text? (If not, then propose an alternate purpose and theme and cite evidence.)

_____
_____
_____
_____
_____

XV. Genre Awareness (select one) –

    ___ Mythology: Symbolically, what does the story reveal about human nature or God?

    ___ Legend / Epic: What themes of Judeo-Christian identity emerge?

    ___ History: What historical events have a practical bearing on the present and future?

    ___ Biography: Why is the subject of the biography worth special attention?

    ___ Drama: What aspects of the play a "hold a mirror up to nature"?

    ___ Short Story: What elements of intentional storytelling contribute to theme and unity?

    ___ Narrative Poetry: Why was the story told via elevated and/or figurative language?

Based on your selection, provide a response to the genre-related question provided above:

_____
_____
_____

LESSON EIGHTEEN STUDY GUIDE

Objective Identification:

John the Baptist, baptism, Jordan River, Pharisees, exorcism, Sabbath, lepers, disciples, Peter, Judas, Jerusalem, Last Supper, Gethsemane, Pontius Pilate, Golgotha (Calvary), Christ Figure

Discussion & Exploration:

1) Recall: Summarize what it means for Jesus to be called the "Christ." Find three different verses where Jesus claims, directly or indirectly, to be the Christ. Find verses where he claims, directly or indirectly, to be the Son of God.

2) Cultural Connections: Select one or two Christ figure characters with which you are familiar, and see if you can identify the elements of their stories which correspond to the sacrificial "lose-to-win" pattern of the Jesus story. Here are some additional Christ figure characteristics:

- Unmarried male
- Association with prophecy
- Association with water and/or the number three
- Miracles
- Humble background or job
- Has disciples or a group of dedicated friends
- Wounded hands and/or outstretched arms (as on a cross)
- Suffering and death (or near-death)
- Resurrection (or apparent resurrection)
- Sacrifices for the lives of others
- Father-son theme

3) Cultural Connections: Can you find a song from your own personal experience that refers to Jesus, Judas, the Jordan River, or any other concrete detail from the Gospel of Mark? See if you can find a song that is secular, not religious.

4) Further Research: Many other world traditions have myths and legends that feature the death and resurrection of a hero. Find one of these stories and share it with your class.

5) Further Research: Research another major world religious figure, like the Buddha and/or Muhammad. Compare him to Jesus in plot and in message. Which story is more profound, in your opinion?

6) Opinion: As you read in the textual footnotes, the last 12 verses of Mark are often debated. It seems that the oldest manuscript copies we have of Mark's Gospel do not include these verses. Several early church fathers and historical sources indicate that ancient Greek manuscripts ended with Mark 16:8. Some scholars have suggested that verses 9-20 were written during the second century, in order to provide a more satisfactory ending to the story. Go back and re-read these passages; if these verses were removed, would the message of the story be changed? What are your opinions about verses 9-20?

7) Opinion: C.S. Lewis is the writer who created Narnia and wrote <u>The Lion, the Witch, and the Wardrobe</u>. What do you think of the quotation from his most famous nonfiction work, <u>Mere Christianity</u>, appearing below? Do you find his argument to be convincing?

QUOTABLE QUOTES

> A man who was merely a man and said the sort of things Jesus said would not be a great moral teacher. He would either be a lunatic — on the level with the man who says he is a poached egg — or else he would be the Devil of Hell. You must make your choice. Either this man was, and is, the Son of God, or else a madman or something worse. You can shut him up for a fool, you can spit at him and kill him as a demon or you can fall at his feet and call him Lord and God, but let us not come with any patronizing nonsense about his being a great human teacher. He has not left that open to us. He did not intend to.

C.S. Lewis
from <u>Mere Christianity</u>

LESSON NINETEEN: CROSS CULTURE

Many of you will readily recognize the above painting by Leonardo da Vinci called <u>The Last Supper</u>. It depicts that final meal shared by Jesus with his disciples in the upper room, right before his arrest. The fame and significance of this image testifies to the cultural potency of the Jesus story. Works of art such as this, as well as music and film and holiday celebrations, are inextricably tied to the gospel narratives. Understanding some of these celebrations and themes will enhance your cultural literacy.

There are several important holidays that are linked to the Jesus story. We've already talked about Christmas as the Christian celebration of Jesus' birth. Easter is the celebration of his resurrection; many churches refer to it, simply, as Resurrection Sunday. Easter is always celebrated on Sunday because the gospel narratives indicate that Jesus' tomb was discovered to be empty on the morning after the Sabbath (Saturday), as you read in Mark 16. The exact date of Easter is a more complicated matter, for Easter is always linked to the dates of Passover (which you read about in Exodus and Lesson 11). It was for Passover that Jesus and his disciples went to Jerusalem in the first place, bringing about the climax of the story. In many languages the words for *Passover* and *Easter* are etymologically linked. Passover, which comes sometimes in March and sometimes in April, is determined by the Hebrew calendar. The Gregorian/Christian calendar (January, February, March...) is a solar calendar, whereas the Hebrew calendar is luni-solar.

Because these calendars differ, the date of Easter on the Gregorian calendar is not constant (unlike Christmas, which always occurs on December 25th). However, the dates for Passover and Easter will always occur very close to one another.

Easter Sunday is always preceded by forty days of Lent, a period in Christian tradition that prepares the faithful for a spiritual contemplation of Jesus' death. You may note the significance of the forty-day designation: the same number is associated with Jesus' temptations in the wilderness, the years of wandering after Exodus, and the days of rain in the great flood. The number forty seems to be associated with finite periods of suffering, followed by salvation or redemption. In the case of Lent, forty days of prayer and fasting are followed by Easter Sunday, which is observed around the world by early morning church services, processions, and celebratory dinners.

Lent begins on Ash Wednesday; on the morning of Ash Wednesday, it is customary for many Christians to attend church and receive a mark of ashes upon the forehead, which signifies the beginning of a period of mourning. The day prior, "Fat Tuesday" or Mardi Gras, is when some Catholic-rooted cultures stage great feasts and festivals, indulging in rich food and drink on the night before beginning their forty-day fast. Some countries refer to this celebration as Carnival.

The final week of Lent, the week leading up to Easter Sunday, is called Holy Week. It begins with Palm Sunday, referring to Jesus' arrival into Jerusalem. Thursday of Holy Week is often called Maundy Thursday. *Maundy* is from the same Latin word as *mandatory* and refers to Jesus' final command

---

HOLY DAYS & CELEBRATIONS

Advent
Period of four Sundays prior to Christmas; a time of preparation marked by lighting candles in an advent wreath

Christmas (December 25)
Commemoration of Jesus' birth in Bethlehem

Epiphany (January 6)
Meaning "appearance," this holiday primarily commemorates Jesus' baptism in the Jordan

Fat Tuesday (Mardi Gras)
The day before Lent begins, typically observed with indulgence

Ash Wednesday / Lent
The first day of Lent, a period of 40 days of fasting prior to Easter

Palm Sunday / Holy week
The Sunday prior to Easter, marking Jesus' entry into Jerusalem and the beginning of Holy Week

Maundy Thursday
Foot washing and communion mark this observance of the Last Supper

Good Friday
Commemoration of Jesus' death

Easter
Commemoration of Jesus' resurrection; Lent fasting ceases

Pentecost
Occurring 40 days after Easter, this holiday commemorates the coming of the Holy Spirit (see Acts 2)

to his disciples at the Last Supper: "that [they] love one another" (John 13:34, not recorded in Mark's gospel). Thus, Maundy Thursday is often observed with ceremonial foot washing, a custom indicating humility and care for one's fellow man. Another tradition associated with the Last Supper is communion, or the *Eucharist*, which is a ritual ceremony of eating bread and drinking wine to signify the sacrifice of Jesus' body and blood on the cross. The Eucharist is reenacted throughout the year in most churches.

The Friday of Jesus' death is called Good Friday, "good" meaning "holy." His death is at the core of the Christian belief system. As you may recall from reading Mark, at the moment that he "gave up the ghost," the curtain to the holiest room of the temple in Jerusalem is said to have been ripped apart, from the top down. Symbolically, this suggests to Christians that Jesus' death permanently opened all barriers between sinful mankind and holy God. For this reason, the most recognizable visual symbol of Christianity is the cross – not the manger or the empty tomb.

Dramas that enact the death of Jesus have been staged across Europe for many centuries and, like the 2004 movie The Passion of the Christ, are called "Passion Plays." In this context, the word *passion* is related to the ancient Greek word for "suffering." The movie received much attention for its realistic depiction of Jesus' crucifixion, and it was also criticized for focusing solely on his violent death while entirely skipping his peaceful lifetime of teaching and healing. However, it should be noted that passion dramas have always been designed to help the audience focus only on Jesus' death and what that death represents.

Jesus' death on the cross ties back to the motif of animal sacrifice in the Old Testament. Let's review some of those sacrifice episodes: 1) Cain and Abel make sacrifices to God, for an unexplained purpose, and only one of them is deemed acceptable. 2) After the flood, Noah makes a sacrifice of thanksgiving, and God promises never to destroy the earth again. 3) Abraham is asked to sacrifice his son Isaac on the mountaintop, but an angel provides a ram at the last minute. 4) Lambs are sacrificed for the first Passover, which saves the Jews from losing their firstborn sons when the angel of death passes over Egypt. Continuing in the tradition of these four Old Testament examples, Jesus on the cross is the sacrificial lamb on an altar. Like all sacrifices from the ancient world, it reminds us that mankind is sinful and in debt to God. Jesus' death is considered by Christians to be the final, ultimate sacrifice – essentially, God sacrificing part of *himself*. This divine sacrifice is the grand finale of sacrifices: "It is finished" said Jesus from the cross, according to John (19:30).

Without the resurrection, however, the story would not be complete. Our protagonist would be very good, but not very triumphant. Jesus' resurrection attests to the Christian belief that God is eternal and all-powerful, and that good triumphs over evil. The celebration of Easter as a holiday of life-affirmation has grown into a secular celebration as well as a religious one. Because the calendar placement of the holiday always occurs near the spring equinox, Easter is associated with spring flowers just as much as Christmas is associated with snow. Thematically, the secular observance of Easter runs parallel to a religious one, the common thread being the idea of renewal and redemption. The eggs that have become synonymous with Easter also tie into the theme of birth and beginnings. Church-going girls get new dresses and white shoes, and anyone who participated in Lent gets to indulge once again in their favorite foods.

These holidays and theological concepts have significantly shaped European and American culture. As a student, you have certainly noticed that your two biggest breaks from school occur at Christmas and Easter. Western commerce thrives on Christmas gifts and Easter baskets. Carnivals, including Mardi Gras, are highlights of the year in places like New Orleans and Rio de Janeiro. Paintings, sculpture, music, and literature based on the gospel narrative include some of the best art in the world. If there is one single-most-influential story in the West, the gospel of Jesus Christ would be it.

LESSON NINETEEN STUDY GUIDE

Key Terms and Names: Easter, Resurrection Sunday, Passover, Gregorian calendar, Lent, Ash Wednesday, Mardi Gras, Holy Week, Maundy Thursday, Good Friday, the cross

Discussion & Exploration:

1) Recall: This lesson makes the case for the cross as the most significant Christian symbol – more important than the manger, the Christmas star, the empty tomb, or even the "Jesus fish" that adorns Christian-themed jewelry and bumper stickers. Summarize the meaning of the cross symbol.

2) Comparison: There is a motif of sacrifice throughout the Bible. From your Old Testament readings, select at least one episode of sacrifice and compare it to the sacrifice of Jesus. Do you think self-sacrifice is indeed the most important spiritual value? If not, which value would you put in first place?

3) Deeper Analysis: The Jesus narrative bears many interesting connections to Old Testament stories and passages, in addition to the sacrifice motif/theme. For each item listed below, see if you can explain the similarity or connection:

- Genesis 3:15
- Abraham and Isaac atop the mountain
- The tenth plague
- Forty days of the flood and 40 years of wilderness wandering
- Jonah's submersion inside the fish
- Psalm 22
- Isaiah 40

4) Cultural Connection: Survey your classmates to see how many of them practice some element of an Easter or Passover tradition, either secular or religious in nature. Are any family traditions particularly unique or creative?

5) Further Research: Look through a book of iconic Western artwork and see how many images are related to the Jesus story. While you're at it, look for other Bible-based scenes. Which are your favorites?

SERMON, EPISTLE & APOCALYPSE

Ye are the light of the world.
A city that is set on a hill cannot be hid.

"THE SERMON ON THE MOUNT"

Matthew 5

The Beatitudes

¹And seeing the multitudes, he went up into a mountain: and when he was set, his disciples came unto him: ²And he opened his mouth, and taught them, saying,

> ³"Blessed are the poor in spirit: for theirs is the kingdom of heaven.
>
> ⁴Blessed are they that mourn: for they shall be comforted.
>
> ⁵Blessed are the meek: for they shall inherit the earth.
>
> ⁶Blessed are they which do hunger and thirst after righteousness: for they shall be filled.
>
> ⁷Blessed are the merciful: for they shall obtain mercy.
>
> ⁸Blessed are the pure in heart: for they shall see God.
>
> ⁹Blessed are the peacemakers: for they shall be called the children of God.
>
> ¹⁰Blessed are they which are persecuted for righteousness' sake:
> for theirs is the kingdom of heaven.
>
> ¹¹Blessed are ye, when men shall revile you, and persecute you, and shall say all manner of evil against you falsely, for my sake.

¹²Rejoice, and be exceeding glad: for great is your reward in heaven: for so persecuted they the prophets which were before you. ¹³Ye are the salt of the earth: but if the salt have lost his savour,[a] wherewith shall it be salted? it is thenceforth good for nothing, but to be cast out, and to be trodden under foot of men.

¹⁴Ye are the light of the world. A city that is set on a hill cannot be hid. ¹⁵Neither do men light a candle, and put it under a bushel, but on a candlestick; and it giveth light unto all that are in the house. ¹⁶Let your light so shine before men, that they may see your good works, and glorify your Father which is in heaven."

Law and Morality

¹⁷Think not that I am come to destroy the law, or the prophets: I am not come to destroy, but to fulfill. ¹⁸For verily I say unto you, till heaven and earth pass, one jot or one tittle shall in no wise pass from the law,[b] till all be fulfilled. ¹⁹Whosoever therefore shall break one of these least commandments, and shall teach men so, he shall be called the least in the kingdom of heaven:

---

[a] Savour = flavor (FI)
[b] Jot = in Greek, the original wording was "one iota," meaning one small word; tittle = translated as "stroke of a pen" in other versions. (BHL)

but whosoever shall do and teach them, the same shall be called great in the kingdom of heaven. ^{20} For I say unto you, that except your righteousness shall exceed the righteousness of the scribes and Pharisees, ye shall in no case enter into the kingdom of heaven.

^{21} Ye have heard that it was said of them of old time, "Thou shalt not kill"[c]; and whosoever shall kill shall be in danger of the judgment: ^{22} But I say unto you, that whosoever is angry with his brother without a cause shall be in danger of the judgment: and whosoever shall say to his brother, "Raca," shall be in danger of the council: but whosoever shall say, "Thou fool," shall be in danger of hell fire.[d]

(5:22-37 additional clarifications of law and morality)

^{38} Ye have heard that it hath been said, "An eye for an eye, and a tooth for a tooth"[e]: ^{39} But I say unto you, that ye resist not evil: but whosoever shall smite thee on thy right cheek, turn to him the other also." ^{40} And if any man will sue thee at the law, and take away thy coat, let him have thy cloak also. ^{41} And whosoever shall compel thee to go a mile, go with him twain.[f] ^{42} Give to him that asketh thee, and from him that would borrow of thee turn not thou away.

^{43} Ye have heard that it hath been said, "Thou shalt love thy neighbour, and hate thine enemy."[g] ^{44} But I say unto you, love your enemies, bless them that curse you, do good to them that hate you, and pray for them which despitefully use you, and persecute you; ^{45} that ye may be the children of your Father which is in heaven: for he maketh his sun to rise on the evil and on the good, and sendeth rain on the just and on the unjust. ^{46} For if ye love them which love you, what reward have ye? do not even the publicans the same?[h] ^{47} And if ye salute your brethren only, what do ye more than others? do not even the publicans so?

^{48} Be ye therefore perfect, even as your Father which is in heaven is perfect.

---

[c] Throughout this segment of his sermon, Jesus quotes from Old Testament law. This of course is a quote from the Ten Commandments. (FI)

[d] Raca = fool. Hell fire = literally, the fire of Gehenna, which refers to the Valley of Hinnon just south of Jerusalem. It was a burial sit for criminals and a place for burning garbage; historically, Gehenna was a place where children were once sacrificed by fire. In Jewish tradition, it was considered a place similar to the Catholic purgatory. Most Christians believe it is an illustration of the eternal fires of hell. (FI)

[e] Again, Jesus quotes from the Old Testament law (Exodus 21:24). You may also recognize this line from Hammurabi's Code, which would have been written several centuries before Moses wrote Exodus. Thus, scholars assume that Moses borrowed this idea from the Sumerians. As discussed in Lesson Six, this principle was a restriction on practices of revenge.

[f] Twain = two. It is believed that there was a Roman law during the time of Jesus that allowed Roman soldiers to force Jewish citizens to carry their belongings for them for one mile. This is the source of the saying "go the extra mile." (FI)

[g] The first part of this verse, about loving your neighbor, comes from the Old Testament law (Leviticus 19:18). The rest of the verse is a casual quotation of what many Jews assumed to be the other side of the coin: that if you are commanded to love only your neighbor, it must be okay to hate your enemies. Jesus counters that assumption here.

[h] Publicans = Roman tax collectors, who were viewed by Jews as corrupt (FI)

Matthew 6

"Take heed that ye do not your alms before men,[i] to be seen of them: otherwise ye have no reward of your Father which is in heaven. ² Therefore when thou doest thine alms, do not sound a trumpet before thee, as the hypocrites do in the synagogues and in the streets, that they may have glory of men. Verily I say unto you, They have their reward. ³ But when thou doest alms, let not thy left hand know what thy right hand doeth: ⁴ that thine alms may be in secret: and thy Father which seeth in secret himself shall reward thee openly.

The Lord's Prayer

⁵ And when thou prayest, thou shalt not be as the hypocrites are: for they love to pray standing in the synagogues and in the corners of the streets, that they may be seen of men. Verily I say unto you, they have their reward. ⁶ But thou, when thou prayest, enter into thy closet, and when thou hast shut thy door, pray to thy Father which is in secret; and thy Father which seeth in secret shall reward thee openly. ⁷ But when ye pray, use not vain repetitions, as the heathen do: for they think that they shall be heard for their much speaking. ⁸ Be not ye therefore like unto them: for your Father knoweth what things ye have need of, before ye ask him. ⁹ After this manner therefore pray ye:

> Our Father which art in heaven, Hallowed be thy name.
>
> ¹⁰ Thy kingdom come, Thy will be done in earth, as it is in heaven.
>
> ¹¹ Give us this day our daily bread.
>
> ¹² And forgive us our debts, as we forgive our debtors.
>
> ¹³ And lead us not into temptation, but deliver us from evil: For thine is the kingdom, and the power, and the glory, for ever. Amen.

(Matthew 6:14-23, continued teachings about religious practices)

Consider the Lilies

²⁴ No man can serve two masters: for either he will hate the one, and love the other; or else he will hold to the one, and despise the other. Ye cannot serve God and mammon.[j] ²⁵ Therefore I say unto you, take no thought for your life, what ye shall eat, or what ye shall drink; nor yet for your body, what ye shall put on. Is not the life more than meat, and the body than raiment?[k]

²⁶ Behold the fowls of the air: for they sow not, neither do they reap, nor gather into barns; yet your heavenly Father feedeth them. Are ye not much better than they? ²⁷ Which of you by taking thought can add one cubit unto his stature?[l] ²⁸ And why take ye thought for raiment? Consider the lilies of the field, how they grow; they toil not, neither do they spin:[m] ²⁹ and yet I say unto

---

[i] Alms = gifts of money for the poor (FI)

[j] Mammon = material wealth (FI)

[k] Raiment = clothing (FI)

[l] Taking thought (*merimnon* in Greek) = being anxious; cubit = a unit of measurement, often translated as "a single hour" in this context; stature (*elikian*) = age, maturity. (BHL)

[m] Spin, as in spin yarn, or make their own clothes (FI)

you, that even Solomon in all his glory was not arrayed like one of these. ³⁰ Wherefore, if God so clothe the grass of the field, which today is, and tomorrow is cast into the oven, shall he not much more clothe you, O ye of little faith?

³¹ Therefore take no thought, saying, "What shall we eat?" or, "What shall we drink?" or, "Wherewithal shall we be clothed?"ⁿ ³² (For after all these things do the Gentiles seek:)ᵒ for your heavenly Father knoweth that ye have need of all these things. ³³ But seek ye first the kingdom of God, and his righteousness; and all these things shall be added unto you. ³⁴ Take therefore no thought for the morrow: for the morrow shall take thought for the things of itself. Sufficient unto the day is the evil thereof.ᵖ

Matthew 7

The Golden Rule
Judge not, that ye be not judged. ² For with what judgment ye judge, ye shall be judged: and with what measure ye mete,ᑫ it shall be measured to you again. ³ And why beholdest thou the moteʳ that is in thy brother's eye, but considerest not the beam that is in thine own eye? ⁴ Or how wilt thou say to thy brother, "Let me pull out the mote out of thine eye"; and, behold, a beam is in thine own eye? ⁵ Thou hypocrite, first cast out the beam out of thine own eye; and then shalt thou see clearly to cast out the mote out of thy brother's eye.

⁶ Give not that which is holy unto the dogs, neither cast ye your pearls before swine, lest they trample them under their feet, and turn again and rend you.ˢ

⁷ Ask, and it shall be given you; seek, and ye shall find; knock, and it shall be opened unto you: ⁸ For every one that asketh receiveth; and he that seeketh findeth; and to him that knocketh it shall be opened. ⁹ Or what man is there of you, whom if his son ask bread, will he give him a stone? ¹⁰ Or if he ask a fish, will he give him a serpent? ¹¹ If ye then, being evil, know how to give good gifts unto your children, how much more shall your Father which is in heaven give good things to them that ask him?

¹² Therefore all things whatsoever ye would that men should do to you, do ye even so to them: for this is the law and the prophets.

¹³ Enter ye in at the strait gate: for wide is the gate, and broad is the way, that leadeth to destruction, and many there be which go in thereat: ¹⁴ Because strait is the gate, and narrow is the way, which leadeth unto life, and few there be that find it. ¹⁵ Beware of false prophets, which come to you in sheep's clothing, but inwardly they are ravening wolves.

ⁿ Wherewithal = with what means (FI)
ᵒ Gentiles = non Jews. This speech was likely made to a Jewish audience. (FI)
ᵖ Sufficient… thereof = Each day has enough trouble of its own. (FI)
ᑫ Mete = measure out, hand out (FI)
ʳ Mote = speck (FI)
ˢ Rend = to tear to pieces (FI)

¹⁶ Ye shall know them by their fruits. Do men gather grapes of thorns, or figs of thistles? ¹⁷ Even so every good tree bringeth forth good fruit; but a corrupt tree bringeth forth evil fruit. ¹⁸ A good tree cannot bring forth evil fruit, neither can a corrupt tree bring forth good fruit. ¹⁹ Every tree that bringeth not forth good fruit is hewn down, and cast into the fire. ²⁰ Wherefore by their fruits ye shall know them.

²¹ Not every one that saith unto me, "Lord, Lord," shall enter into the kingdom of heaven; but he that doeth the will of my Father which is in heaven. ²² Many will say to me in that day, "Lord, Lord, have we not prophesied in thy name? and in thy name have cast out devils? and in thy name done many wonderful works?" ²³ And then will I profess unto them, "I never knew you: depart from me, ye that work iniquity."

Conclusion
²⁴ Therefore whosoever heareth these sayings of mine, and doeth them, I will liken him unto a wise man, which built his house upon a rock: ²⁵ And the rain descended, and the floods came, and the winds blew, and beat upon that house; and it fell not: for it was founded upon a rock. ²⁶ And every one that heareth these sayings of mine, and doeth them not, shall be likened unto a foolish man, which built his house upon the sand: ²⁷ And the rain descended, and the floods came, and the winds blew, and beat upon that house; and it fell: and great was the fall of it.

²⁸ And it came to pass, when Jesus had ended these sayings, the people were astonished at his doctrine: ²⁹ For he taught them as one having authority, and not as the scribes.

LESSON TWENTY:
RHETORIC ON THE MOUNT

Chapters 5-7 of the Gospel of Matthew, although they are excerpted from Jesus' life story in the gospels, are non-narrative in nature. Here, Matthew pauses in his storytelling to capture the most famous preaching episode of Jesus, commonly known as the "Sermon on the Mount." In this lesson, we will explore the structural and rhetorical elements in the sermon as well as some of its most iconic passages and phrases, like "Blessed are the meek," "Consider the lilies," "Judge not lest ye be judged," and "Do unto others as you would have them do unto you."

A MUSICAL OVERTURE

The sermon begins with a passage known to Christians as the Beatitudes. The word "beatitude" is Latin in origin and means, essentially, *happy* or *fortunate*. The Beatitudes establish a theme of spiritual principles that will be carried throughout the entire sermon, functioning as a sort of overture to the entire message. These principles lay out the source of happiness and good fortune. Rhetorically speaking, it is interesting that Jesus begins his talk with an arrangement of words that sounds like a song. Note the obvious parallelism achieved through repetition of the phrase "Blessed are" as well as the balanced structure of each line. It is an artistic prelude, not to mention a positive, inviting introduction. It is somewhat jarring, in that Jesus' definition of a "blessed" life is rather different from what could be described as a "successful" life. In ancient times, it was assumed that a successful life happened as a result of the blessing of the gods. Jesus' description of blessing would have appealed strongly to an audience of common workers.

EVERYDAY IMAGES & SIMPLE METAPHORS

After Jesus' speech has engaged our ears and our hopes, he proceeds to engage our minds with a collection of metaphors, all of which are earthy and common, never "highbrow" or inaccessible to an average audience member. They are designed to help the audience connect everyday images and concepts to spiritual lessons. In these metaphors we find some of the most quotable phrases (and paraphrases) of Jesus: "You are the salt of the earth," "You are the light of the world," "Turn the other cheek," and "Give us this day our daily bread." Daily bread, for instance, is probably representative of both physical and spiritual needs, not just food and drink.

APPEAL TO AUTHORITY

In the second section of the sermon, Jesus reminds his primarily Jewish audience that he does not intend to contradict the Old Testament in any way. This is an important part of establishing credibility with the crowd. As we saw in the Gospel of Mark, Jesus often taught in the temple and would have been viewed as a rabbi, complete with his contingent of disciples. As such, he would not have received any respect from a Jewish audience if he did not demonstrate an agile command of Old Testament texts. When Jesus says "Ye have heard that it was said of them of old time" or "You have heard that it hath been said," he is always prefacing a quote from the Old Testament prophets. During this sermon, Jesus does this six times (some instances which were skipped in our excerpt). Each time, he asserts his knowledge of the Hebrew scriptures and then provides a stricter re-interpretation of each law. In rhetorical terms, this is called an "appeal to authority," and it builds the confidence and trust of his audience.

POETIC PRAYER

Perhaps the best known passage from the Sermon on the Mount is the Lord's Prayer. Like the Beatitudes, the prayer is rhythmic and parallel, featuring qualities of Hebrew poetics as studied in previous passages like Genesis 1, the Psalms, and Proverbs. Rendered in English, particularly in the King James translation, the prayer contains not only parallel structure but also alliteration and off-rhyme: "Thy *king*dom *come*, thy will be *done*." Can you hear the musicality of the word choices? For this reason, the prayer is easy to memorize and easy to chant chorally.

DEDUCTIVE LOGIC & RHETORICAL QUESTIONS

The remainder of the sermon is full of continued metaphors and imagery as well as deductive logic and rhetorical questions. Note how many of Jesus' propositions hinge on the ideas before and after them, forming a ladder of logical thought that leads to spiritual conclusions. These short, logical discourses build simple arguments that a casual audience can digest without having to take notes. Rhetorically, this is achieved with subordinating

> **RHETORICAL DEVICES & STRATEGIES**
>
> **Appeals to Logos:**
> Appeals to authority
> Argument by analogy
> Logic (deductive or inductive)
>
> **Appeals to Pathos:**
> Appeals to desire, pride, fear, etc.
> Rhetorical questions
> Imagery
> Humor through irony or exaggeration
>
> **Appeals to Ethos:**
> Presentation of a speaker's credentials or trustworthiness
>
> **Appeals to the Senses/Memory:**
> Parallelism
> Repetition
> Rhythm

conjunctions like "for," "therefore," "if/then," and "lest." Here is an example: "No man can serve two masters: *for either* he will hate the one, and love the other; *or else* he will hold to the one, and despise the other. Ye cannot serve God and [material wealth]" (6:24). The logic is simple: 1) He states a very simple principle that a First Century listener would immediately agree with, that a servant cannot have two masters. 2) He breaks the problem down into two options. 3) He uses these options to demonstrate a conclusion. This is a three-part deductive argument known as a syllogism.

Often, rather than just laying out an objective argument, Jesus will make just as strong a point by calling his listeners to think for themselves. This is achieved by asking questions that have obvious answers, called rhetorical questions: "Are you not much better than [the birds]?" "Is not the life more than meat, and the body than [clothes]?" Furthermore, the *combination* of rhetorical questions, simple logic, and repetitive musical phrasing helps communicate his points in a memorable and accessible fashion, much like politicians and advertisers do with today's catch phrases and slogans. Jesus' ideas are delivered in bite-size, tightly-constructed, quotable chunks.

APPEALS TO EMOTION

This sermon, as we've already discussed, opened with a warm invitation, an appeal to the audience's desire to be blessed. Throughout the passage, Jesus continues to appeal to natural human emotions, from desire to fear. Aristotle called this an appeal to *pathos,* which occurs when an audience enjoys a speech or feels warmly toward the message, or when they feel anger or fear regarding the speech's antithesis – consider how advertisers cause you to desire a certain product or hate an opposing candidate. Jesus uses both methods in the Sermon on the Mount. In addition to hopeful promises, sometimes he warns his listeners about hell, using the fear of punishment to inspire compliance. You might even say that he flatters his audience when he calls them "the light of the world" and a "city on a hill," perhaps inspiring them, through feelings of pride, to serve God with special diligence due to their special status.

Jesus also uses humor to enhance the sermon… Where, you ask? Consider that humor is often found in exaggeration and incongruity (as discussed in Lesson 13 when even the cows and dogs of Ninevah dress in sackcloth and ashes in a ridiculous display of mourning). It is completely possible that Jesus uses the ridiculous image of a log in your eye – picture it now, a log big enough for your fireplace sticking out of your head – to communicate truth through humor. Immediately after the log image, Jesus speaks of throwing precious pearls to filthy pigs, and then he describes a child who asks his father for bread, and is given a rock. Exaggeration and irony are used to create images that play like silly cartoons. They are highly creative and designed to appeal to the audience through means of humorous entertainment. Keep in mind that this is a long, heavy speech, and humor lightens the tone while still teaching important lessons.

UNIVERSAL PRINCIPLES

You may have noticed that Jesus brings his sermon toward conclusion with a concept common throughout Western culture, what we have come to know as the Golden Rule: "Do unto others as you would have them do unto you." This idea of reciprocity can be found in Christianity, Confucianism, Buddhism, Hinduism, Islam, and humanism. Although the theology of the New Testament is largely focused on the singular idea of Jesus' divinity and sacrificial death, ideas such as the Golden Rule connect Christianity to moral and ethical norms around the world and throughout history. Much (but not all) of what Jesus preaches is just good old fashioned common sense: simple reminders to do what is just and wise and healthy.

CLOSURE

Jesus ends his sermon with a final argument that reflects the best of all his rhetorical strategies. Basically, he says, *Follow these precepts, and your house will stand. Ignore them, and it will fall.* It is metaphorical, built on an everyday image, deductively logical, rhythmically balanced, and emotionally jarring. It is Jesus at his quotable best. And, like all good speeches, the concluding thought brings us back to his introductory thoughts, like a pair of bookends. He began with a poetic invitation to a beautiful, successful spiritual life that promises to bring on the "kingdom of heaven." He ends with a warning about the opposite scenario – what might cause your spiritual house to fall in a worthless heap: "And the rain descended, and the floods came, and the winds blew, and beat upon that house; and it fell: and great was the fall of it" (7:27). He says that if you want to build a heavenly kingdom, you'd better heed his building codes or expect catastrophe.

STUDYING EXPOSITION AND RHETORIC

Before we conclude our study of the sermon, let's treat the text to one more literary sifting with our **Inventory for Exposition**. This is our third and final version of the literary inventory, designed specifically to uncover the unique artistic qualities of expository nonfiction prose, or, in other words, literature that explains an idea. First of all, exposition requires attention to a *main idea* rather than a *plot* or a *theme*. Secondly, attention must be given to the structure of the supporting ideas, because exposition should be organized logically. Finally, analysis of exposition demands more emphasis on audience, occasion, and historical context than do other genres (like narrative and poetry) because it is inextricably linked to its originating situation – explanations are always delivered to a particular audience for a particular reason, and readers outside the intended audience must adjust their interpretations accordingly. For instance, a book about feminine manners written in the 1950's would not be fully relevant to a modern woman; likewise, a letter of parental advice written from a mother to her teenage son would be irrelevant to an old man who received the letter by mistake; and a religious discourse written 2000 years ago for a Jewish or Greek audience could be misunderstood by a 20th Century American. For this reason, our **Inventory for Exposition** combines our historical criticism question with our genre analysis item, since the two are so inextricably linked. As always, a blank copy of this inventory is located in the appendices of this book.

BIBLICAL LITERARY INVENTORY — EXPOSITION

Passage: Sermon on the Mount (excerpts) **Book/Chapter:** Matthew 5-7

I. Speaker and Tone – Jesus is the speaker; his tone is warm but firm. What other adjectives would you use to describe his tone or style? _____

_____

II. Audience and Occasion – Matthew himself provides most of what we need to know about the context of this sermon. It was delivered in the region of Galilee to an audience of people who were suffering from disease and demon-possession (Matthew 4:23-24). Jesus spoke directly to his disciples (5:1) whom he had recruited very recently (4:18-22). It is very early in his ministry, and people are still trying to figure out what sets Jesus apart from other rabbis. Given this scenario, we can presume that everyone in attendance at this sermon needed a basic primer of Jesus' message. Indeed, this is the longest, most cohesive speech recorded in the New Testament, something like a manifesto of Christian morality.

III. Purpose and Main Idea – Simply stated, the purpose of the sermon is <u>to teach</u> the disciples and gathered crowds about the precepts of Jesus' unique message. The sermon takes place as part of a campaign throughout the region of Galilee to "preach the gospel (good news)." Taking a cue from his opening words, the Beatitudes, we might summarize his main idea as "HOW TO BE BLESSED BY GOD."

IV. Structure of Supporting Ideas – The sermon is composed of loosely connected "discourses" (units of discussion) that fall under the main idea of HOW TO BE BLESSED BY GOD: (1) The first discourse lasts for 16 verses, including the Beatitudes, followed by further description of what blessed and godly people should look like in society. (2) The next discourse re-defines key aspects of Old Testament laws and morals, such as murder and divorce. (3) The third discourse, which includes the Lord's Prayer, outlines several spiritual practices including prayer, charity and fasting. (4) Next comes a long section that describes appropriate attitudes and behaviors of believers, including the lily analogy which argues against worrying, and the Golden Rule. (5) The sermon ends on a note of promise and warning – what will happen to those who follow Jesus and those who don't.

V. Rhetorical / Persuasive Devices – Jesus' speech draws in the audience with a pleasant, musical introduction and an appeal to desire. He explains his ideas with everyday metaphors, deductive logic, and rhetorical questions. Furthermore, he appeals to authority as well as humor, fear, and flattery in order to put his audience in a receptive state of mind.

VI. Additional Literary Devices -- Some scholars see Jesus' ascension up the mountain as an allusion to Moses, who gave the first spiritual laws to the Jews atop Mount Sinai. You could also see the mountain as symbolic, bringing the listeners closer to God and giving them a higher perspective.

VII. Historical Criticism / Genre Awareness – Few historians debate the historicity of Jesus, but many scholars debate the intent of his sermons. We can assume that because this sermon was delivered in a Jewish region, his teachings should be interpreted within the context of the Old Testament God, and the Old Testament Messiah prophecies. However, we should also be aware that there would have been other philosophical backdrops for a First Century traveling preacher, namely that of Cynicism. Cynics in the First Century believed in living a simple and virtuous life that was in harmony with nature; they favored poverty, condemned materialistic attitudes, and defied social conventions. There are many quotations from ancient Cynics that closely parallel the teachings of Jesus in the Sermon on the Mount. See how many verses from the Sermon you find that seem aligned with Cynicism; then, see how many verses seem specifically Jewish and/or monotheistic. Based on this sermon (and the gospel narrative), do you think a Cynical interpretation of Jesus is justified? _____

_____
_____
_____
_____

LESSON TWENTY STUDY GUIDE

Objective Identification:

Beatitudes, deductive logic, syllogism, rhetorical question, pathos

Discussion & Exploration:

1) Cultural Connection: When and where have you come across some of the more well-known sayings from this text? For example: the Beatitudes, "salt of the earth," "light of the world," the Lord's Prayer, "conider the lilies," "seek and ye shall find," and a "house upon the sand."

2) Opinion: Do you think Jesus purposefully employed persuasive strategies when he taught? Do you think he rehearsed his delivery? Do you think he was intentionally flattering or humorous?

3) Deeper Analysis: The easy "quotability" of Jesus' teachings have made it possible for people to sometimes speak his words without understanding their contextual meaning. A perfect example is the moment when he supposedly tells his followers to *judge not, lest ye be judged*. This common quotation, as worded here, is actually a mis-quotation. Look up Matthew 7:1-2 in two different Bible translations and note the actual wording of the verse. Then continue reading through the end of the argument (verse 5) and make sure you grasp the full meaning in context. Jesus is not prohibiting judgment here – in fact, think back to how Jesus himself judged the Pharisees in the Gospel of Mark. What is Jesus actually saying about the dangers of judgment and self-righteousness?

4) Further Research and Recall: Look up "rhetoric" and record a full definition of the word. Beneath the definition, list all the rhetorical strategies discussed in this lesson. Then circle or star the two devices that you found most effective or interesting in the Sermon on the Mount.

5) Creative Response: Write a thirty-second advertisement for an everyday product or a political candidate that uses three rhetorical strategies. You might consider applying this exercise to an object from "Bible times." Use the rhetorical devices sidebar as a checklist if you wish.

EXCERPTS FROM THE EPISTLES

I Peter 1

¹Peter, an apostle of Jesus Christ, to the strangers scattered throughout Pontus, Galatia, Cappadocia, Asia, and Bithynia,[t] ² elect according to the foreknowledge of God the Father,[u] through sanctification of the Spirit,[v] unto obedience and sprinkling of the blood of Jesus Christ:[w] Grace unto you, and peace, be multiplied.

³ Blessed be the God and Father of our Lord Jesus Christ, which according to his abundant mercy hath begotten[x] us again unto a lively hope by the resurrection of Jesus Christ from the dead, ⁴ to an inheritance incorruptible, and undefiled, and that fadeth not away, reserved in heaven for you, ⁵ who are kept by the power of God through faith unto salvation ready to be revealed in the last time.

⁶ Wherein[y] ye greatly rejoice, though now for a season, if need be, ye are in heaviness through manifold temptations: ⁷ that the trial of your faith, being much more precious than of gold that perisheth, though it be tried with fire, might be found unto praise and honour and glory at the appearing of Jesus Christ: ⁸ whom having not seen, ye love; in whom, though now ye see him not, yet believing, ye rejoice with joy unspeakable and full of glory: ⁹ receiving the end of your faith, even the salvation of your souls.

¹⁰ Of which salvation the prophets have enquired and searched diligently, who prophesied of the grace that should come unto you:[z] ¹¹ searching what, or what manner of time the Spirit of Christ which was in them did signify, when it testified beforehand the sufferings of Christ, and the glory that should follow. ¹² Unto whom it was revealed, that not unto themselves, but unto us they did minister the things, which are now reported unto you by them that have preached the gospel unto you with the Holy Ghost sent down from heaven; which things the angels desire to look into.

¹³ Wherefore gird up the loins of your mind,[aa] be sober, and hope to the end for the grace that is to be brought unto you at the revelation of Jesus Christ; ¹⁴ as obedient children, not fashioning yourselves according to the former lusts in your ignorance: ¹⁵ but as he which hath called you is holy, so be ye holy in all manner of conversation; ¹⁶ because it is written, "Be ye holy; for I am holy."[bb]

---

[t] These are Roman provinces in Asia Minor
[u] Elect = selected by fate or God's foreknowledge to be followers of Jesus (FI)
[v] Sanctification = purification, being made holy (FI)
[w] The blood of Jesus is often used as a symbol of his sacrificial act and is often referred to as a cleansing agent, i.e. being "washed in the blood."
[x] Begotten = given birth to, created (FI)
[y] Wherein = although (FI)
[z] He is referring to Old Testament messianic prophecies, like those from Isaiah
[aa] Wherefore = therefore. Gird up your loins = put on your pants, prepare yourself. (FI)
[bb] Leviticus 11:14. This line is a quote from Moses' Law.

17 And if ye call on the Father, who without respect of persons judgeth according to every man's work, pass the time of your sojourning here in fear: **18** forasmuch as ye know that ye were not redeemed with corruptible things, as silver and gold, from your vain conversation received by tradition from your fathers; **19** but with the precious blood of Christ, as of a lamb without blemish and without spot: **20** who verily was foreordained before the foundation of the world, but was manifest in these last times for you, **21** who by him do believe in God, that raised him up from the dead, and gave him glory; that your faith and hope might be in God.

22 Seeing ye have purified your souls in obeying the truth through the Spirit unto unfeigned love of the brethren, see that ye love one another with a pure heart fervently: **23** being born again,[cc] not of corruptible seed, but of incorruptible, by the word of God, which liveth and abideth for ever. **24** For all flesh is as grass, and all the glory of man as the flower of grass. The grass withereth, and the flower thereof falleth away: **25** but the word of the Lord endureth for ever. And this is the word which by the gospel is preached unto you.

I Corinthians 13

The Love Passage

1 Though I speak with the tongues[dd] of men and of angels, and have not charity,[ee] I am become as sounding brass, or a tinkling cymbal.[ff] **2** And though I have the gift of prophecy, and understand all mysteries, and all knowledge; and though I have all faith, so that I could remove mountains, and have not charity, I am nothing. **3** And though I bestow all my goods to feed the poor, and though I give my body to be burned,[gg] and have not charity, it profiteth me nothing.

4 Charity suffereth long,[hh] and is kind; charity envieth not; charity vaunteth not itself,[ii] is not puffed up, **5** doth not behave itself unseemly, seeketh not her own, is not easily provoked, thinketh no evil; **6** rejoiceth not in iniquity,[jj] but rejoiceth in the truth; **7** beareth all things, believeth all things, hopeth all things, endureth all things.

8 Charity never faileth: but whether there be prophecies, they shall fail; whether there be tongues, they shall cease; whether there be knowledge, it shall vanish away. **9** For we know in part, and we prophesy in part. **10** But when that which is perfect is come, then that which is in part shall be done away. **11** When I was a child, I spake as a child, I understood as a child, I thought as a child: but when I became a man, I put away childish things. **12** For now we see through a glass, darkly;[kk] but then face to face: now I know in part; but then shall I know even as also I am known. **13** And now abideth faith, hope, charity, these three; but the greatest of these is charity.

[cc] Born again = biblical metaphor for spiritual renewal, redemption, or salvation (FI)

[dd] Tongues = languages (FI)

[ee] The King James translators render the Greek word *agape* as "charity" in this passage. Today, the more familiar translation of this passage uses the word "love." Another synonym might be "goodwill."

[ff] A better translation of this phrase is "noisy gong and clanging cymbal," as found in the NIV. The Greek word *alalazon* which the KJV renders "tinkling," means something closer to "a battle cry." (BHL)

[gg] Christians were often persecuted in Paul's day, sometimes being burned to death. (FI)

[hh] Suffereth long = is patient during troubles (FI)

[ii] Vaunteth not itself = does not boast (FI)

[jj] Iniquity = sin, wrongdoing (FI)

[kk] Glass = a looking glass, or mirror

LESSON TWENTY-ONE:
SINCERELY, PETER & PAUL

An epistle is a formal letter, and the New Testament is composed largely of epistles written from the first Christian missionaries to the early churches across First Century Europe. Epistles echo the themes established by Jesus in the gospels, and they also interpret the theology behind Jesus' biography and teachings. Often, epistles speak directly toward the context of specific early church concerns, for instance, withstanding persecution and living righteously within a pagan empire. In this lesson, we will focus on two selected chapters, presumably written by the two most significant founders of the Christian religion, Saints Peter and Paul.

PETER ON SALVATION

The first excerpt preceding this lesson is attributed to Peter, the disciple you read about in the Gospel of Mark. Because he was a firsthand witness to Jesus' ministry, he was and is revered as one of the most important conveyers of Jesus' message in the early days of Christianity. Catholics recognize him as the first pope. The church in Vatican City, presided over by the pope for 1700 years, is called Saint Peter's Basilica. Peter's writing is more overtly theological than Jesus' Sermon on the Mount because it was written after Jesus' death and resurrection, so Peter is able to interpret those events and put them into a larger religious context. Because Peter was a disciple and apostle, his writings were considered authoritative and thus copied and spread across the region, eventually treated as scripture by Christians.

In Peter's first epistle – written for the Christians living in Roman provinces – we see that he and his readers were suffering from persecution: their faith was being "tried by fire" (1:6). He also describes deep-seated concerns about remaining pure and set apart from pagan culture: he and his followers are in "heaviness through manifold temptations" (1:5) and are exhorted by Peter to "gird up the loins of [their] mind…as obedient children, not fashioning [themselves] according to the former lusts in [their] ignorance" (1:13-14). They are learning to see themselves as distinctly different from not only their Jewish predecessors but also from their Gentile neighbors and relatives. Few Christians at this time were born into the faith – rather, they were converts to a new and politically dangerous religion. So it comes as no surprise that Peter, in the opening chapter of his first letter, addresses the fears of his followers. He acknowledges their trials and challenges and tells them that, through Jesus, there is a promise of hope and salvation. He describes for them a light at the end of a very dark tunnel.

Peter uses the word "salvation" three times in chapter one. He says that salvation is the end result of faith (1:9), that it is connected to the Old Testament messiah prophecies (1:10), and that it will be available in heaven (1:5). It is associated with sanctification (1:2) and holiness (1:15-16) and Jesus Christ's death on the cross (1:19). Peter also uses the phrase "born again" (1:23) as a synonym for salvation – if you've ever seen a street corner evangelist, you have likely read these words painted on a sign and accompanied by a call for sinners to repent and believe. In the context of the epistle's original First Century audience, Peter seems to be telling his readers that even though their bodies will suffer and their minds will struggle, their souls will be saved. Furthermore, a reward of "joy unspeakable" (1:8) will come in the afterlife.

Although modern Christians in the West are no longer the victims of persecution like Peter's first readers, salvation remains a core concept in Christianity. Some denominations believe that Jesus will save believers from hell; others believe that spiritual faith saves humanity from earthly despair. Different churches therefore prescribe different methods for individuals to personally receive salvation – prayer, baptism, righteous living, charity – but the theme of being saved, reborn, and renewed is the common theme of every Christian creed.

PAUL ON LOVE

Another apostle who echoes and interprets Jesus' life is Paul. You did not meet Paul in Mark's gospel, for he was not a disciple. In fact, Paul was a Pharisee! According to several other New Testament books, he was a powerful enemy of the Jesus movement, persecuting and killing Christians until God struck him with a miraculous vision of Jesus and then temporary blindness (Acts 9). After this dramatic conversion, the man once known as Saul was re-named Paul and became one of the most well-travelled missionaries and prolific writers for the cause of Jesus Christ. Paul's epistles form the bulk of the New Testament. His education as a Pharisee and a Roman citizen make him a particularly gifted author, and a close study of his preaching and writing reveals his great rhetorical skill and broad knowledge of Greek literature and Jewish scripture.

We will focus our study of Paul upon one chapter from his first epistle to the Corinthians. Corinth was a bustling Greek port city during Paul's lifetime, featuring temples to the god

Apollo and the goddess Aphrodite. The worship of Aphrodite, the goddess of love, was significant in Corinth. It is interesting to note that the Bible's most famous description of love is written for a Corinthian audience; perhaps Paul had in mind a comparison between Christian ideals of love and Greco-Roman ideals of love, as personified in Aphrodite. Since Paul personifies love in this passage, a comparison is easily justified. According to Paul, love is patient, kind, not envious, and not prideful. This is in stark contrast to Aphrodite, known for many acts of jealousy, pride, and cruelty throughout Greek mythology. It is possible that Paul wished to draw a stark contrast between Christian ideals and popular Hellenistic culture.

Furthermore, the nature of love is another recurrent theme in the New Testament – consider what Jesus said about loving God and loving your neighbor, as well as the words of Peter you just read: "see that ye love one another with a pure heart fervently" (I Peter 1:22). Paul says in I Corinthians 13 that without love, good preaching and good words are worthless. He concludes at the end of the passage that love is the greatest virtue of all. The commandment to love others is perhaps the most significant common ground of all the world's religions. Love makes the world go 'round, as they say! Because of its poetic beauty, this chapter is often called the "love hymn" and is frequently recited at weddings.

PETER AND PAUL ON HEAVEN

Peter and Paul also express one more theme common to all strains of Christianity: anticipation of heaven. Both of the excerpts you read for this lesson in some fashion address the end of the world and the beginning of the next. Peter suggests that earthly suffering is temporary and that the word of God is eternal (1:24-25). Paul talks about a time when perfection will come, when he shall "know even as also I am known" (13:12). He suggests that he will know God in the same way that God knows him, but that in the present time, his earthly knowledge is incomplete. One of the most famous lines from this chapter is in verse 12: "For now we see through a glass, darkly." As indicated in the footnotes, a "glass" is a mirror. Paul is saying that when he (metaphorically) looks at himself, he sees a cloudy image – in contrast to the clarity that will come at the End. In your next lesson, we will take a closer look at the Bible's description of the end of the world. For now, let's apply our literary inventory to Peter and Paul.

BIBLICAL LITERARY INVENTORY — EXPOSITION

Passage: I Peter I

I. Speaker and Tone – _____
_____

II. Audience and Occasion – Re-read the first verse of I Peter and look up I Peter in an encyclopedia or a Bible reference book. To whom was Peter writing? When and why?

_____
_____
_____

III. Purpose and Main Idea – The purpose and main idea of the entire letter are presented in the first chapter: to lay out the basic tenets of Christian beliefs for new Christians across a broad region.

IV. Structure and Supporting Ideas – Peter's first epistle begins by describing the nature of salvation and then moves into exhortation about Christian behavior. He concludes with words of encouragement to churches suffering from persecution.

V. Rhetorical / Persuasive Devices – Peter uses strings of *if's, then's*, and *therefore's* to build his points in a logical progression. He also quotes from the authority of the Old Testament. Do you see any other rhetorical strategies at play? Consider the rhetorical devices discussed in our study of the Sermon on the Mount (Lesson 20). _____
_____
_____

VI. Additional Literary Devices – Peter establishes a direct and confident style with his use of declarative and imperative sentences, almost entirely free of figurative or poetic language. He achieves unity and clarity in his argument through a motif of sacrificial blood.

VII. Historical Criticism / Genre Awareness – It is widely accepted that Peter became a martyr for Christianity during the period of persecution following the Great Fire that reportedly tore through Rome during the reign of Nero (a catastrophe which was blamed on the Christians and caused them to be treated as criminals). What details in I Peter 1 indicate that the author was concerned with issues of persecution? _____
_____
_____

BIBLICAL LITERARY INVENTORY — EXPOSITION

Passage: "The Love Hymn" **Book/Chapter:** I Corinthians 13

I. Speaker and Tone – _____

_____

II. Audience and Occasion – The title of the book indicates the audience of the letter: the church in Corinth. For more information about ancient Corinthians and the occasion of the letter, look up I Corinthians in an encyclopedia, a Bible reference book, or the *Archaeological Study Bible* (NIV). _____

_____

_____

III. Purpose and Main Idea – The purpose of the letter as a whole is to respond to specific issues and questions from the Corinthian church (see I Cor. 7:1). What is the main idea within Paul's discourse on love? _____

_____

_____

IV. Structure and Supporting Ideas – The structure of the letter is topical. The love passage in chapter 13 is part of a larger section on spiritual gifts (12-14) including specific exhortation about the gift of "speaking in tongues" (when the Holy Spirit comes upon someone and inspires them to speak in a foreign language) and the gift of prophecy. Note how the beginning of chapter 13 refers specifically to these two gifts and then comes back to the issues of tongues and prophecies at the end of the chapter as well. Someone with these two gifts would almost certainly have been a preacher, and preachers in Paul's day were always at risk of martyrdom in "flames" (13:3). Paul's points about love fit into the larger topic of spiritual gifts. What is he saying to preachers who have the gifts of "tongues" and prophecy?

_____

_____

_____

V. Rhetorical / Persuasive Devices – Paul is a gifted writer, and he employs artistic strategies in his letter to Corinth; he is particularly poetic during the love discourse. In what ways does he appeal to his audience and strengthen his message rhetorically? _____

VI. Additional Literary Devices – Specifically identify the poetic techniques evident in the passage: _____
_____

VII. Historical Criticism / Genre Awareness – It is common to hear I Corinthians 13 read at weddings, which puts this famous "love hymn" into a romantic context. However, we have discovered that this was not Paul's original context at all. He was writing a letter of instruction to a church located in the midst of a thriving pagan culture, one that was presumably hostile to Christian sects. And he used the Greek word *agape*, which can also be translated as "goodwill" or "brotherly love" (as opposed to the Greek word *eros*, which refers to love in a romantic sense). If Paul were delivering this segment of his letter to a modern audience, he would probably not deliver it to newlyweds. To whom, in a modern context, would Paul most likely deliver this message? Why? _____
_____
_____

LESSON TWENTY-ONE STUDY GUIDE

Objective Identification:
epistle, Saint Peter, pope, Saint Peter's Basilica, Saul, Saint Paul

Subjective Expression:

1) Further Research and Comparison: In this and the previous lesson, much time has been devoted to clarifying the Christian point of view. Select another world religion, do some basic research, and find out how it compares to Christianity in the matter of "salvation" or "redemption." What would someone of this alternative faith do in order to find peace, forgiveness, enlightenment, or approval from God? Which point of view do you prefer?

2) Opinion: How do you feel about Peter's blood motif and the Christian reverence for the shed blood of Jesus? Some people find it to be barbaric. Others see blood as a natural aspect of human mortality, a reality that can't be ignored when putting together a comprehensive philosophy of life. What do you think?

3) Deeper Analysis and Creative Response: Take another look at the Corinthians passage and note its many poetic devices. Re-copy it as if it were a poem, and label the parallelism, the figurative language, and any other poetic devices you notice. Decorate the page with images that complement the content of the passage.

4) Opinion: Do you feel that most churches model Paul's teachings about *agape* well? Give specific examples from your local church or the American Christian community in general, and apply specific points from I Corinthians 13.

5) Further Research: Allusions to the phrase "through a glass darkly" are common in Western culture, and they usually have something to do with mankind's search for truth, or the limited perspective of human beings. Do an Internet search on this phrase along with a *minus sign* followed by the word *bible*, and you will get a list of website mentions of this phrase minus all the sites that mention the Bible. If you are still getting religious sites, add in a "–God" to your search command.

> "through a glass darkly" –bible

In this fashion, you can peruse a sampling of the many places where this phrase is used in a secular context: book titles, names of companies and organizations, news articles, etc. Also, if you search images you can find t-shirts, jewelry, and cartoons that contain the phrase. Find an interesting allusion to "through a glass darkly" and share it with the class. (Obviously you can do the same thing with any famous Bible passage, like "love is patient," and find out how the line has been used in non-biblical contexts.)

EXCERPTS FROM REVELATION

Revelation 1

The Second Coming of Jesus

The Revelation[ll] of Jesus Christ, which God gave unto him, to shew unto his servants things which must shortly come to pass; and he sent and signified it by his angel unto his servant John:[mm] ² who bare record of the word of God, and of the testimony of Jesus Christ, and of all things that he saw. ³ Blessed is he that readeth, and they that hear the words of this prophecy, and keep those things which are written therein: for the time is at hand.

⁴ John to the seven churches which are in Asia: Grace be unto you, and peace, from him which is, and which was, and which is to come; and from the seven Spirits which are before his throne; ⁵ and from Jesus Christ, who is the faithful witness, and the first begotten of the dead, and the prince of the kings of the earth. Unto him that loved us, and washed us from our sins in his own blood, ⁶ and hath made us kings and priests unto God and his Father; to him be glory and dominion for ever and ever. Amen.

> ⁷ Behold, he cometh with clouds;
> and every eye shall see him,
> and they also which pierced him:
> and all kindreds of the earth shall wail because of him.
> Even so, Amen.[nn]

⁸ "I am Alpha and Omega, the beginning and the ending," saith the Lord, "which is, and which was, and which is to come, the Almighty."[oo]

⁹ I John, who also am your brother, and companion in tribulation, and in the kingdom and patience of Jesus Christ, was in the isle that is called Patmos, for the word of God, and for the testimony of Jesus Christ.[pp]

¹⁰ I was in the Spirit on the Lord's day, and heard behind me a great voice, as of a trumpet, ¹¹ saying, "I am Alpha and Omega, the first and the last:" and, "What thou seest, write in a book, and send it unto the seven churches which are in Asia; unto Ephesus, and unto Smyrna, and unto Pergamos, and unto Thyatira, and unto Sardis, and unto Philadelphia, and unto Laodicea."

[ll] The Greek word for Revelation is *Apocalypse* (FI)

[mm] The revelation is being given from God through Jesus, and it is being sent to John via an angel. Keep in mind that John is the primary speaker in this book, but there are quotes from the angel and from Jesus. As with the reading of Isaiah, it may be difficult to sort through the sequence of quotations. Such is the nature of prophecy.

[nn] John is quoting from the prophets Daniel (7:13) and Zechariah (12:10). The quotation after this verse contains the words of Jesus.

[oo] Alpha and Omega = the first and last letters of the Greek alphabet, signifying the beginning and end of the universe. (FI)

[pp] He is in prison on Patmos *because of* [for] the word of God. In other words, he was exiled for preaching the word of God. (FI)

¹² And I turned to see the voice that spake with me. And being turned, I saw seven golden candlesticks; ¹³ and in the midst of the seven candlesticks one like unto the Son of man, clothed with a garment down to the foot, and girt about the paps with a golden girdle.[qq] ¹⁴ His head and his hairs were white like wool, as white as snow; and his eyes were as a flame of fire; ¹⁵ And his feet like unto fine brass, as if they burned in a furnace; and his voice as the sound of many waters. ¹⁶ And he had in his right hand seven stars: and out of his mouth went a sharp two-edged sword: and his countenance was as the sun shineth in his strength.[π]

¹⁷ And when I saw him, I fell at his feet as dead. And he laid his right hand upon me, saying unto me, "Fear not; I am the first and the last: ¹⁸ I am he that liveth, and was dead; and, behold, I am alive for evermore, Amen; and have the keys of hell and of death. ¹⁹ Write the things which thou hast seen, and the things which are, and the things which shall be hereafter; ²⁰ The mystery of the seven stars which thou sawest in my right hand, and the seven golden candlesticks. The seven stars are the angels of the seven churches: and the seven candlesticks which thou sawest are the seven churches."

*Next, John is told to write seven letters to the seven churches. After this, he describes the throne of heaven and a scroll that has been ratified by seven royal seals; Jesus alone has the authority to break the seven seals and does so with an accompaniment of storms and earthquakes and fear upon the earth, ushered in by the **Four Horsemen** of the Apocalypse, and followed by seven angels who sound seven horns that bring more storms, fire, locusts, and plagues. At the seventh horn, John observes a great **Dragon** (identified as Satan) being thrown out of heaven and down to earth, followed by the appearance of two **Beasts**.*

Revelation 13

The Two Beasts
And I stood upon the sand of the sea, and saw a beast rise up out of the sea, having seven heads and ten horns, and upon his horns ten crowns, and upon his heads the name of blasphemy. ² And the beast which I saw was like unto a leopard, and his feet were as the feet of a bear, and his mouth as the mouth of a lion: and the dragon gave him his power, and his seat, and great authority. ³ And I saw one of his heads as it were wounded to death; and his deadly wound was healed: and all the world wondered after the beast.[ss]

⁴ And they worshipped the dragon which gave power unto the beast: and they worshipped the beast, saying, "Who is like unto the beast? Who is able to make war with him?" ⁵ And there was given unto him a mouth speaking great things and blasphemies; and power was given unto him to continue forty and two months. ⁶ And he opened his mouth in blasphemy against God, to blaspheme his name, and his tabernacle, and them that dwell in heaven. ⁷ And it was given unto

---

[qq] Son of man = recurrent phrase used to refer to Jesus, acknowledging his humanity; "girt about the paps" = wrapped around the breast; Jesus is wearing a golden sash. (FI)
[π] Countenance = facial expression (FI)
[ss] The Beast coming up out of the sea with seven heads is often referred to by Christians as a man called the "Antichrist." The word *Antichrist* is derived from other New Testament texts. The Dragon is Satan. (FI)

him to make war with the saints, and to overcome them: and power was given him over all kindreds, and tongues, and nations.[tt] **8** And all that dwell upon the earth shall worship him, whose names are not written in the book of life of the Lamb slain from the foundation of the world.[uu]

9 If any man have an ear, let him hear.

> **10** "He that leadeth into captivity
> shall go into captivity:
> he that killeth with the sword
> must be killed with the sword." [vv]

Here is the patience and the faith of the saints.

11 And I beheld another beast coming up out of the earth; and he had two horns like a lamb, and he spake as a dragon. **12** And he exerciseth all the power of the first beast before him, and causeth the earth and them which dwell therein to worship the first beast, whose deadly wound was healed. **13** And he doeth great wonders, so that he maketh fire come down from heaven on the earth in the sight of men, **14** and deceiveth them that dwell on the earth by the means of those miracles which he had power to do in the sight of the beast; saying to them that dwell on the earth, that they should make an image to the beast, which had the wound by a sword, and did live.

15 And he had power to give life unto the image of the beast, that the image of the beast should both speak, and cause that as many as would not worship the image of the beast should be killed. **16** And he causeth all, both small and great, rich and poor, free and bond, to receive a mark in their right hand, or in their foreheads: **17** And that no man might buy or sell, save he that had the mark, or the name of the beast, or the number of his name.[ww] **18** Here is wisdom. Let him that hath understanding count the number of the beast: for it is the number of a man; and his number is Six hundred threescore and six.[xx]

After the appearance of the two Beasts, John sees seven angels pour out seven bowls of God's wrath upon the earth: disease, water turned into blood, a scorching sun, darkness, and a great battle commonly referred to as **Armageddon.** *The seventh angel then shows him the destruction of a woman known as the Whore of Babylon.*

[tt] Kindreds = ethnicities. Tongues = languages. (FI)
[uu] Book of Life = God's book listing the names of all who are destined for heaven. The Lamb = Jesus. (FI)
[vv] John quotes from the prophets Daniel and Zechariah
[ww] Mark of the Beast = this passage describes how the Beast will physically mark his subjects so that their buying and selling can be controlled, thereby extending his power from religion and politics to the economy as well. (FI)
[xx] Six hundred threescore and six = 666. This number is known as the Number of the Beast and associated with Satan. (FI) Several explanations exist. Archetypally, 6 is the number of man and of imperfection (in contrast with 7, the number of God and perfection), and 3 is a holy number of unity; therefore, three 6's could signify the ultimate unholy trinity of imperfection. Some scholars have suggested that 666 is code for the emperor Nero – each letter of the Greek and Hebrew alphabets had numerical equivalents, and this type of coded numerology was commonly used in the ancient world (it is called *gematria*). John may be inviting informed readers "that hath understanding" to decipher this secret code for Nero, who was the world's first political opponent to Christianity.

Revelation 17:1-11

The Whore of Babylon

And there came one of the seven angels which had the seven vials, and talked with me, saying unto me, "Come hither; I will shew unto thee the judgment of the great whore that sitteth upon many waters: [2] with whom the kings of the earth have committed fornication, and the inhabitants of the earth have been made drunk with the wine of her fornication."

[3] So he carried me away in the spirit into the wilderness: and I saw a woman sit upon a scarlet coloured beast, full of names of blasphemy, having seven heads and ten horns. [4] And the woman was arrayed in purple and scarlet colour, and decked with gold and precious stones and pearls, having a golden cup in her hand full of abominations and filthiness of her fornication: [5] And upon her forehead was a name written, "Mystery, Babylon The Great, The Mother Of Harlots[yy] And Abominations Of The Earth." [6] And I saw the woman drunken with the blood of the saints, and with the blood of the martyrs of Jesus: and when I saw her, I wondered with great admiration.

[7] And the angel said unto me, "Wherefore didst thou marvel? I will tell thee the mystery of the woman, and of the beast that carrieth her, which hath the seven heads and ten horns. [8] The beast that thou sawest was, and is not; and shall ascend out of the bottomless pit, and go into perdition: and they that dwell on the earth shall wonder, whose names were not written in the book of life from the foundation of the world, when they behold the beast that was, and is not, and yet is.[zz]

[9] And here is the mind which hath wisdom. The seven heads are seven mountains, on which the woman sitteth. [10] And there are seven kings: five are fallen, and one is, and the other is not yet come; and when he cometh, he must continue a short space. [11] And the beast that was, and is not, even he is the eighth, and is of the seven, and goeth into perdition."[aaa]

*Following the defeat of the Whore of Babylon, Jesus appears as a warrior on a white horse and defeats the Beast and his armies. He then binds up the Dragon (Satan) for a 1000-year period (which has become known to contemporary theologians as the **Millennium**). At the close of the Millennium, the Dragon and his remaining followers are permanently cast into a lake of fire, and a new heaven and earth come into view.*

[yy] A harlot is a prostitute; Babylon hearkens back to the tower of Babel as well as the great enemy of Israel who brought about the Babylonian Exile. (FI)

[zz] Perdition = damnation. (FI)

[aaa] The seven heads/mountains are directly associated with the seven literal hills upon which Rome was built; the meaning of the seven heads as "kings" is open for debate – some think it refers to seven emperors of Rome including the infamous persecutor, Nero. Some think it refers to seven kingdoms or empires (perhaps Egypt, Assyria, Babylon, Persia and Greece as the five fallen empires, and Rome as the living empire, with the future seventh and eighth undetermined at the time of John). Alternatively, the count of seven could archetypally signify a totality of emperors or empires, with John's historical point of view placed near the end of times (concurrent with number 5 of 7).

Revelation 22

A New Eden and a New Jerusalem

And he shewed me a pure river of water of life, clear as crystal, proceeding out of the throne of God and of the Lamb. ² In the midst of the street of it, and on either side of the river, was there the tree of life, which bare twelve manner of fruits, and yielded her fruit every month: and the leaves of the tree were for the healing of the nations.

³ And there shall be no more curse: but the throne of God and of the Lamb shall be in it; and his servants shall serve him: ⁴ And they shall see his face; and his name shall be in their foreheads. ⁵ And there shall be no night there; and they need no candle, neither light of the sun; for the Lord God giveth them light: and they shall reign for ever and ever.

⁶ And he said unto me, "These sayings are faithful and true: and the Lord God of the holy prophets sent his angel to shew unto his servants the things which must shortly be done. ⁷ Behold, I come quickly: blessed is he that keepeth the sayings of the prophecy of this book." ⁸ And I John saw these things, and heard them. And when I had heard and seen, I fell down to worship before the feet of the angel which shewed me these things.

⁹ Then saith he unto me, "See thou do it not: for I am thy fellowservant, and of thy brethren the prophets,[bbb] and of them which keep the sayings of this book: worship God." ¹⁰ And he saith unto me, "Seal not the sayings of the prophecy of this book: for the time is at hand.[ccc] ¹¹ He that is unjust, let him be unjust still: and he which is filthy, let him be filthy still: and he that is righteous, let him be righteous still: and he that is holy, let him be holy still."

¹² "And, behold, I come quickly; [ddd]and my reward is with me, to give every man according as his work shall be. ¹³ I am Alpha and Omega, the beginning and the end, the first and the last. ¹⁴ Blessed are they that do his commandments,[eee] that they may have right to the tree of life, and may enter in through the gates into the city. ¹⁵ For without are dogs, and sorcerers, and whoremongers, and murderers, and idolaters, and whosoever loveth and maketh a lie.[fff] ¹⁶ I Jesus have sent mine angel to testify unto you these things in the churches. I am the root and the offspring of David, and the bright and morning star."

¹⁷ And the Spirit and the bride say, "Come."[ggg]
And let him that heareth say, "Come."
And let him that is athirst come.

[bbb] The angel does not want John to worship him. He says that he is a fellow servant of God, just like John and the prophets.
[ccc] The angel tells John not to seal this book of revelation closed, as a scroll would have been sealed with clay.
[ddd] Jesus is the speaker here.
[eee] Where the KJV says "do his commandments," the original Greek words say "Blessed are those who wash their robes." (BHL)
[fff] This city is commonly referred to as the New Jerusalem. "Without" should be read as "outside" the city gates. (FI)
[ggg] Spirit = Holy Spirit; bride = the church (throughout the New Testament, the church is often called the bride of Christ) (FI)

And whosoever will, let him take the water of life freely. ⁱ⁸ For I testify unto every man that heareth the words of the prophecy of this book, if any man shall add unto these things, God shall add unto him the plagues that are written in this book: ¹⁹ And if any man shall take away from the words of the book of this prophecy, God shall take away his part out of the book of life, and out of the holy city, and from the things which are written in this book. ʰʰʰ

²⁰ He which testifieth these things saith, "Surely I come quickly."

Amen. Even so, come, Lord Jesus.
²¹ The grace of our Lord Jesus Christ be with you all. Amen.

ʰʰʰ This book = the Book of Revelation, not the entire Bible. Remember, the New Testament had not even been assembled at the time of John's writing.

LESSON TWENTY-TWO:
APOCALYPSE!

"It's the end of the world as we know it, and I feel fine" says the rock band R.E.M. According to <u>The Book of Eli</u>, a 2010 blockbuster adventure film, the world as we know it ends in a nuclear catastrophe, and the only hope for mankind is Denzel Washington, who plays Eli. At the initial writing of this lesson (in 2013) Steve Carell starred in a comedic drama called <u>Looking for a Friend at the End of the World</u> last year, and currently the comedy <u>This is the End</u> is in theatres. This type of literature, be it film or song or novel, is known as *apocalyptic* or *post-apocalyptic*. The word *apocalypse* comes from the Greek, meaning "the revelation of something hidden," and the trend is rooted in the Judeo-Christian tradition of prophesy. Today, the word has come to be associated with the End of Days, or "the end of the world as we know it." Apocalyptic and post-apocalyptic fiction can be a lot of fun, very intense and imaginative, for instance the popular <u>Hunger Games</u> series, set during the brutal aftermath of an apocalyptic war. Other manifestations of the apocalyptic genre include the video game Wasteland, the movie <u>Zombieland</u>, and the classic novella <u>Anthem</u> by Ayn Rand.

The Book of Revelation contains the canonical Christian apocalypse story. It describes the return of Jesus from heaven and the final war on planet earth that ends in the defeat of Satan. Much of the book is written in poetry and contains dramatic, supernatural imagery that is clearly symbolic in nature, for instance the description of Jesus with a sword coming out of his mouth (1:16). Some passages are expressly symbolic, for instance the identification of the seven candlesticks as representative of the seven churches in Asia Minor to whom John was writing (1:4 and 1:20). Furthermore, there is an abundance of literary archetypes throughout the book, including frequent use of the number seven (God's number, signifying totality or perfection) and the number six (mankind's number, symbolizing imperfection) as well as light (candlesticks) and snakes (Dragon and Beast) and the classic Crone or Witch (Whore of Babylon). As in all ancient apocalyptic literature, the complex symbolism is cryptic, and interpretation highly subjective. In fact, Christians of different historical eras have looked at Revelation in a variety of different ways.

Let's begin our survey of interpretations in the year 96, when most scholars believe Revelation was written. The presumed author, John (the disciple of Jesus also credited with writing the Gospel of John), identifies himself in verses 1 and 4 and claims to be recording a prophetic vision. It is encased in a letter written to seven churches in Asia Minor, his primary preaching territory. In verse 9 he says he is on the Island of Patmos, presumably exiled there due to illegal preaching of the Christian gospel within the Roman Empire.

ORIGINAL AUDIENCE

First of all, the Emperor Nero (54-68 C.E.) was well known for his flagrant persecution of Christians. Domitian, the emperor in power at the time Revelation was written, did not have the same reputation for persecution, but the cult of emperor worship was alive and well and in direct opposition to Christianity. According to the text, John himself was in prison because of his faith. The Christian community certainly viewed Rome as a threat and the Roman Empire as the antithesis of God's kingdom on earth. John's "Whore of Babylon" is clearly a symbol of Rome: "that great city, which reigneth over the kings of the earth" (17:18) and which was in fact built upon seven literal hills, identified in the King James text as "seven mountains" (17:9). The seven-headed beast that rises from the sea was likely associated with Roman emperors including Nero and Domitian: "the Dragon [Satan] gave [the Beast from the sea] his power, and his seat, and great authority" (13:2) in which case the beast from the land would have been a priest or provincial governor who required "the earth and them which dwell therein to worship the first beast" (13:12). The original readers – those letter recipients in the seven churches – therefore interpreted Revelation as a story about the inevitable destruction of the Roman Empire, the dissolution of which they assumed would signal the end of the world, and they read the book as a warning to be faithful and an encouragement to be patient. They clearly believed that the events of Revelation "must shortly come to pass" (1:1) and that "the time [was] at hand" (1:3).

Well, as we know now, apocalyptic events did not come to pass as Revelation's original readers believed they would. Rome fell, but it was about four centuries later than expected, and the world did not come to an end. Furthermore, Rome eventually became the seat of the Catholic Church. Thus, for many Christians of latter eras, the Book of Revelation required new interpretations.

MIDDLE AGES

Theologians in the early Middle Ages thought that the Whore of Babylon referred only to *pagan* Rome (not *Catholic* Rome). Dramatic events like the bubonic plague and the invasions of Genghis Khan's horsemen were interpreted as signs of the coming apocalypse. The Millennium was taken to be the "era of the church," during which time Satan was being restrained so that the gospel could be spread worldwide. Although many people expected the world to literally end in the year 1000, many church scholars including Saint Augustine believed that the stories in Revelation were purely allegorical, that the Millennial designation of 1000 years simply represented an epoch of time, and that the plagues and battles of Revelation were metaphors for the individual spiritual struggles of everyday Christians.

RENAISSANCE

Once the Reformation got underway, Protestant Christians began to identify the Whore of Babylon as the Roman Catholic Church, and the first Beast (the Antichrist) as the Pope. After the Reformation, perspectives on Revelation became highly political, pitting the Catholic and Anglican "Beasts" against the truly righteous Puritans, who saw themselves as aligned with the New Jerusalem. Furthermore, during the scientific revolution, the authority of the Bible was often extended from spiritual matters to natural and scientific matters, resulting in controversies like the trial of Galileo, during which the Bible was used to insist that the earth did not move around the sun but remained stationary, as described in the Psalms: "the world…shall not be moved" (96:10).

REVELATION GLOSSARY

Dragon = Satan, aligned with the Serpent from Genesis

The (First) Beast = from the sea, with seven heads aligned with the seven hills of Rome, seven Roman emperors, and/or seven pagan empires

Second Beast = from the land; serves the first one and enforces worship

666 = the number of the Beast

Mark of the Beast = required by the second Beast as a means of economic control

Antichrist = the Beast

Whore of Babylon = originally symbolized Rome, with an allusion to Israel's ancient foe, Babylon

Armageddon = the final climactic battle on earth, in which Satan's forces are conquered

Millennium = a 1000-year period during which time Satan is temporarily bound up and after which he is eternally defeated by Jesus

AMERICAN REVOLUTION

Rhetoric based on the Book of Revelation fueled the American rebellion in that the Mark of the Beast was associated with the Stamp Act; King George was identified as the Antichrist; and the new nation itself was conceived as the Millennial kingdom. However, by the 19th Century it became fully apparent that the Millennium, if taken literally, could not possibly correspond to past or ongoing church history (since the church was well over 1000 years old) and must therefore be understood as a prophecy yet-to-be-fulfilled. Thus, many Christians within the last two centuries have identified the images of Revelation as future events that will take place after Jesus' literal return to earth, through the clouds, as vividly described in Revelation 1.

TODAY

Many events of the past century have supported the perspective that we are currently living in the End Times, as described in Revelation and other biblical books of prophecy. For instance, Isaiah 66:8 suggests that the nation of Zion will be "born at once," and thus when the State of Israel was established in 1948, many Christians saw this as direct confirmation of prophetic truth. For biblical literalists, the proliferation of weapons of mass destruction and the development of technology that could potentially track all human movement (Internet, GPS, bio-chips) seems to lay the groundwork for Revelation's global warfare narrative and the Mark of the Beast. As examples of this trend, we may consider that the "Y2K" frenzy was largely apocalyptic in nature, and that Tim LaHaye's best-selling Left Behind series also speaks to a literal and imminent expectation of the apocalypse.

TIMELESS LITERARY QUALITIES

Modern readers thus have a broad variety of opinions to choose from when interpreting Revelation: historical, literal, allegorical, political, literary, or even psychologically archetypal. Whatever your interpretation might be, Revelation obviously functions as a final bookend for the entire biblical library, with the first bookend being, of course, Genesis. Note the significant reappearance of the Tree of Life from the Garden of Eden. Also, the Bible starts with seven days of creation and concludes with seven angels who show John the apocalypse. Genesis 3 tells us that a Serpent will be crushed, and Revelation 20 describes the defeat of the Dragon. With this big picture in mind, we might say that Genesis is the Bible's exposition, Revelation is its resolution, and the gospels function as the climax upon which the entire Christian story hinges. Chapter 22 is not a bad way to wrap up one of the most powerful books in the world: "the leaves of the tree were for the healing of the nations. And there shall be no more curse: but the throne of God and of the Lamb shall be in it; and his servants shall serve him" (22). The End.

BIBLICAL LITERARY INVENTORY — EXPOSITION

Passage: Revelation 1

I. Speaker and Tone – John is the primary speaker, although there are many quotations from an angel (who provides the vision) and Jesus (who is in the vision). What tone does John take overall? _____

_____

II. Audience and Occasion – John claims to have received a vision from God and is writing his document from prison on the island of Patmos, where he is being held for the crime of Christian preaching. His audience is the seven churches established in Asia Minor (currently Turkey). As you know, seven is an archetypal number, perhaps suggesting that the audience is God's Church in its entirety. In fact, a seven-branched menorah has long been recognized as a symbol of Israel and Judaism (a Hanukkah menorah uses 9 branches). What else do you know about the situation of thee Christians in Nero's and Domitian's Rome? _____

_____

_____

III. Purpose and Main Idea – Why do you think John wrote such a highly-symbolic letter to the churches that he had pastored? What do you think he most wanted to communicate to them?

_____

_____

IV. Structure and Supporting Ideas – Most critics see seven distinct sections within the Book of Revelation: 1) Prologue and seven churches/candlesticks 2) Vision of heaven and the seven seals on the scroll held by Jesus, 3) Seven trumpets, which announce the wrath of God, 4) Dragon and Beasts, 5) Seven bowls/plagues, which run parallel to the trumpets and "pour" judgment upon earth, 6) Babylon falls, and 7) Triumph in New Jerusalem.

V. Rhetorical / Persuasive Devices – The primary communicative device in Revelation 1 is the bold, supernatural imagery. How would you describe the emotional impact of the way John portrays Jesus? _____

_____

VI. Additional Literary Devices – Secondary to the imagery is the use of archetype. Find and explain one or more examples of archetype in chapter 1: _____

_____

VII. Historical Criticism – Revelation has been interpreted differently in each successive era of the church, each one expecting that Jesus' return and the end of the world was imminent. Given the symbolism of the seven hills and the Whore of Babylon, we can safely assume that John intended his readers to see the Roman Empire as the antagonist of his vision. If you were reading Revelation from your home in Ephesus in the year 100, what would you believe John's meaning to be? What sort of impact do you think he wanted to make upon you and your local church?

_____

_____

_____

_____

VIII. Genre Awareness – The Book of Revelation is actually a unique combination of apocalypse, epistle, and prophecy. We could just as easily have applied the **Inventory for Narrative** to your reading, although we did not read the entire story, only the beginning, middle, and end. Even so, can you identify the protagonist(s), antagonist(s), conflict, and resolution of the story? You might want to take your cues from the summative structural list in item IV.

_____

_____

_____

_____

LESSON TWENTY-TWO STUDY GUIDE

Objective Identification: apocalypse, Patmos, Whore of Babylon, the Beast, the Mark of the Beast, 666, the Antichrist, Armageddon, Millennium

Subjective Expression:

1) Cultural Connections: Where have you seen or heard of the number 666? Can you remember the two explanations for the meaning of this number?

2) Cultural Connections: Describe an apocalyptic book, movie, or TV show that you have seen. How does it explain the end of the world? Additional suggestions: <u>The Restaurant at the End of the Universe</u> (book), <u>Planet of the Apes</u> (movie), <u>Dark Angel</u> (TV), <u>The Walking Dead</u> (TV), and <u>I Am Legend</u> (movie).

3) Creative Response: Create a color drawing or painting of the images you read in our Revelation excerpts. Alternatively, you could make up your own version of how you envision the eventual end of planet earth. Your artwork should use color and style to capture a distinct mood. Don't worry about being too realistic. After all, Revelation is very symbolic, and your work can be representational as well.

4) Opinion: How do you interpret the Book of Revelation? Do you think John experienced an actual vision from God, or do you think John composed his story using evocative imagery and encoded symbolism? Do you think it's a spiritual allegory or a literal prediction of End Times?

QUOTABLE QUOTES

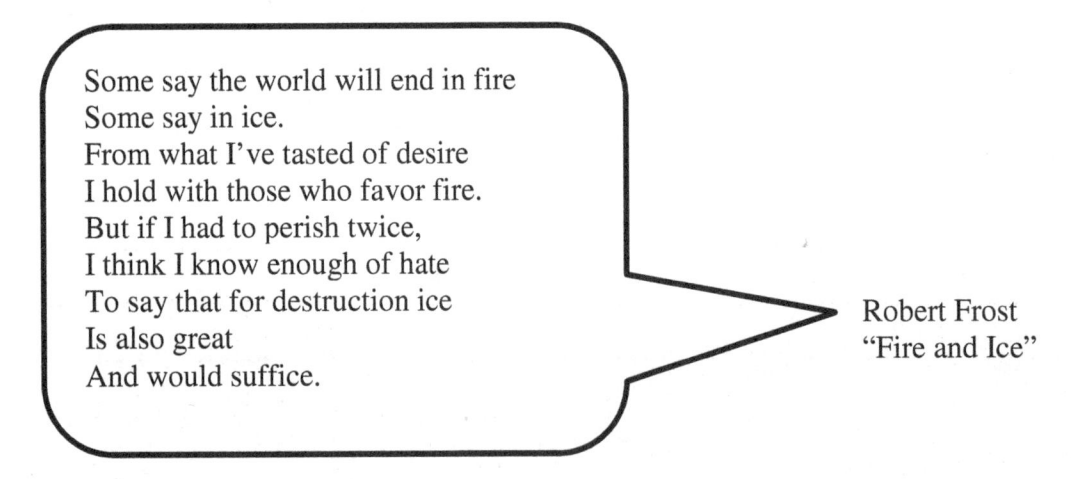

> Some say the world will end in fire
> Some say in ice.
> From what I've tasted of desire
> I hold with those who favor fire.
> But if I had to perish twice,
> I think I know enough of hate
> To say that for destruction ice
> Is also great
> And would suffice.

Robert Frost
"Fire and Ice"

LITERARY INVENTORIES & APPENDICES

BIBLICAL LITERARY INVENTORY / NARRATIVE

Story – _____ Book/Chapters – _____

I. Protagonist and Antagonist – _____
_____

II. Inciting Incident – _____
_____

III. Rising Action – _____
_____

IV. Climax – _____
_____

V. Falling Action – _____
_____

VI. Resolution – _____
_____

VII. Theme – _____
_____
_____
_____

VIII. Symbolism – _____
_____
_____
_____

IX. Motif – _____
_____
_____
_____

X. Character Development - _____
_____
_____
_____
_____

XI. Narrative Persona – _____
_____
_____

XII. Irony, Contrast, Foil and/or Reversals – _____
_____
_____

XIII. Additional Literary Devices – _____
_____
_____
_____
_____

XIV. Historical Criticism – _____
_____
_____
_____
_____
_____
_____

XV. Genre Awareness (select one) –

　　　___ Mythology: Symbolically, what does the story reveal about human nature or God?

　　　___ Legend / Epic: What themes of Judeo-Christian identity emerge?

　　　___ History: What historical events have a practical bearing on the present and future?

　　　___ Biography: Why is the subject of the biography worth special attention?

　　　___ Drama: What aspects of the play a "hold a mirror up to nature"?

　　　___ Short Story: What elements of intentional storytelling contribute to theme and unity?

　　　___ Narrative Poetry: Why was the story told via elevated and/or figurative language?

_____
_____
_____
_____

BIBLICAL LITERARY INVENTORY / POETRY

Poem: _____ Book/Chapter: _____

I. Imagery and Mood – _____

_____

_____

_____

_____

_____

II. Persona and Tone – _____

_____

_____

_____

III. Interpretation of Figurative Language and/or Analysis of Diction – _____

_____

_____

_____

_____

_____

IV. Structure and Movement – _____

_____

_____

_____

V. Theme – _____

_____

_____

_____

VI. Additional Literary Devices – _____

_____

_____

_____

VII. Historical Criticism – _____
_____
_____
_____
_____
_____

VIII. Genre Awareness (select one) –

    _____ **Lyric Poetry** (expressing personal emotions of the speaker): Can you relate to the emotions of the speaker? How do the speaker's emotions interact with his faith?

    _____ **Prophetic Poetry** (spoken on behalf of God as a call to faith and/or action; frequently cryptic): What warning, promise, or prediction is being proclaimed to whom?

    _____ **Narrative Poetry** (a story set down in poetic lines rather than prose): Why do you think the storyteller chose elevated, poetic language for the telling of this particular story?

    _____ **Proverbs** (short, wise, folk sayings heavy in figurative language, imagery and/or parallelism): How does this reflect universal truth and/or faith-based common sense?

_____
_____
_____
_____
_____

NOTES ABOUT IDENTIFYING AND ANALYZING POETRY

Poetic passages are often figurative in nature; therefore, you should often consider a non-literal interpretation for poetic passages. Poetry is also intentionally precise in diction; therefore, an especially close look at word choice is merited.

A portion of text suitable for poetic analysis should display two out of three of the following qualities:

1) Written in poetic **lines**, not paragraphs

2) Features significant **repetition** and/or **parallel structure**, producing a **musical rhythm**

3) Uses a significant amount of **figurative language**: metaphor, simile, personification

BIBLICAL LITERARY INVENTORY / EXPOSITION

Passage: _____ Book/Chapter: _____

I. Speaker and Tone – _____

_____
_____
_____

II. Audience and Occasion – _____

_____
_____
_____
_____
_____
_____
_____

III. Purpose and Main Idea – _____

_____
_____
_____
_____
_____
_____

IV. Structure and Supporting Ideas – _____

_____
_____
_____
_____
_____

V. Rhetorical / Persuasive Devices – _____

_____
_____

VI. Additional Literary Devices – _____

VII. Historical Criticism – _____

VII. Genre Awareness – Our focus on expository prose is already a fairly specific genre label; within this category you will find **epistles, sermons** (within the gospel narratives), and the Old Testament **laws**. For an enhanced appreciation of expository genres, particular attention to historical criticism is recommended.

TYPES OF RHETORICAL DEVICES

- Appeals to authority
- Argument by analogy (metaphors and similes included)
- Logic (deductive or inductive)
- Appeals to desire, pride, fear, etc. (pathos)
- Rhetorical questions
- Imagery
- Humor through irony or exaggeration
- Parallelism, repetition, rhythm

APPEARANCE/FORMAT OF THE BIBLICAL TEXT

The biblical text in this textbook comes word-for-word from the King James Version of the Holy Bible. All biblical text appears in single-space paragraphs, unlike the 1.5 spacing of lessons and inventories.

Paragraph breaks and section titles were inserted by the author/editor of this textbook, Caryn Kirk. She also provided original section titles, which appear in bold. The King James translators provided neither of these helpful conventions. They were added for ease of reading.

The author/editor also added quotation marks as needed to designate secondary speakers. Capital letters from the beginnings of verses that begin mid-sentence were changed to lower-case letters. These alterations were done for the purpose of meeting contemporary standards in English punctuation and capitalization. No words have been changed, and meaning has not been altered in any way.

In the Moses story, from Exodus-Deuteronomy, there are several passages that include quotations within quotations within quotations. In these cases, the text is arranged in a "block format" to facilitate easier reading. Again, no words have been changed, and meaning has not been altered. Other translations were consulted to confirm quotation boundaries.

Poetic strophes were determined and formatted in accordance with the NIV Bible. The King James translators did not format poetic passages into Hebrew strophes (stanzas).

Books and passages chosen for inclusion in this textbook were selected by the author/editor and do not always include entire chapters. Selected chapters and verses are clearly labeled so that all omissions from the original text are obvious to the reader (for example, note the omitted genealogies from Genesis, done for the sake of narrative continuity). No single words or phrases were omitted, and therefore no sentence meanings have been altered in any way. All omissions amount to large chunks of sequential verses and complete sentences (for example, the omission of the first half of Proverbs 31, leaving the complete "Epilogue to the Noble Wife" intact). Large omissions between selected chapters have been summarized in italics. All omissions were made for the purpose of brevity, genre focus, or topical focus. Books and passages may be read in their entirety by consulting any KJV Bible, and students are free and encouraged to do so if preferred.

Footnotes were composed by the author/editor in order to enhance comprehension, clarify context, or paraphrase KJV wording. The following abbreviations were used to denote the sources of footnoted information. Please note that footnotes with no parenthetical ID's may contain editorial interpretation.
- (FI) = Factual information confirmed in 2-3 general reference sources such as encyclopedias, dictionaries, or maps
- (EP) = Editor's paraphrase of the biblical text
- (BHL) = Bible Hub lexicon (www.biblehub.com, which hosts a Strong's lexicon)
- (BHC) = Bible Hub commentary; the source of the commentary will also appear in the footnote (www.biblehub.com also hosts a wide assortment of traditional commentaries)
- (WBD) = Wycliffe Bible Dictionary
- (ASB) = Archaeological Study Bible (an NIV publication)

ANNOTATED BIBLIOGRAPHY

"Apocalypse! The evolution of apocalyptic belief and how it shaped the western world." Frontline. WGBH Educational Foundation, 2014. Web. 15 Feb. 2014. Compendium of written reports, interviews, primary sources, and a two-hour PBS special called "Apocalypse." Resource for Lesson 22.

Archaeological Study Bible (NIV). Grand Rapids, Michigan: Zondervan, 2005. Print. This source was often used for historical reference material throughout the textbook. It is a beautiful rendering of the Holy Bible with ancient maps, photographs of artifacts, and extensive historical and archaeological commentary. It was used frequently to fact-check and write footnotes for the biblical text; footnotes are marked as (ASB).

Bible Hub. Biblos, 2014. Web. This source was often used for footnotes; such references are marked as (BHL) for the lexicon and (BHC) for commentary. The Hebrew and Greek lexicon at Bible Hub uses traditional Strong's numbers, definitions, and cross-references. Strong's Exhaustive Concordance of the Bible (1890) is a classic non-interpretive index of all the words in the Bible; it assigns a number to each Hebrew and Greek root word, and it cross-references each word's use throughout the Bible. The commentaries featured at Bible Hub include a wide array of popular concordances from the past 400 years; when referenced in textbook footnotes, the name of the commentary is provided in parentheses.

Catholic Encyclopedia. Robert Appleton Company, 1905. New Advent.org. Kevin Knight, 2009. Web. This encyclopedia was used for factual information throughout the textbook. The online version was pioneered by Kevin Knight and transcribed from the 1913 15-volume edition. This source was used extensively for fact-checking and clarification on essentials of theology.

Covington, Michael A. Notes on the Original Greek Text of the New Testament. 13th draft, 2003 Sept 28. Program in Linguistics, UGa. <www.covingtoninnovations.com/nttext.pdf>. Excellent research paper with 14 scholarly sources including multiple Greek "minority text" manuscripts and seminal works by notable Princeton and Harvard authors. This paper was a resource for Lesson 1 and the Bible Resources and Recommendations page.

Early Christian Writings: New Testament, Apocrypha, Gnostics, Church Fathers. Peter Kirby, 2014. Web. This site offers an extensive online collection of Christian texts written during the first three centuries, including translations and commentaries. It was a resource for the sidebars in Lesson 17, regarding textual criticism and author ID's of the gospels.

Eerdman's Handbook to the History of Christianity. Ed. Tim Dowley, John H.Y. Briggs, David F. Wright, and Robert D. Linder. Hertforshire, England: Lion Publishing, 1977. This book was used as a general reference in matters of Christian history, from the First Century through the Twentieth.

From Jesus to Christ: The First Christians. Frontline. WGBH educational foundation, 2014.
    Web. This PBS program website includes a wealth of historical and critical information.
    It was a resource for lessons on the gospels, and cited in one of the sidebars in Lesson 17.

Israel Ministry of Foreign Affairs. State of Israel, 2013. Web. <mfa.gov.il> This site was used
    as a resource for Lesson 8, in reference to Israel's "covenant" identity.

Rich, Tracey. Judaism 101. Tracey R. Rich, 2011. Web. <www.JewFAQ.org> This website,
    although not sponsored or written by a notable scholar, has proven to be a reliable, user-
    friendly site with well-written articles about matters of Jewish tradition and religious
    observance. It was a resource for Lesson 16, in reference to the Jewish concept of
    the Messiah, and for additional fact-checking regarding Jewish theology and customs.

Wycliffe Bible Dictionary. Ed. Charles F. Pfeiffer, Howard F. Vos, and John Rea. Peabody,
    Massachusetts: Hendrickson Publishers, Inc., 1975. Print. This source was often used for
    general fact-checking and footnotes to the biblical text; footnotes are marked as (WBD).

FREE WEB/APP BIBLES

Biblegateway.com
Easy passage and verse look-up with dozens of translation options, including foreign languages. Parallel format available, with two translations appearing side by side for easy comparison. Religiously-sponsored with Christian theological supplements and ads.

The Bible by UBS (iPad app)
Offers KJV, ESV (English Standard) and The Message versions as well as an atlas of biblical geography, media images to accompany selected passages, reading plans, personal notes and bookmarks/highlights, and a "share" feature.

BIBLE VERSIONS/TRANSLATIONS

King James Version (KJV)
The classic "authorized" version of the Bible, translated in 1611, based on the Biblia Hebraica, with a Septuagint influence, and the Textus Receptus. It is the most influential English version.

New International Version (NIV)
This is the current best-selling version of the English Bible, due to its easy-to-read contemporary style. Between 1965 and 1978, more than 100 evangelical Bible scholars translated the Biblia Hebraica and the Novum Testamentum Graece using a "thought-for-thought" translation philosophy that attempts to render complete thoughts fluently into the new language rather than working word-for-word. The NIV omits or alters more than 50 verses (compared to older versions like the KJV) partially due to textual discrepancies between the Novum Testamentum Graece and the Textus Receptus (used in older versions). Many notable theologians and denominations have criticized the NIV for alleged inaccuracies such as interpretive wording and changes in pronoun gender. The NIV was revised in 2011 and the copyright is owned by Biblica (formerly the New York Bible Society).

New Revised Standard Version (NRSV)
This is a widely-respected "word-for-word" translation of the Biblia Hebraica and Novum Testamentum Graece. Completed in 1989, the NRSV also contains the Apocrypha (translated from the Septuagint)

New King James Version (NKJV)
This 1982 "word-for-word" revision of the classic King James Bible was based on the Biblia Hebraica (with a Septuagint influence) and the Textus Receptus, as was the 1611 original. It updates 17th Century vocabulary and grammar, adds paragraph breaks and quotation marks, and arranges poetic passages into strophes, while preserving the noble literary style of its predecessor.

The Message
This Bible is a paraphrase rather than a translation. It goes far beyond the "thought-for-thought" philosophy and strives for a modern-day American idiom that takes creative and interpretive liberties. Completed by author Eugene Peterson in 2002, this Bible is very easy to understand and appeals to open-minded Bible readers.

ANCIENT MANUSCRIPT TYPES & TERMS

Biblia Hebraica: the Tanakh, written in Hebrew. The oldest and best copies we have today are the Masoretic texts, which date to around 1000 C.E.

Septuagint: a Greek version of the Tanakh, translated around 200 B.C.E.

Textus Receptus: Greek version of the New Testament, based on Byzantine manuscripts.

Byzantine manuscripts: Greek manuscripts dating back to the 400's and possibly commissioned by Constantine – our most numerous collection of texts and thus the "majority texts." However, they contain more verses than the older Alexandrian manuscripts, and scholars argue over which group is more accurate to the originals.

Novum Testamentum Graece: Greek version of the New Testament, based on Alexandrian manuscripts. They are considered "new" (novum) because they were discovered later than the Textus Receptus.

Alexandrian manuscripts: Greek manuscripts dating back to the school at Alexandria, Egypt (as far back as the 200's). These are our oldest copies of New Testament text and are often called the "minority texts" because we have fewer of them.

SIDEBAR TOPICAL INDEX

BIBLE BASICS

Books of the Bible	17
Biblical Canon	18
Translation Comparison	19

LITERARY LISTS

Literary Terms Glossary	31
Criticism Definitions	32
Genre Types	33
Three Steps for a Literary Analysis of Biblical Text	34
Archetypes in the Bible	71
Narrative Genres of the Torah	89 (also see page 121)
Rhetorical Devices and Strategies	241

TEXTUAL CRITICISM & LITERARY CONNECTIONS

Literary Sources for the Flood Story	72
Prophetic Characters in Literature with Impaired Vision	176
Did Matthew the Apostle Write the Gospel of Matthew?	187
Did Mark the Apostle Write the Gospel of Mark?	188
Biographies in the Ancient World	189
Movies About Jesus	216
Christ Figures in Books & Film	219

THE TORAH & JUDAISM

Judaism Glossary	15
Universal Truths from Eden	41
Timeline of Morality & Law (in Genesis)	59
"Young Earth" Timeline of Biblical History	60
Ancient Covenants and Modern Weddings	92
Art or History? (in the Torah)	120
Possible or Impossible? (events of the exodus)	121

THE NEW TESTAMENT & CHRISTIANITY

A Christian Reading of the Eden Story	42
Holy Days and Celebrations	228
Revelation/Apocalypse Glossary	264

A COMPREHENSIVE BIBLE TIMELINE

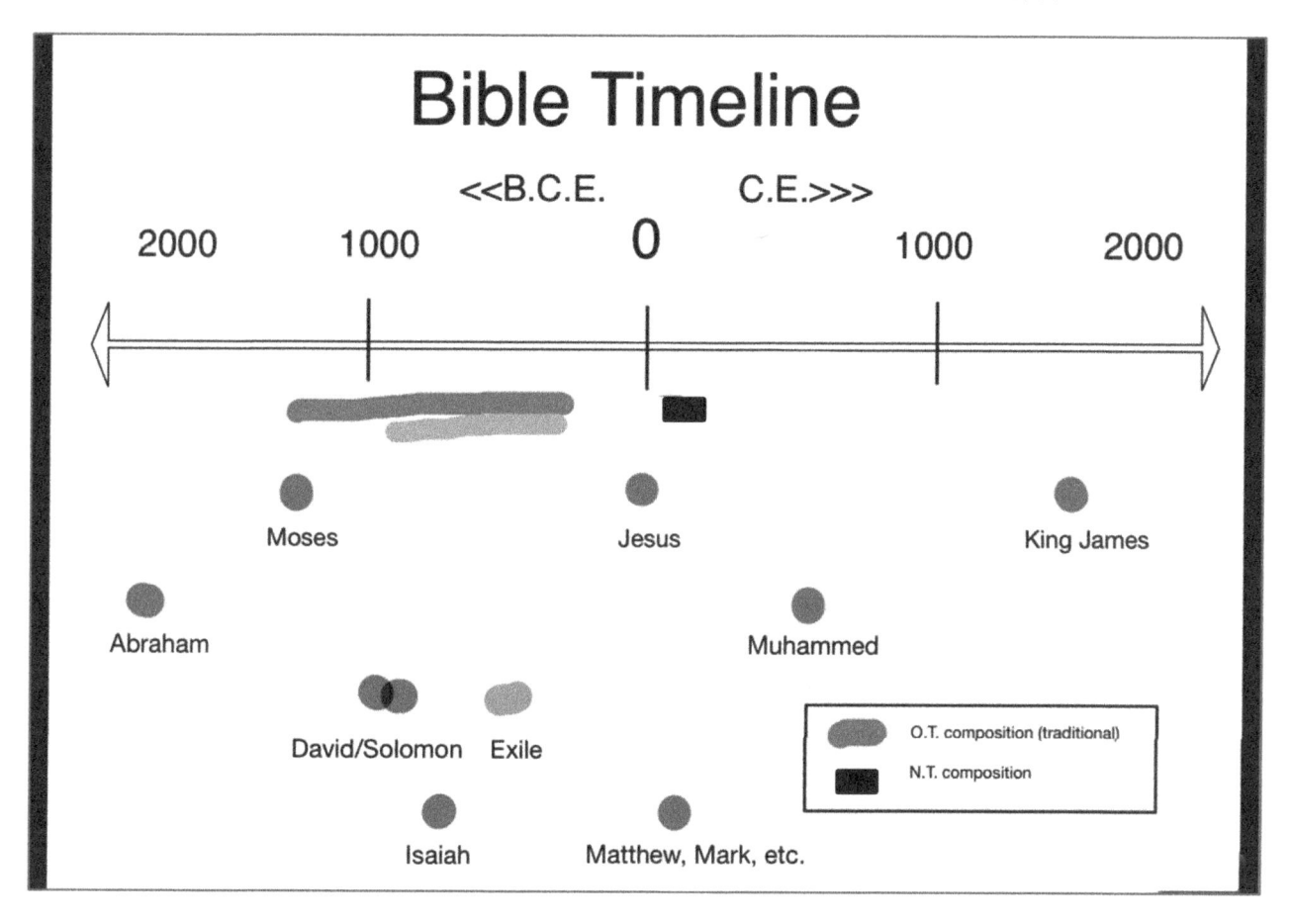

Bible Timeline

<<B.C.E.   C.E.>>>

2000   1000   0   1000   2000

- Moses
- Jesus
- King James
- Abraham
- Muhammed
- David/Solomon
- Exile
- Isaiah
- Matthew, Mark, etc.

Legend:
- O.T. composition (traditional)
- N.T. composition

A VERBAL TIMELINE / METANARRATIVE

- Mythical era: Creation through the Tower of Babel
- Abraham and the covenant (beginning of Jewish family tree)
- Isaac fathers Jacob, whose name is changed to Israel
- 12 tribes of Israel (12 sons of Jacob) – the eldest being Judah, the tribe of kings
- Nation of Israel migrates to Egypt
- Moses leads exodus from Egypt into Promised Land
- Hebrew nation becomes a kingdom
- David and Solomon preside over golden age of Israel; the temple is built
- Hebrew nation splits into northern kingdom (Israel) and southern kingdom (Judah)
- Political turmoil, Assyrian invasion (Jonah preaches to Ninevah prior to invasion)
- Babylonian Exile, destruction of Jerusalem and temple
- Return to Jerusalem and re-building of the temple ("second temple")
- Final prophecy (Malachi) given to post-exilic Jerusalem and conclusion of Old Testament
- Life of Jesus
- Early church narrative (Acts) and missionary preaching
- Composition of the New Testament gospels and epistles
- Final revelation: John's vision at Patmos

ALLUSIONS TO THE BIBLE IN POP CULTURE

These items are provided as a sample of the broad array of biblical allusions throughout Western culture, in books, movies, art, advertising, music, political speeches, etc. Can you identify and interpret these examples?

- The cover of the book Twilight features a hand holding an apple, suggesting the theme of temptation and "forbidden fruit."

- An Illinois tattoo parlor is called Mark of Cain Tattoos. Find their website on the Internet.

- In Douglas Adams' book The Hitchhiker's Guide to the Galaxy, a Babel Fish is a creature one can insert in the ear in order to understand alien languages.

- From the song "Viva la Vida" by Coldplay:
  One minute I held the key / Next the walls were closed on me
  And I discovered that my castles stand / Upon pillars of salt and pillars of sand

- "Gangsta's Paradise" by Coolio begins with a reference to the valley of the shadow of death.

- "By the Waters of Babylon" is a post-apocalyptic short story by Stephen Vincent Benét in which the main character, John, and his family appear to be exiled from the forbidden land across the river to the East.

- John Grisham's novel A Time to Kill explores the ethics behind a father who kills his daughter's rapists.

- From a World War I poem by Rudyard Kipling called "Gethsemane":

  And all the time we halted there
  I prayed my cup might pass.
  It didn't pass—it didn't pass-
  It didn't pass from me.
  I drank it when we met the gas
  Beyond Gethsemane!

- A poster that reads: "Blessed are the weird people, for they teach us to see the world through different eyes."

- A bumper sticker with both Clemson and Gamecock designs on it that says "a house divided" (the Clemson Tigers and USC Gamecocks are South Carolina rivals)

- Caption of a cartoon featuring men wearing ancient-styled robes while playing basketball: "In a lively game of pick-up basketball, Peter denies Jesus three times."

- The Faith-Hope-Love Foundation sponsors children born into the slums of India, providing them with education and a place to live.

PERSPECTIVES ON GENESIS AND EVOLUTION

VIEW-POINT	Age of the earth	Darwinian evolution	Genesis 1 Creation	Genesis 2-3 Adam and Eve	Genesis 6-10 Noah/Flood
Young Earth Creation	6,000 years old, as determined by genealogies throughout the Bible	Macro evolution did not occur. God put Adam on the earth. Man did not come from apes.	Literal reading. The universe was created in 6 24-hour days.	Literal reading. Adam and Eve historically existed in Eden.	Literal reading. The flood covered the entire planet, killing all life.
Old Earth Creation	Billions of years old, as determined by modern science.	Macro evolution did not occur. God put Adam on the earth. Man did not come from apes.	Symbolic reading, in keeping with the figurative properties of poetry. The days of creation may symbolize eons of gradual creation. OR Literal reading but with the Hebrew word for "day" translated as "age"	Literal reading. Adam and Eve historically existed in Eden.	Literal reading, but possibly interpretive. The flood may have been regional, only <u>seeming</u> global from Noah's perspective.
Theistic Evolution	Billions of years old, as determined by modern science.	Humans evolved from lower life forms, as posited by Darwin.	Symbolic/mythical reading. The days of creation symbolize eons of God-shaped evolution.	Symbolic/mythical reading. Adam and Eve represent humanity in a cultural and spiritual manner.	Symbolic/mythical reading. There was likely a catastrophic regional flood, but Noah himself is fictional or legendary at best, symbolically representing mankind's need for cleansing and rebirth.
Atheism / Evolution	Billions of years old, as determined by modern science.	Humans evolved from lower life forms, as posited by Darwin.	Fictional reading.	Fictional reading, though the tale contains archetypal and thematic truth in the same way that a short story would.	Fictional reading. The tale probably evolved from earlier Sumerian myths and was inspired by a catastrophic regional flood.

Recommended books:
YOUNG EARTH: <u>In Six Days: Why 50 Scientists Choose to Believe in Creation</u>, Ed. John F. Ashton
OLD OR YOUNG EARTH: <u>Creation & Evolution 101</u>, by Bruce Bicknel and Stan Jantz (Christianity 101 Series)
THEISTIC EVOLUTION: <u>The Language of God: A Scientist Presents Evidence for Belief</u>, by Francis S. Collins

IMAGE CREDITS

All black-and-white photography on cover pages and section header pages (except for the hero stories image) are the original work of the author/editor, Caryn Kirk.

All diagrams, time lines, and maps are original images created by the author/editor.

The following images have been licensed or are in the public domain:

- Image of Lexi ("Red Haired Teen Girl 1" by Lisafx, royalty free license from StockFreeImages, 8/18/13)
- Image of Fatima ("Beautiful Teen Latina Headshot" by Csproductions, royalty free license from Dreamstime, 8/18/13)
- Image of Scott ("Teen Boy" by Goodynewshoes, royalty free license, Dreamstime, 8/18/13)
- "Eliza Codex 23 Ethiopian Biblical Manuscript" from the Hill Museum and Manuscript Library**
- "Creation" from the Sistine Chapel ceiling by Michelangelo**
- "The Temptation of Eve" by John Roddam Spencer Stanhope **
- "Pandora" by Jules Joseph Lefebvre **
- "Vitruvian Man" by Leonardo da Vinci **
- "The Tower of Babel" by Peter Bruegel the Elder **
- "NOAH'S ARK" cartoon by Nem4a, royalty free liceense, Dreamstime, 8/29/13
- "The Dove Sent Forth from the Ark" by Gustave Dore **
- Photograph of the Kaaba ("Mecca" by Ariandra03 from Wikimedia Commons, licensed under the Creative Commons Attribution-Share Alike 3.0)
- Image of hero's hand ("Old Man With Walking Stick" by Sqback, royalty free license, Dreamstime, 9/22/13)
- "Charleston Heston in The Ten Commandments film trailer" (published without a copyright notice)
- "Odysseus-Sirens" **
- "Jonah and the Whale" by Pieter Lastman**
- "The Judgment of Solomon" by Raphael **
- "Tiresias Appears to Ulysses" by Henry Fuseli **
- "The Adoration of the Kings" by Jan Mabuse **
- "The Last Supper" by Leonardo DaVinci**

**These images are faithful photographic reproductions of original two-dimensional works of art. The works of art themselves are in the public domain because they never held a copyright or the copyright has expired.

A WORD TO THE TEACHER

Thank you for selecting this textbook for use in your English classroom. I hope you will find it to be a useful resource in structuring your Bible-related curriculum. Here are a few ideas and recommendations that may prove helpful:

TWO PADAGOGICAL APPROACHES TO USING THE LESSONS

- **Coaching:** Have students read both the biblical text and accompanying lessons for homework. You might have them write definitions, construct outlines, or prepare answers to assigned study questions. Afterward, you can facilitate class discussion and assign follow-up activities using the "Subjective Expression" items as a reference bank.

- **Lecturing:** Have students read the biblical text as homework. You can then freely use and adjust lesson content for custom-designed lectures that suit the specific needs of your classroom. With this approach, the textbook lessons can be used as a reference for absentees and for study/review purposes.

FORMS OF ASSESSMENT

- **Quizzing recommendation:** I recommend quizzing practices that are as objective as possible. See the "Objective Identification" lists for assistance.

- **Testing recommendation:** Lesson study guides are provided to inspire class discussions and test creation/preparation. Let students know which items are most important to you, and allow them to respond to subjective test questions from their individual religious or non-religious points of view; provide clear guidelines for what constitutes a thorough and well-supported subjective response. Tests might also require identification and explanation of biblical allusions from a variety of sources – see page 276 for a list of examples.

- **Project recommendations:** Have students collect biblical allusions from secular music, art, movies, advertising, etc. Consider forming project teams with diverse groupings of faith perspectives.

A WORD FROM THE AUTHOR

Greetings from South Carolina, and thank you for reading! I am a teacher of high school literature and composition currently employed at Hammond School, a private secular K-12 academy in the capital city of Columbia. For me personally, the Bible is a holy book, and my interest in its artistic qualities is a natural result of many years in the study of literature combined with many years of Christian faith. My passion for teaching Bible stories and poetry starts with the power of the text itself and is expressed through a desire to engage each and every student in my classroom, many of whom do not share my religious convictions. In writing this book, my goal has been to convey a deep appreciation for the Bible's narrative and poetic richness. Of course, it is nearly impossible to keep one's personal opinions completely out of a discussion of literature, much less religious literature, and I am sure I came to the task with a certain amount of bias. Therefore, an excellent chance exists that you, the reader of this text, will find something herein to disagree with. In that case, please be my guest, for that is part of the purpose of sending teenage students to a secular school: so that they will emerge with broad horizons. Teens are entering a time in their lives when encountering new ideas, asking questions, and seeking answers will be part of their character formation.

    Dear readers, if you are Christian or Jewish, then I hope you will take your questions about the Bible straight to the family dinner table and into your church or synagogue. If you are not religious at all, I hope that you might find something interesting and thought provoking herein that will help you relate better to Judeo-Christian culture at large. If you are a follower of another faith, I hope you will discover many similarities between Judeo-Christian literature and your own. There is a great marketplace of ideas in modern culture, and knowing about the Bible is an important part of that exchange. My own experience in public school, private Christian school, and private secular school has enabled me to keep a broad audience in mind, and I hope there is something positive in these pages for all my readers. I hope that you will permit me, throughout these 22 lessons, the privilege of speaking from my head and my heart, for I think it virtually impossible to separate the two when discussing great literature.